From Trocchi to Trainspotting:
Scottish Critical Theory Since 1960

For Robert and Catherine Gardiner

From Trocchi to Trainspotting

Scottish Critical Theory Since 1960

Michael Gardiner

Edinburgh University Press

© Michael Gardiner, 2006

Edinburgh University Press Ltd
22 George Square, Edinburgh

Typeset in 10.5/13 Adobe Sabon
by Servis Filmsetting Ltd, Manchester, and
printed and bound in Great Britain by
MPG Books Ltd, Bodmin, Cornwall

A CIP record for this book is available from the British Library

ISBN-10 0 7486 2232 2 (hardback)
ISBN-13 978 0 7486 2232 0 (hardback)
ISBN-10 0 7486 2233 0 (paperback)
ISBN-13 978 0 7486 2233 7 (paperback)

Contents

Acknowledgements

In the various processes that went towards the writing of this book, I would particularly like to thank: Jackie Jones, Alan Riach, Willy Maley, Robert Crawford, Scott Hames, Kenneth White, Claudia Kraskiewicz, Margery Palmer McCulloch, Duncan Jones, Duncan Petrie, Berthold Schoene, Aaron Kelly, Edwin Morgan, Stuart Kelly, Kirsti Wishart and William Miller.

Introduction

Even today it is common to come across the assumption that there has never been any Scottish literary theory. In part this has to do with the explosive word theory, which is typically taken to mean a collection of jargon which spoils literature for everyone else, and which peaked among boffins between the late 1970s and early 1990s, producing excitement among some and fear and loathing among others. Abuse of the term has always been far greater than actual use. 'Theory' has, nine times out of ten, never been the playground bully it has been portrayed as. We can test this by rephrasing theory, seen as either dated or precocious, scary or imperative, as literary thought, which is a staple.

Even more worthy of suspicion is the idea that theory has nothing to do with Scotland. One of the legacies of the Scottish Enlightenment, which I date more strictly than most, from about the 1740s to the 1780s, is the separation out of academic disciplines and objects of study via a nexus of vision/knowledge, and the attempt to master each in the new British Union. If France's Enlightenment concepts were unravelled by theory, Scotland invented the very concept of discrete concepts. Yet in the latter part of the twentieth century many in 'English Literature', itself largely a Scottish idea, stood and watched as France reworked its own Enlightenment in the form of big names, which meant theory *sui generis*. If there are two countries in the world where there should be a body of theory, they are France and Scotland. And yet the silence in Scotland has been deafening.

The general idea behind the apparently disparate chapters which follow is very simple: where we have witnessed theory thread its way through English Studies and acknowledged that this is an effect of the French Enlightenment rethinking itself, the recent literary-political developments for which Scotland has become world known – devolution and a huge leap in literary prestige – are in large part correlates of the Scottish Enlightenment going through a similar process of auto-deconstruction. This has been happening for some time, but we haven't looked straight at it. Rather, in a country this small, the Enlightenment must remain a beacon (etc.) of fame for Scotland, and we should play down anything that looks as if it might threaten the memory of the Edinburgh *philosophes*. Thus, there has been no Scottish Derrida. But then there was no French Derrida either: he was an Algerian, and it's vital to remember that the whole post-Enlightenment project is also a postcolonial one. Scotland is also emerging from a colonial mindset which it helped create.

There were rumblings of change during the Scottish Renaissance which, in phases, most critics today think of as a movement stretching from Patrick Geddes to the later Hugh MacDiarmid, from the 1890s to the 1960, rather than the earlier 1920s–1930s model. To an extent the Renaissance was working in the dark, without any concrete idea of how national literary thought could dovetail with imperial, constitutional and representational matters. Theoretical movement only came post-war, after the jewel in the imperial crown had been lost, and the Cold War had kicked in. The shadow-theory of Scotland is what this book aims to chart, using figures who have in the past been mostly subject to biographical criticism. Indeed, some of what follows may prove troubling to disciplinary fundamentalists, since some of the theorists described here are known as 'creative writers', whatever that means.

In the most comprehensive overview of the situation of Scottish literature in recent years, Alan Riach (2005) has listed seven key features in the negotiation of national literary thought. The seventh he doesn't give a number: it remains a supplement which haunts the other six, yet is, for the purposes of my study, the most significant. The six qualities are: voice, place, nation, language, people and humour, and all of these will come up frequently in my study. They might seem obvious to any national literature at first glance; a closer association with the history of Scottish literature, though, shows that in the past, and sometimes in the present, these qualities have been highly problematic and subjects of intense debate, or worse, silence. The conjunction of these six unknowables is extraordinary, and in a time of great literary optimism offers immense opportunities for crossover and rethinking, where in the past some of them have been seen as a handicap. The missing term in Riach's Seven Types of Ambiguity, following hard on the heels of the first six, is genre: the undoing the flexibility and the radical rethinking of, as a means of organising texts. And this will to keep typologies open is what will really separate Scottish literature from Eng. Lit. in coming decades.

My study is not exhaustive by any means; far from it. It tends rather to take specific lines in Scottish thought and demonstrate that they were already 'doing' theory, despite the *faux* debate about whether theory should be 'used' in Scottish literature. More generally, the book suggests, within time-frames that are colonial and postcolonial, that there has been a movement within Scottish thought to disassemble the universalist ideas of Enlightenment, a movement which works within what we ought to call theory. The key Scottish Enlightenment figure David Hume, who stresses sympathy over the contract, yet like Jean-Jacques Rousseau still prepares the ground for an aesthetics which is pragmatic and imperialistic, has never been drawn into Scottish theory in the way that the French have gnawed at Montesquieu, Voltaire and the other *philosophes*.

The first two chapters here are to an extent 'stand-alone' and bring up concepts which will resound throughout the book. Chapter 1 may prove conceptually gristly and not yet to the point, but the ideas behind it will prove central and the promise (yes, that's a trick word) of a Scottish Literature standing on its own feet, unbeholden to notions of genre, omniscience and empire. The first two sections of Chapter 2 to an extent describe what post-1960 Scottish literature is *not*: in a semi-conscious state of doubt as to whether a language, a 'people' and a nation can be reconciled. After the 'Second Renaissance' debate which concludes Chapter 2 I move on to recognisable names: Chapter 3 suggests that Muriel Spark was a key figure in rethinking many of the central ideas of Enlightenment, and, with Alexander Trocchi, who occupies much of Chapter 4, was behind an alliance with French thought which her Anglo-British image belies. Chapter 4, the longest, looks at activities from novel-writing to pamphleteering undertaken by Trocchi, his collaborators, and similar figures, and puts these in the context of a *nouvelle alliance*, particularly in relation to the question of Paris 1968. Chapter 5, despite its title, takes the experimental work of Edwin Morgan and shows how he alters the position of the author in a way that can be read as direct criticism of Enlightenment. Chapter 6 looks at Ian Hamilton Finlay, a figure who can't be excluded from any discussion of how post-Enlightenment thought puts violence and reason back together, apparently separated out in glorious modernity, demonstrating how the tenets of Enlightenment mean that we are still living through cruelty. Chapter 7 looks at the important critical work of James Kelman from two periods, the first concerned with specific injustices, often a stone's throw from 'Merchant City', Glasgow's centre of Enlightenment, the second linking the ethics of his own narration in fiction to that of Franz Kafka, via Gilles Deleuze. The last chapter imagines a situation in which Scotland is not dependent on genres at all, the separation and seeing-knowing process of Enlightenment, and suggests that times when 'a batch of new' novelists or poets arises may not be such a cause for celebration as is typically thought. Instead, Scotland can help inaugurate an entirely genre-free way of looking at literature, where a text's 'literariness' inheres in the effects it has, rather than how saleable it is.

Chapter 1

The Idea of Resistance

The idea of resistance

Resistance can be read here in two ways, one of which should be immediately obvious, and will probably be taken to be the single meaning by those who don't bother to finish the chapter. Scottish literature emerged into the 2000s in a strong position relative to the embattled discipline of Eng. Lit., which itself had largely grown from the ban the Edinburgh Enlightenment *literati* levied on Scottish literary language. Scottish literature was not saddled with a holy canon of Great Works – there were few specifically national 'models' at all – or a central position to the remains of an imperial bureaucracy which Eng. Lit.'s remit was to represent culturally. Scottish literature was formally forward-looking rather than backward-looking, and had access to a range of languages, none of which was considered correct in the older Eng. Lit. sense; read like this it has *resisted* Eng. Lit. for over four decades, and that difficult process of resistance is part of what this book describes. This can take global significance; as I have suggested, in Deleuzian terms, Scotland and England are *minor* nations within the UK state, and are forced into *becoming*, a process which has long seemed much more urgent in Scotland – despite the importance of starting to define a post-Union English culture.[1]

Less obviously, *resistance* can be linked to the psychosocial backbone of this transition: the notion of persons in mutual resistance, sharing a present time in tactile communication, as against the visual – which causes a split in the time it takes light to move – is something shared by both Scottish literary thought since about 1960 and what we have known as theory. In this sense, much theory is deeply related to Scotland. The manifestos that the French thinker Paul Virilio produced with Claude Parent, representing the *Architecture Principe* group in 1966, overlapped with Kenneth White's Jargon Group papers, the Sigma Group manifestos of the by now fairly established Alexander Trocchi, the popular and underrated mid-1960s phase of R. D. Laing, and numerous other counter-cultural experiments in Scotland.

In the early part of the innocuous-looking yet explosive conversation between Paul Virilio and Sylvère Lotringer, *Crepuscular Dawn*, Virilio describes early architectural experiments to create non-orthogonal buildings in which the floor is not flat, but *resistant* to the footstep, and in which obstacles are placed around rooms.[2] For Virilio, since the perception of space is 'plagiarised' in technoculture,[3] a force of repulsion against the terrestrial is necessary to be grounded in space at all; thus '[t]he topological system, the "oblique function," amounted to using oriented surfaces rather than ruled surfaces'.[4] The classically flat surface, via the appropriation of light-time in modern logistics, can offer a seamless illusion of depth in endless repetition of itself, as in the skyscraper, *virtual* groundedness: thus 'New York is a catastrophe in slow motion'.[5] Part of the (back)ground to the following chapters is the way in which Enlightenment and neo-Enlightenment Scotland aimed at the visual in communications, and how, in a recent converse movement, literary thought during the period of theory partly reinstated the primacy of the tactile, the resistant.

It is widely acknowledged that Virilio has become established over the last decade or so as a theorist of speed – more accurately, as a theorist of how light-speed is tied to polity via logistics. Less well known is that he was once a theatrical set designer, and that he saw May 1968, along with White, Trocchi and other members of the French diaspora, as a literary revolution, rather than a revolution of the older, pre-Situationist, regime-change variety.[6] His historical motion is from revolutions to wars to 'accidents', as was vividly demonstrated a year before *Crepuscular Dawn* was published (in 2002).[7] Virilio's stress on the need for mutual physical repulsion to replace the highly manipulable 'cinema' of remote visual presentation is very close to the Scottish thinker John Macmurray's idea of resistance: there is no valid experience 'in itself', as Anglo-British logical positivism had been trying to convince philosophers throughout Macmurray's career; there is only experience in contact with an other.[8]

For Virilio, the spectacle – as in 1968ist thought – has a deadly dual function of integration ('bringing together' a society) and separation (the creation of social isolation via television, the car, and so on).[9] The stress on the speed of light – the fact that light has a limiting velocity and that nearing light-speed is more indexical of power than is 'knowledge' – is highly analogous to the slightly earlier Macmurray: since light takes time to travel across distance, visual experience will always be separated into 'old' and 'new' – the 'colonial time-lag' as we now say in postcolonialism, or, as Virilio might think through it, the 'digital divide'. For both, only persons who are *in touch* can share experience, yet experience is speeding away in the specular technology of the military-industrial complex.[10] In Virilio there is thus a 'pollution' of the experience of distance in travel at speeds which are too high, which he ingeniously terms 'grey pollution': the foreclosure of the physical world and its exhaustion.[11] The compression of time destroys the sequentiality of tactile experience which makes up history, and the world which is constructed in terms of space within the self becomes modified and open to solipsistic individuation.[12] In the Scottish case, the state capital has for three centuries been conceptually far away when measured in terms of extensive Humean space, or the space of power/knowledge; things change, though, after the 'technological accident' ushered in by the Cold War era and the demonstration of the explosive power of light in Hiroshima. When, after the Scottish-imperial push towards London and towards light-speed had withered, and the seeing-knowing notion of race in empire with it, the state of everything happening simultaneously appears as a real danger. Resistance, on the other hand, ensures that persons share a time, by pushing against one another physically, and that experience is not purely individual or subjective. Virilio thus sets himself against hands-off digitisation – a position which will become more important as this book goes on.[13]

Virilio also poetically describes the concerns of *Architecture Principe* as 'making waves', both politically and on architectural surfaces, making the classically flat ambivalently resistant, a notion which strongly recalls Ian Hamilton Finlay's wave-form sculptures of the early 1970s.[14] Finlay's use of super-flat surfaces (marble, for example) is typically broken by some form of resistance – by the rough of the earth itself, by physically discordant angles, by the 'conceptual discordance' of the cruelty which inhabits the Enlightenment, a world away from the Marvellian garden of Eng. Lit. Virilio takes as an example one of Finlay's favourite images, the sailboat:

> *In a way, the function of the oblique is to make weight perceptible again, to give it back its gravity, its resistance . . .*

And to work with gravity, with heaviness, the way a sailboat works with the wind . . .

With the orthogonal plane, the flat plane, as in the entire history of architecture, there is no difference between making one movement or another. On an inclined plane, climbing and descending are radically different; but climbing diagonally or descending diagonally are different *again*; and walking laterally is different *as well*. Every dimension, every direction of space becomes a modification of the body.[15]

For Virilio, speed as the removal of resistances (rather than money, or, in Foucauldian terms, knowledge) should increasingly be understood as the measurement of power.[16] The arms race, for example, which, in the 1980s, was largely carried out in Scotland against its wishes, is really speed-based rather than weapons-based, as war *response* approaches *reflex*, and defence approaches light-speed detection.[17] In Cold War and post-Cold War environments, the ultimate aim, accelerated by the 'Star Wars' use of lasers, is to eliminate reaction time altogether by conducting war at the speed of light.[18] A cornerstone of the present book is that a desire to reach light-speed was exactly an enterprise pushed by the Scottish Enlightenment *literati*, newly remote from the state capital, leading to technocrats of communications through James Watt to John Logie Baird, and imaged in the *Starship Enterprise*'s Scotty, the only crew member among a cringe-worthy multicultural-but-American crew to speak with, as they say, 'an accent'. Only he could take the ship to warp speeds, using light-speed technology.[19]

When war thus becomes automated – at light-speed – it also becomes pure deterrence: absolute globalised security equals total war – approximately the current state of affairs.[20] Thus Virilio speaks not of deterrent weapons but of a *deterred people* – and a deterred people are behind the resistant culture growing from around new nuclear bases such as Faslane from the 1980s. The nuclear targeting of Scotland, of course, hardly tallies with the idea of 'Union' as double-nationed: Scotland has been seen as far away from the 'centre', and therefore empty for nuclear programmes, which only deter *local* populations, not from a specific enemy, but *generally*.[21] Non-physical enclosure manifests itself as glocalisation – an individuation which happens at the same time as the closing down of space – as well as by the model of the Foucauldian panopticon, in which everyone is always open to surveillance.[22] Douglas Gordon, an artist highly interested in both light and Scottish literature, in 'Under Darkness, Between Shadows', critiques the control of light-speed and technocracy in 2000, in a proposal to cut all light in Glasgow for one hour.[23]

Both Virilio and Macmurray, partly for the reason that a mild Catholicism is behind their critiques, align themselves with the human (Virilio makes a compelling case that genetic engineering creates a new, non-human species), and with the importance of action and reaction.[24] While it is perhaps more possible to read Macmurray in sympathetically post-humanist fashion, for the apocalyptic Virilio, the human is the end and can never be improved upon.[25] And yet the human is, literally, eclipsed. Virtual reality means that we are already witnessing the beginning of 'teleportation', and simultaneous occurrence of everything.[26] In this sense of a total vision, even the training of the eyes in advertising, typically seen as a type of art, is a form of censorship – or as the Scottish playwright Tom McGrath has put it, narrative realism in

TV is brainwashing, since TV trains us to imagine a totality of physical possibilities, whereas it only involves one narrow set of conventions.[27] As Derridean critics have noted, such a simultaneity implies a supplementarity at work in Muriel Spark's early novels, in which, for example, characters telepathically read one another's thoughts (*Memento Mori*) or even discern an untouchable narrator (*The Comforters*).[28] We are left, then, with the central problem of the gap between presence and tele-presence, or, as Macmurray would have put it, action (which is mutual) and activity (which is subjective).[29]

Virilio's dystopia is one in which everyone has already arrived; it is over, and 'home', the Scottish imperialist's guilty dream, has become meaningless. The 'resident' has the upper hand over the nomad, but – and here begins the critique of extensional space which Scots have inherited from David Hume – this difference is not by played out in space at all: residents, with superior access, are at home everywhere (painfully, since they have no 'elsewhere'), even during high-speed transportation.[30] And thus, since the Greek 'metaphor' itself means transport, for fellow '68ist Gilles Deleuze literariness, in the sense of halting the spectralisation of the human, has no metaphor. Literature is resistance itself, refusing the split between nomad and resident.

> Communication without resistance is communication without leaving a trace . . .[31] Action at a distance without interaction (resistance) is a form of pollution, a 'second greenhouse effect', while the ideal is a simultaneous collective interactivity . . .[32]
>
> The revolution in *physical transmission* came first: movement and acceleration up to supersonic speeds. The revolution in *transmissions*, which comes second, is the revolution of live transmission. It is the cybernetic revolution. It is the ability to reach the light barrier, in other words, the speed of electromagnetic waves in any field, not only television and tele-audition, but also tele-operation.[33]

The latter parts of *Crepuscular Dawn*, and Virilio's movement throughout his long career, see another major crossover point between him and Macmurray: the proposal that 'the arts', understood in the widest sense, precede science, and that when science tries to become prior it reverts to the status of myth, performing a kind of auto-cannibalism.[34] Virilio has often expressed his horror at artists imitating science, drastic body mutilation and the undoubtedly dubious idea of 'genetic art', the creation, as art, of species from the increasingly accessible genome pool.[35] Macmurray similarly, anticipating G. E. Davie's 1962 identification of a long-running generalist strain in Scottish thought, stresses, *contra* logical positivism, that even activity that can be seen as 'purely' scientific must be driven by emotional and spiritual impulses, otherwise science would have become automated (and Macmurray has no qualms about setting up the hierarchy spirituality–art–science).[36] For Virilio, when science is subject to over-specialisation, it breaks free from ethics and destroys itself.[37]

Virilio also identifies contemporary biotechnology ('the genetic bomb') as a new form of colonisation: with the rationalisation of genes comes the possibility not only of the obvious eugenic dream of a super-race,[38] but also its necessary correlate, a sub-race of service-sector slaves (to an extent, some would argue, already set in place by the Eng. Lit.-inspired differential of English as a 'world language'), and different species.[39] This is a racism beyond racism, since the integrity of any given race in the old terminology[40] is undermined by the fact that there now is no stable 'human' referent upon which to mark different forms of the species; genetic engineering makes 'human species' plural, not singular.[41] The 'genetic bomb' accident has yet to come, but as with every accident, it is *unimaginable*;[42] the cyber-bomb, or information bomb, is however already central, since, for example, nuclear weapons contain computers, and in any case, electronic warfare is no longer territorial – extensive Enlightenment space has been collapsed.[43] Thought is led to conform to state apparatus (in our case, the UK state), and the form of the war-machine follows the form of the state machine.[44] The cyber-bomb and the genetic bomb are also, of course, open to DIY warfare, or 'terrorism', in which the enemy is undeclared or 'general'. The attack is the accident.[45]

Thus, the pursuit of speed is dehumanising, as in communications in the British empire; my point is that these communications were pushed ahead by Scots, who not only built post-1746 roads, but arranged path-ways in panoptical fashion in institutions.[46] But this 'street culture' is actually *reversed* by the inclined plane, by resistance, by, for example, the uphill mountain path of Alan Warner's *The Man Who Walks*.[47] Where the schizo *is* his proactive stroll in Deleuze and Guattari, and, as Deleuze and his commentator Timothy S. Murphy point out, is equally so in Beckett, the walker in *The Man Who Walks makes* history by encoun-tering the resistance of the upwards slope of a hill, on a comically dubious quest, nevertheless pointedly low-tech and ploughing on along Virilio's inclined plane.[48]

The idea of 'the accident' is also, of course, a sign of a population held in place by the promise of social betterment.[49] During the current Scot-tish literature boom, stretching from the mid-1980s (let's say 1984, the year of James Kelman's *The Busconductor Hines* and Edwin Morgan's 'Sonnets From Scotland') to the declaration of Edinburgh – a city in which, symptomatically, neither of these writers works – as World City of Literature in 2005, the nature of literary resistance has changed, and with it our idea of resistance must stay attuned to the post-Enlightenment significance of Macmurray's idea of resistance as mutual experience, and away from colloquial ideas which see the Scots language as in itself a blow against powers vaguely defined as Eng. Lit. In the murky and often embarrassing past of the early twentieth century, 'resistance' was often taken to mean 'against England' – itself logically problematic, since Scotland is in a nominal Union with England and England is, like Scotland, a nation with no state or foreign policy. Indeed, part of the point of literature in the period under study as I see it is, far from scoring points for Scottish literature, to act as a prolegomenon to the tidal wave of resistant literature which will arise in England, the *unheimlich* home of Eng. Lit., a nation in which that discipline has never really belonged, but which has always been taken as its reference point. At the time of Edwin Morgan's early experimentations, which would open the floodgates to 1960s and 1970s Scottish experiment, England was still buckled under Kingsley Amis's now famous ban on foreign cities and fancy ideas.[50] This was cultural suicide, but it was also the act of a culture (Anglo-British) which had forgotten about the resistance of its own borders, via the imperial habit of expanding Englishness. The aim, then, is not just to reinstate Scotland after Eng. Lit., but to reinstate England.

Deleuze's doctorate

The title of this section, which sounds as if it should be the name of a strip in *Viz* comic, in fact says something very important about Scots' place in 'French' theory. Published in 1953, the book that arose from Gilles Deleuze's doctoral thesis on David Hume was one of his last to be translated into English, in 1991.[51] But here are to be found the seeds of Deleuze's 'transcendental empiricism', and also an important early Franco-Scottish theorisation of Enlightenment.

For Deleuze's Hume, as for Macmurray, experience is a principle of nature.[52] Thence Deleuze's transcendental empiricism: 'not only are perceptions the only substances, they are also the only objects'.[53] And as in Macmurray, in Deleuze's Hume we have to restrict ourselves to experience:[54] '[t]here are no objects in the world other than impressions which are themselves not referable to other objects.'[55]

However, in stressing Hume's idea of causality as an association of ideas formed in the imagination, Deleuze can also be seen as retrospectively hinting that structuralism's use of 'connotation', or imaging at a 'vertical' tangent, is outmoded; he certainly points towards a later idea for which he will become known, that great literature has no 'metaphor'.[56] For Deleuze's Hume, nature implies a form of causality which is only watered down as 'culture'. And the famous teacup can never be guaranteed to break when dropped, but is assumed to do so by association, cultural habit, which works through the assembly of men, or the institution. Thus for Hume history-as-association becomes part of human nature (the universal sympathy that isn't so universal), where 'nature itself' is its residue.[57] However, although 'under the influence of association, imagination becomes reason', imaginative reason cannot be referred back to another morality.[58] Morality is a construct of the imagination. Certainly, for the later Deleuze, the power of a critique is based on its fictionality, where fiction does not 'stand for' something else.[59] The laws of association, for which Hume is so famous for rendering contingent, really come into play in the imagination – culture – to which the drives are directly related, and which are more open than Hume would have liked to think.[60]

One of the ways in which the post-Humean Deleuze most resembles mid-century Scottish thought – as we can now see better from a devolutionary perspective – is in his insistence on action, even within thought. And '[t]o act is to assemble means in order to realise an end'.[61] The un-French (and un-Scottish) method of empiricism would be used via utilitarianism and logical positivism, until Scottish theory began to take it back.[62] A transcendental super-category is needed for causes to meet effects, and if 'reason' is the name given to this process, Hume is willing to go along with this.[63] For Hume reason was open-ended – causes could never finally be linked to effects – yet reason's stake in 'sympathy' ensures something like universality – a universality which will be exploded later in Scottish thought. This causal repetition by 'sympathy' or 'fancy' would also much later be critiqued by the mature Deleuze in un-Humean terms of consistent displacement rather than similitude.[64]

Hume, then, the bedrock of Scottish Enlightenment, self-styled historian and political theorist, is really best approached via the cultural and the literary. And Deleuze's reading of Hume is proactive (one is tempted to say 'deconstructive') in stressing 'a divorce between speech and thought'.[65] *Pace* Derrida's Rousseau, there is no sense that writing is a mature reflection of speech; each has direct effects particular to each.[66] And in his 1989 Preface to the English-language edition, Deleuze reminds us that Hume, by replacing knowledge with belief, underscores the cultural founding of association: '[h]e gave the *association* of ideas its real meaning, making it a practice of cultural and *conventional* formations (conventional rather than contractual), rather than a theory of the human mind'.[67] The mind fleetingly comes into being via belief, anticipation and inventiveness.[68]

Deleuze's Hume is certainly suspicious of the French penchant for the *contractual*, as opposed to the more Scottish *sympathetic*, Enlightenment, the former making society seem abstract and false. Morality thus becomes political and psychological.[69] Deleuze's Hume, though, is also one which, as the hard-fought doctoral thesis of a soon-to-be-major French theorist should tell us, contains within it the seeds of its own downfall; what was left of Hume's universalism has silently fallen apart in culture (and we are now in the luxurious position of seeing how 'universal' isn't really universal: Hume and his peers were riding high on a wave of finance made possible by a horrifically cruel slave trade). Or in more Derridean terms, sympathy has always been inhabited by its own supplementarity: if the person behind the contract isn't clear-cut, then neither is the person behind sympathy.[70] And as Hume's Enlightenment wore on, both the UK and France would play out the drama of this un-universal universality over two centuries in their huge empires. Until, that is, the time of modern Scottish literature.

Culture, to recap, is in Deleuze's Hume a reflection of the passions (sympathy), which transcend and thus fix the mind.[71] Imagination tries to extend its own stability infinitely, making essential use of association.[72] Thus, 'reason is imagination which has become nature'.[73] In the 1740s, during high Unionism among the *literati*, this might have seemed like a neat explanation for natural justice; today, it looks open-ended, theoretical. Even more problematically, the state makes 'general interest', the bogus universal, an object of belief, but commerce is the affirmation of the power of the state, and property requires a state.[74] The fallacy of causality, we can now see, works in the same way as the principle of association becoming reason:[75] reason, rather, should be seen as contingent.[76] Thus Hume makes statehood – and we should rid ourselves of any lingering temptation that Hume was not a thoroughly British Unionist – a prerequisite of converse between property-owning men, the small proportion of the public who constituted the polity. Crucially, property is the driving force for Humean reason:

> The convention of property is the artifice by means of which the actions of each one are related to those of the others. It is the establishment of a scheme and the institution of a symbolic aggregate or of the whole. Hume thus finds property to be a phenomenon which is essentially political – in fact, the political phenomenon par excellence. Property and conversation are joined at last, forming the two chapters of a social science. The general sense of the common interest must be *expressed* in order to be efficacious. Reason presents itself here are the conversation of proprietors.[77]

For Deleuze, writing in 1953, this can be read in terms of a nascent structuralism via which reason is continuously reconstituted. And yet already, '[t]he structuralist *doxa* is fissured and cracked; it envelops lines of flight and plateaus of [invented] compossibilities'.[78] Personhood, moreover, is a struggle for difference (economic, ethical), and is better thought of in terms of 'collective assemblages', 'the qualification of a collection of ideas'.[79] Deleuze's subject is already defined merely by its own movement,[80] and the subject itself, the observer of the cup which may or may not smash the millionth time you drop it, is an invention, a habit formed over time by association.[81] Subjects are made via moral, aesthetic and social judgement; the subject believes and invents, and transcends the given ('the flux of the sensible').[82]

For Deleuze, then, reading deep into Scottish polity against the grain, the problem of the self is moral, political and active in a very different way from the pragmatic uses to which Hume has been put; it is a 'synthesis of the affection and its reflection'.[83] Again, this is close to Macmurray's idea of resistance, in which the subject is constituted through an endless push and pull which never finds a stable resting place.[84] Resonating (unintentionally, one assumes) with Macmurray, the Deleuze scholar Ronald Bogue reminds us that all bodies are simultaneously active and reactive.[85] Hume's double-sidedness rings throughout Scottish theory, especially where reason comes to rest on the institution. John Macmurray, in Deleuze's early days, staunchly set himself against Anglo-British logical positivism and stressed the importance of the tactile where vision-centred theories of perception had tended to dominate.[86] Scottish literature since the early 1960s, like Scottish polity, has struggled to get back *in touch*.

Notes

1. Michael Gardiner, *Modern Scottish Culture* (Edinburgh: Edinburgh University Press, 2005), pp. 1–8.
2. Paul Virilio and Sylvere Lotringer, trans. Mike Taormina, *Crepuscular Dawn* (New York: Semiotext (e), 2002), pp. 13–14.
3. See, for example, Paul Virilio, *Architecture Principe* (1996 [1966]), as excerpted in Steve Redhead, ed., *The Paul Virilio Reader* (Edinburgh: Edinburgh University Press, 2004), pp. 87–92.
4. Virilio and Lotringer, *Crepuscular Dawn*, p. 22.
5. Ibid., p. 34.
6. Ibid., pp. 31, 50.
7. Ibid., pp. 177, 179; cf. Paul Virilio, trans. Chris Turner, *Ground Zero* (London: Verso, 2002).
8. John Macmurray, *The Form of the Personal II: Persons in Relation* (London: Faber and Faber, 1991 [1961]), pp. 66–79.
9. Virilio and Lotringer, *Crepuscular Dawn*, p. 14.

10. Macmurray, *Persons in Relation*, pp. 15–17; cf. Michael Gardiner, ' "A Light to the World": British Devolution and Colonial Vision', *Interventions: International Journal of Postcolonial Studies* 6.2, June 2004, pp. 264–81.
11. Virilio and Lotringer, *Crepuscular Dawn*, pp. 63, 79, 85, 90, 150; for speed as the death of science itself, p. 160; cf. Paul Virilio, *The Lost Dimension* (1991 [1984]), excerpted as 'The Overexposed City', in Redhead, ed., *The Paul Virilio Reader*, pp. 83–99.
12. Virilio and Lotringer, *Crepuscular Dawn*, p. 76.
13. Ibid., p. 141; cf. Paul Virilio, trans. Julie Rose, *The Art of the Motor* (Minneapolis: University of Minnesota Press, 1995 [1993]).
14. Virilio and Lotringer, *Crepuscular Dawn*, p.30; see Ian Hamilton Finlay, in Yres Abrioux, ed. *Ian Hamilton Finlay: A Visual Primer* (Edinburgh: Reaktion, 1985), p. 229.
15. Virilio and Lotringer, *Crepuscular Dawn*, p. 36; ultra-flatness in sculpture is also ironised in Finlay's *Nuclear Sail*, recalling Virilio's description of Mutually Assured Destruction as the technological accident, and Scotland's status as a nuclear target in the nuclear stand-off: Abrioux, ed., *Ian Hamilton Finlay*, p. 179.
16. Virilio and Lotringer, *Crepuscular Dawn*, pp. 66, 162.
17. Ibid., p. 150.
18. Ibid., p. 59.
19. Cf. Michael Gardiner, 'Endless Enlightenment: Eye-Operated Technology and the Political Economy of Vision', *Reconstruction* 4.1, Winter 2004: http://www.reconstruction.ws/041/gardiner.htm.
20. Paul Virilio and Sylvere Lotringer, trans. Mark Polozzitti, *Pure War* (New York: Semiotext(e), 1997 [1983]).
21. Virilio and Lotringer, *Crepuscular Dawn*, pp. 58, 127, 136–40, 163.
22. Ibid., p. 63.
23. Douglas Gordon, *Under Darkness*, discussed variously in Gordon, *Kidnapping* (Eindhoven: Setedlijk Van Abbesmuseum, 1998).
24. Virilio and Lotringer, *Crepuscular Dawn*, pp. 73, 123.
25. Ibid., pp. 151–5, p. 157–9.
26. Ibid., p. 86; cf. Virilio, 'The Overexposed City'.
27. Virilio and Lotringer, *Crepuscular Dawn*, p. 157; Tom McGrath and Gavin Selerie, *The Riverside Interviews* (London: Binnacle Press, 1983), p. 120.
28. Muriel Spark, *Momento Mori* (New York: New Directions, 2000) p. 40; Spark, *The Comforters* (New York: New Directions, 2000); cf. Nicholas Royle, 'Memento Mori', in Martin McQuillan, (ed.) *Theorizing Muriel Spark: Gender, Race, Deconstruction* (Basingstoke: Palgrave, 2002), pp. 189–203.
29. Virilio and Lotringer, *Crepuscular Dawn*, p. 87.
30. Ibid., pp. 70–1; cf. Virilio, 'The Overexposed City'.
31. Virilio and Lotringer, *Crepuscular Dawn*, p. 8.
32. Ibid., pp. 80, 83.
33. Ibid., p. 99.
34. Ibid., pp. 126, 142.
35. On genetic art see, for example, Paul Virilio, trans. Julie Rose, *Art and Fear* (London: Continuum, 2003); cf. Virilio and Lotringer, *Crepuscular Dawn*, pp. 114–15, 117–22, 124–5.

36. G.E. Davie, *The Democratic Intellect* (Edinburgh: Edinburgh University Press, 1981 [1961]); John Macmurray, *The Form of the Personal I: The Self As Agent* (London: Faber and Faber, 1991 [1957]), pp. 196–202; Macmurray, *Persons in Relation*, pp. 176–85; cf. Virilio and Lotringer, *Crepuscular Dawn*, p. 149.
37. Virilio and Lotringer, *Crepuscular Dawn*, p. 156.
38. Cf. ibid., p. 147.
39. Ibid., pp. 101–8.
40. Ibid., p. 127.
41. Ibid., pp. 109, 144.
42. Cf. Jacques Derrida, trans. Peggy Kamuf, ed. Elisabeth Weber, 'Passages – From Traumatism to Promise', in Derrida, *Points . . . Interviews 1974–1994* (Stanford CA: Stanford University Press, 1995), pp. 372–95; cf. Paul Patton, 'Future Politics', in Paul Patton and John Protevi, eds., *Between Deleuze and Derrida* (London: Continuum, 2003), pp. 15–29.
43. Virilio and Lotringer, *Crepuscular Dawn*, pp. 137–8.
44. Gilles Deleuze and Felix Guattari, trans. Brian Massumi, *A Thousand Plateaus: Capitalism and Schizophrenia* (London: Athlone, 1988 [1980]), p. 374; cf. light-speed interfaces 'inhabiting' the body in Paul Virilio, *Polar Interia* (2000 [1990]), especially as excerpted in Redhead, ed., *The Paul Virilio Reader*, pp. 135–53.
45. Virilio and Lotringer, *Crepuscular Dawn*, pp. 172–3.
46. Ibid., p. 162; Miles Glendinning and Aonghus MacKechnie, *Scottish Architecture* (London: Thames and Hudson, 2004) pp. 95–125.
47. C.f. Berthold Schoene, 'The Walking Cure: *Heimat*, Masculinity, and Mobile Narration in Alan Warner's *The Man Who Walks*', *Scottish Studies Review* 7.1, Spring 2006, pp. 95–109.
48. Gilles Deleuze and Felix Guattari, trans. Robert Hurley, Mark Seem and Helen R. Lane, *Anti-Oedipus: Capitalism and Schizophrenia* (Minneapolis: University of Minnesota Press, 1983 [1972]), pp. 1–9; Gilles Deleuze, trans. Daniel W. Smith and Michael A. Greco, *Essays Critical and Clinical* (Minneapolis: University of Minnesota Press, 1997 [1993]), pp. 152–74; Timothy S. Murphy, 'Only Intensities Subsist: Samuel Beckett's *Nohow on*', in eds. Ian Buchanan and John Marks, eds., *Deleuze and Literature* (Edinburgh: Edinburgh University Press, 2000), pp. 229–50; Alan Warner, *The Man Who Walks* (London: Cape, 2002); c.f. Schoene, 'The Walking Cure'; Virilio and Lotringer, *Crepuscular Dawn*, pp. 36–7.
49. See, for example, Paul Virilio, *The Aesthetics of Disappearance* (1991 [1980]), excepted in Redhead, ed., *The Paul Virilio Reader*, pp. 57–81: 66, and many other examples of the 'plagiarism of vision' in Virilio, especially developed in *Polar Inertia* (London: Sage, 2000 [1990]; James Kelman, *A Chancer* (Edinburgh: Polygon, 1985), and many other stories by Kelman; Cairns Craig's discussion of Kelman in 'Resisting Arrest: James Kelman', in eds. Gavin Wallace and Randall Stevenson, eds., *The Scottish Novel Since the Seventies* (Edinburgh: Edinburgh University Press, 1993), pp. 99–114: 106; Michael Gardiner, *The Cultural Roots of British Devolution* (Edinburgh: Edinburgh University Press, 2004), pp. 140–2.

50. See Robyn Marsack, 'A Declaration of Independence: Edwin Morgan and Contemporary Poetry' in. Robert Crawford and Hamish Whyte, eds., *About Edwin Morgan* (Edinburgh: Edinburgh University Press, 1990), pp. 25–38.
51. Gilles Deleuze, trans. Constantin V. Boundas, *Empiricism and Subjectivity: An Essay on Hume's Theory of Human Nature* (New York: Columbia University Press, 1991 [1953]), p. 1.
52. Ibid., p. 67; cf. Macmurray, *The Self as Agent*, pp. 114–15.
53. Deleuze, *Empiricism and Subjectivity*, p. 88.
54. Ibid., p. 88.
55. Ibid., p. 124.
56. Ibid., pp. 68, 67.
57. Ibid., p. 44.
58. Ibid., p. 123.
59. Ibid., p. 9.
60. Ibid., pp. 48–9.
61. Ibid., p. 124; cf. effects posited as an end to action – an implicit critique of utilitarian uses of Hume, p. 125.
62. Ibid., p. 6; cf. Macmurray, *Persons in Relation*, pp.17, 20, 30–3, 184; Macmurray, *Reason and Emotion* (London: Faber, 1992 [1935]), pp. 92–3, 105–8, 113–14.
63. Deleuze, *Empiricism and Subjectivity*, p. 126.
64. Ibid., p. 70; cf. Gilles Deleuze, trans. Paul Patton, *Difference and Repetition* (London: Athlone, 1994 [1968]).
65. Deleuze, *Empiricism and Subjectivity*, p. 3.
66. Cf. Jacques Derrida, trans. Gayatri Chakravorty Spivak, *Of Grammatology* (Baltimore, MD: Johns Hopkins University Press, 1976 [1967]), pp. 142–4; Derrida, 'Dialanguages', trans. Elisabeth Weber, in Derrida, *Points . . . Interviews*, pp. 132–55: 140.
67. Deleuze, *Empiricism and Subjectivity*, p. ix.
68. Ibid., p. 14, cf. p. 67.
69. Ibid., pp. 39, 41, cf. p. 57; but cf. p. 37 on sympathy as aversion to the other's pain.
70. Cf. Jacques Derrida, trans. Peggy Kamuf, *Spectres of Marx: The State of the Debt, the Work of Mourning, and the new International* (London: Routledge, 1994 [1993]).
71. Deleuze, *Empiricism and Subjectivity*, pp. 56–63.
72. Ibid., pp. 59–61.
73. Ibid., p. 65.
74. Ibid., p. 62.
75. Ibid., p. 66.
76. Ibid., pp. 51–3.
77. Ibid., p. 42.
78. Ibid., p. 10.
79. Ibid., pp. 12, 64.
80. Ibid., p. 85; cf. Deleuze and Guattari, *A Thousand Plateaus*, pp. 232–309.
81. Deleuze, *Empiricism and Subjectivity*, pp. 12, 16.
82. Ibid., pp. 86–7.
83. Ibid., p. 64.

84. Macmurray, *Persons in Relation*, pp. 64–85.
85. Ronald Bogue, *Deleuze on Literature* (London: Routledge, 2003), p. 12.
86. Macmurray, *The Self as Agent*, pp. 105–11.

Chapter 2

The Paradox of Scottish Culture: The Twentieth-Century Experience

In the beginning was the word, and the word was *antisyzygy*.

A few decades before the beginning, Patrick Geddes, returning from France, was imagining cities which were effectively made of culture; the term 'Scottish Renaissance' is his. As early as 1877–78 he was attending lectures by *the* nineteenth-century thinker on nations as revived by British theory, Ernest Renan.[1] His contemporaries, the Celtic Revivalists, were rebelling against their immediate predecessors' having been co-opted into kailyard culture, and the labour movement was establishing Glasgow as the socialist capital of Britain, later to culminate in the events of 1919, just before the 'beginning'. Geddes has only fairly recently been recognised as the interdisciplinary thinker he was, to be linked, for example, to G. E. Davie's 1961 *The Democratic Intellect*.[2]

This term antisyzygy was coined in 1919 by G. Gregory Smith,[3] but 'stuck with' the work of the overwhelmingly canonised poet Hugh MacDiarmid. This word was perfect for MacDiarmid, because not only did it sound clever and scientific, no one knew what it meant. More recent critics, having grown up through various waves of this antisyzygy, have tried rethinking the word via theory as *ambivalence*, *ambiguity* or, with reservations, *dialogics*. Whatever twists the term takes (and originally it concerned the alignment of sun, earth and moon, though whether MacDiarmid would have buzzed for this on *University Challenge* is odds-against), in the twenty-first century a retrospective reading might boil it down to the difference between the culture of a nation-state and the culture of a stateless nation, within both of which the people of Scotland live (one can no longer say 'both cultures', since the UK state no longer has anything unified enough to be called a culture). This situation has probably been given its most influential gloss over the intervening decades by Tom Nairn's *The Break-up of Britain*, usually cited as 1979 but actually reaching back via the *New Left Review* to the early 1970s, and describing how a robust national Romanticism failed to appear along with German or even English Romanticism, and collapsed into sentimentality within the security of Union.[4]

MacDiarmid casts his shadow across this whole book, but much of the thought attributed to him, apart from his flawed 'Synthetic Scots' linguistic experiment, can be seen as an amplification of the ideas surrounding the generation of Patrick Geddes after his intellectual travels, his magazine *The Evergreen* (1895–96), interdisciplinary and international, the disingenuously ('ethnically') named 'Celtic Revival' of the 1890s and 1900s, the four-artist group later renamed 'Charles Rennie Mackintosh', and the growth of the labour movement. Here, for the sake of space and the fact that so much time in Scottish Studies has been attributed to the man himself, we will assume that many turn-of-the-century cultural-nationalist ideas pass through the MacDiarmid of the 1920s, to the turn of the 1950s and 1960s, when the man was both rediscovered and questioned. It is worth remembering, moreover, that the evolutionary Geddes was a primary influence behind MacDiarmid's first book, *Annals of the Five Senses* (1923).[5]

Synthetic Scots, as is now recognised, was an attempt to create a grammar and lexicon from archaic forms – a 'language', in other words, which no one spoke. Today, a compromise solution exists in that Broad Scots, as a continuum from the language disappearing when King James I/VI moved his court to London, is seen as having gone underground in 'non-literary' use, and is now used as an umbrella term for the many variations spoken across the country and often described by sociolinguists as dialects.[6] Synthetic Scots was highly problematic, not to say elitist, and found a powerful adversary coming from the un-Scots position of Standard English, in 1936, in one of MacDiarmid's many arch-foes, Edwin Muir.

Edwin and Willa Muir have become best known throughout Ukania and beyond as translators of Franz Kafka.[7] Eleanor Bell nevertheless notes that much of the Kafka translation was done modestly by Willa Muir,[8] a simple fact that warps the entire history of modern Scottish literature, since Kafka's mixture of existentialism and socialism has stayed with Scottish literature through Alexander Trocchi and R. D. Laing to James Kelman. As a reading of antisyzygy, Edwin Muir applies Kafka's aphorism of the man tied to both heaven and earth (where presumably, British imperial diction is heaven and Scottish speech is earth).[9] But Smith's antisyzygy, for Muir, also describes the division between the commonplace, the all-too-present and the literary-mythical, which had been lost, and could never be revived by Synthetic Scots.[10] For Muir, since the Reformation, Scottish fantastic writing (these days we might just say 'fiction') had been mere escapism.[11]

The irony of the twentieth-century situation is that both these consciousness-raisers are saying more or less the same thing. A problem to match Muir's faith in Standard English (SE) arises with MacDiarmid's 'Synthetic Scots' experiment, in trying to set up a standard artificial language on which to base 'a culture': since it relied so heavily on the archaic, it paradoxically had less in common with the way Scottish people spoke than did SE.[12] It was Scots, captain, but not as we know it: it was like expecting present-day inhabitants of Rome to speak like Caesar (or like Caesar using bizarre anachronisms), and then denouncing non-Caesarian linguistic communities as unliterary and unpatriotic and, most damningly, un-Roman. The *mauvaise foi* of Synthetic Scots is exemplified by the way in which a letter 'missing' from SE is shown in MacDiarmid by an apostrophe (for example takin' instead of takin); in fact, this apostrophe dates right back to Allan Ramsay's immediately post-Union 1720s (Ramsay is a classic figure of Nationalist/Unionist wavering), and suggests that Synthetic Scots is less a radical formalist writing than an apologetic realist one in a self-consciously inferior dialect – common among Anglicising Scots of the late eighteenth century. The apostrophe, despite MacDiarmid's overtly Marxist and nationalist stance, *underlines* a belonging to a highly British SE which was dying out fast in speech anyway – suggesting that Muir was right about the impossibility of overcoming the linguistic split under present circumstances. Doubtless large publishers influenced the orthography, but even at the level of later small publishers like Akros, MacDiarmid couldn't resist the SE signifier. The apostrophe for MacDiarmid's Renaissance was a purloined letter which marked a strong British *loyalism* against its best intentions. This haunts the diegetic in Scottish literature right up to the 1970s, always there and not there, proving Britishness at the very moment when it most loudly shouts Scottishness.[13] And man, could MacDiarmid shout.

The irony inhering in this accidental loyalism marks the beginning of the reverse of the eighteenth-century experience. We know that MacDiarmid and writers of the inter-war Renaissance were ferociously pro-Scottish, often active in the nascent SNP, and yet broadly pro-empire, which was thoroughly based on Anglo-British culture. But by the end of MacDiarmid's lifetime most of this empire had decolonised, especially the most long-standing and culturally critical parts, such as India and the Caribbean. Scots were, as we know, at the centre of empire in almost every field, and in the literary field MacDiarmid stands up to be counted in empire – a stance that would undoubtedly alienate him from post-1960s Scottish thought. Does the vertiginous shift in imperial fortunes help to explain MacDiarmid's bitterness towards the Francophile 'vermin' he saw rising up around 1960[14] – the fact that the imperial ideal, and finally not even the consensual British Welfare Statist ideal, could avoid its own unravelling?

From Chapter 1's reading of Hume, we know that culture *is* politics, or, in Scotland at least, should be. And when Britain disappeared, it disappeared culturally, fading with empire and leaving shadow-selves, cardboard people fixated to retro-spectacle, bolting down Ealing comedies with the pleasurable distance of 2000s' eyes, millennial, Saatchi-type Britons, some of whom shared the stomach-turning gravitas of Tony Blair who posed Churchill-style with a bulldog for campaign ads,[15] dined with Oasis and behaved like a normal Third Way guy who could take tough decisions as he went on with Thatcher's dismantling of the Welfare State. And while this book is nominally about Scotland, 85 per cent of the population of Ukania are English, and the 'information bomb' is planted in the proportion of those 85 per cent who either think that Britain is still culturally viable in some way in which the once-imperial borders can still move, like the living-room walls in a 1950s chuckle-flick, or, more commonly, simply fail to comprehend the break-up. Who are these residual 'Britons' and what do they want? Perhaps they feel some empathy with the ancient kingdom of Britain of a thousand years ago. And yet they walk among us, these 'ordinary British folk. What is them? Who do they? And why?'[16]

Edwin Muir was unusual for his time, in that he already had experience of stateless nations via his interest, and residence, in Central Europe. *The* major source of late Renaissance conflict is that, although he agrees with MacDiarmid's edict that poets should go 'back to Dunbar' instead of the post-Union and more pliable Burns, between which two moments the possibility of a Scottish art poetry was Shakespeared away within Eng. Lit.[17] – as indeed was the possibility of any dramatic poetry[18] – Muir remains staunchly opposed to the 'revival' logic of Synthetic Scots. This, of course, is largely what MacDiarmid's experiment was – an idealistic way of looking through old sources and creating a *new* language which would only ever be open to those educated enough to learn it – scarcely a Marxist move, far less a nationalist Marxist one. For Muir, MacDiarmid's Synthetic Scots was narcissistic, underlining the lack of any working Scots which was not confined to a small group. This is the 'twentieth-century condition', and it will lead us to the painful revival of Scots writing in the 1960s and beyond.

The disheartening part of Muir's counter-MacDiarmid argument is that it is also strikingly Eliotic – modern poets experienced a 'dissociation of sensibility' (this is in the SE phrasebook under 'antisyzygy'), a demeaning reading of the bogeyman himself, Burns, who manipulated pop and art registers. In other words, *feeling* was linguistically torn apart from *expression* – in this case corresponding to the languages of Scots and English – so that 'since some time in the sixteenth century Scottish literature has been a literature without a language'.[19] Muir's take on anti-syzygy is insoluble in Scotland, except that he (more properly, 'they') bring(s) experience from Central Europe. He/they then, though, fit(s) the Scottish duality to a terminology which is embarrassingly Eliotic/New Critical, in his/their worry that what has been lost is an 'organic' community. The 'organic' community was famously a favourite fantasy of F. R. Leavis (and indeed of Arthur Quiller-Couch before him: you couldn't fit a razor blade between the two, however excited Leavis was by D. H. Lawrence), and survived all the way through to John Major's fruit-cake version of a pub–church–village green England. But 'organic' is a term to be highly wary of after the advent of theory, with the assumption that communities do not grow 'naturally', but are engineered by institutions ripe for criticism.[20] It is telling that the word *organic* appears repeatedly in Muir's *Scott and Scotland* (1936), as is the loudly voiced worry that 'Scotland was not an organic society'.[21] Muir is almost more Leavisite than Leavis when he states that:

> [t]he reality of a nation's history lies in its continuity, and the present is its only guarantee. English history is real to us, because England as a living organic unity is real to us . . .[22]

Muir's reading of the poetic (that is, early) Walter Scott sets the critical tone for the mid-century: dissociation was already a source of frustration as Scott set about trying to 'save' the ballad tradition, and would remain so.[23] Muir's later novelistic Scott has sensibly recognised that the division can't be fixed, and is already working out his Unionist-Nationalist allegiances in the *Waverley* novels and settling into a failed national Romanticism of the kind later diagnosed by Nairn as setting the tone for the early to mid-nineteenth century.[24] Thus for Muir, 'Scott wrote in a vacuum',[25] or to borrow Cairns Craig's more combative term, was 'out of history'.

Muir even follows Eliot's *Tradition and the Individual Talent* (1919) by demanding that a language express the feelings of 'a whole people',[26] and that the 'national' language is in the representative genius-of-the-race: 'the lack of a whole language . . . finally means the lack of a whole mind'.[27] (Bizarrely, yet still in the key of Eliot, it remains a source of regret to Muir that there was no Scottish Marvell.)[28] The end of the un-dissociated *audience* is, of course, the central theme of *The Waste Land* (and do we need reminding that the Scottish anthropologist J. G. Frazer provided its sourcebook?), and 'a high culture of the feelings as well as the mind', is placed by Muir *and* Eliot in the late sixteenth/early seventeenth century, when the court moved and the Edinburgh *literati* began to adapt to Anglo-Britishness.[29]

For Muir, 'harmony' (another classic Eliotic term) of feeling and thought requires a certain intellectualism, one which we would retrospectively describe as classist, despite similar tendencies in the 'Marxist' MacDiarmid.[30] This harmony fundamentally requires that poetry and prose are to share one canonical language.[31] For Muir, writing in 1936, Robert Fergusson had come closest to creating a critical language in Scots, after which the project had become impossible.[32] Fergusson, nevertheless, leads to Burns, who – and this is one point of contention – keeps Scots alive in folk garments. Yet for the *literati*, Eng. Lit. was built around a Scottish writing so hell bent on becoming correctly English that, as Robert Crawford has described, the origins of the discipline of the discipline of Eng. Lit. itself can largely be described as Scottish.

In the introduction to his 1998 *The Scottish Invention of English Literature*, Crawford stresses that a tradition of English linguistic correctness was part of the Scottish educational mainstream in the late eighteenth century, while in England this was still marginalised in 'dissenting schools', and thus 'how crucial to the origins of the university discipline were issues of perceived marginality in space, gender, and genre'.[33] He reminds us that this whole issue has been missed by Eng. Lit. study, as in Gauri Viswanathan's failure to realise the development of Eng. Lit. in Scotland.[34] (Viswanathan is, of course, a mere sampler: try talking to most postcolonialists about Scotland and they usually only hear the Eric Idle-like cry 'I'm being oppressed!') In late eighteenth-century Scotland, the discipline of 'Rhetoric and Belles Lettres' formed a continuum with later English Eng. Lit. and French antecedents (and Crawford writes from St. Andrews, founded through pressure from the diasporic relationship with Paris, bypassing Oxbridge).[35] William Barron then provided a bridge to James Beattie's famous demolition of Scotticisms in his 'colonization, improvement and rhetoric', stressing 'the superior refinement of the English ear', and his linking of reform in agriculture to reform in literary culture – a common trope in the nascent British empire.[36]

Muir's 1936 book is ostensibly about Walter Scott, but his diagnosis of Scott's dissociation of sensibility became a historiographical standard in Scottish criticism. The book is even more widely about the Renaissance's inevitable petering out, using Scott as an example of the impossible, and giving the lie to the idea of Muir as a Renaissance participant, though he is often cited as such. Muir notes the now commonplace argument that the turn to Union was a pragmatic and thus a selfish one,[37] but since this phase for him is over and Scots language has ceded its ability to communicate, he argues for a conscious turn to SE to express a Scottish sensibility. Thus far, Muir's 'twentieth-century condition' repeats the 'eighteenth-century condition' – but the late twentieth century would move towards a fusion, rather than the eighteenth-century fission which forced writers to take linguistic sides (English for the majority of the ambitious); post-war criticism would be more aware of social contexts, in terms of 'representation' in politics and language.

This section of the chapter, of course, takes its name from David Daiches' seminal *The Paradox of Scottish Culture: The Eighteenth-Century Experience (1964)*, a book with Muir in mind, and in which is identified the political turn to English when Scots fragmented and stopped being the language of choice of the Edinburgh *literati*.[38] The 'problem' of Scots' disappearance is here dated to the middle of the eighteenth century and seen as amplified by educated Edinburgh's overwhelming tendency to side with 'good English'.[39] Here, though, there is a rethinking of the dissociation of sensibility: after Scott's 'sentimental' Jacobitism, if such an epithet must be granted centre stage, Scots was still used in folk culture, and Burns was pressed between a literary hierarchy and a grass-roots activism – since which, for Daiches, rescuing Burns has been a recurrent theme of Scottish criticism.[40] Both MacDiarmid and Muir, we might say, failed to spot this.

Of course, the most illustrious of the Edinburgh *philosophes* was, even while professing patriotism in Scotland and France, caught up in the Anglophilia Daiches identifies as the eighteenth-century Scottish disease: for David Hume, Scots was a 'very corrupt dialect', an attitude which was passed down via his and Adam Smith's students, through the examples Crawford cites, to produce the schism between speech and feeling of which Muir never stops talking – that is, writing.[41] For Daiches, at some point 'Scottish nationalism in the eighteenth century inevitably became associated with antiquarianism' (note the 'associated with', not 'equal to'), and 'if the Union of 1707 made possible a special kind of national feeling, it also created conditions which restricted its effective working in Scottish culture'.[42] Daiches wrote this around the time when it started to be undone.

Daiches is also keen to stress that the Edinburgh *literati* did believe in natural good – their switch to the more international language of English was not simply Machiavellian – and moreover that they saw Scotland as vindicated by its moral duty in Union (a point that a look at educational traditions will back up).[43] Daiches' Burns moves deftly between lowlands oral literature and the emerging English Literature of Edinburgh. Gaelic makes up the third term of the triumvirate, paid lip-service but ignored by Edinburgh – just before idiot readings of Smith's free trade would almost wipe out the language.[44] For Daiches the attitude of the encyclopaedising

Edinburgh Enlightenment fitted the contintental fascination between the primitive and the polished, and he duly cites Adam Smith's 1767 *Considerations concerning the first Formation of Languages* as something like what would become philology (an Anglo-British origin of the study of English Literature).[45] Hume, in his paradoxical double role as a sceptical humanist and a thoroughgoing racist, amplifies this contrast, and his death before Burns (and thus the loss of the chance to put right any notion of Burns as noble savage) accounts for the misreading of Burns as yokel, and inaugurates the period from Hume to Scott as the death-knell for a native Romantic literature in Scots.[46] Alan Riach's 2005 study has gone much of the way to filling this perceived gap, seeing Scott's heroes' duality developing in multiple, modern ways.[47]

But in retrospect we can see how for Muir, Burns, the anachronistically national poet but a product of his time, was already 'dissociated'; his thought and his emotion were split, and he was unable to use Scots as *prose*. (Burns' cottage is for Muir a suburban eyesore, the Burns cult a heritage-based movement rather than a literary one).[48] Although Muir states that Burns was 'the greatest individual genius of Scottish poetry', by the time Burns came on the scene the un-dissociated lyric had already perished, and he was relegated to 'folk poetry' or 'song', nullifying his literary effect.[49] For Muir there was simply no viable literary Scots prose available, whether creative or academic. This now seems a dubious statement, especially given that Muir was writing directly after the publication (1932–34) of Lewis Grassic Gibbon's *A Scots Quair*, now recognised as a highly successful attempt to create a narrative Scots prose.

Muir, though, saw Scotland, somewhat cryptically, Eliotically and within the mentality of Eng. Lit. – which took poetic greatness as a marker of civility – as 'civilized but without that living spirit of civilization which creates its own centre of life'.[50] Because of the dissociation, for Muir Scots prose could not be sufficiently 'poeticised'[51] – a contentious argument which, even if true, was, as I hope to show, exploded in the 1960s – my first example being Muriel Spark. For Muir, unlike Daiches, the dissociation goes way back to the pre-Union of Crowns, not merely pre-Enlightenment, but to the 'strict surveillance of Calvinism' and the Reformation in general;[52] from the late 1950s, though, Spark shows that a Catholic poeticism, and one with a sense of humour, has remained perfectly possible.[53]

If the separation of language and aesthetic intention represents dissociation, there is definitely a 'reassociation' in the 1970s, when a common 'language' (albeit a more various one than that envisaged by either MacDiarmid or Scott) begins to return in writers such as Alan Spence, Tom Leonard, and then Agnes Owens and James Kelman. As the

Eliotic tone suggests, Muir's work on Scott is double-edged: it may have been a necessary correction to any remaining self-congratulation over the Renaissance of the 1920s, but it becomes disingenuous when it strengthens its insistence on English over Scots 'dialect' as a (Freudian) return to civilisation, equating the use of Scots dialect with an infantile regression:

> Dialect is to a homogeneous language what the babbling of children is to the speech of grown men and women . . . it is blessedly ignorant of the wider spheres of thought and passion . . . Scottish dialect poetry is a regression to childhood . . .[54]

and thus:

> when we insist on using dialect for restricted literary purposes we are being true not to the idea of Scotland but to provincialism, which is one of the things that have helped destroy Scotland.[55]

Muir moreover links the infantilisation of the language to geographical splits in Scottish thinking (thus anticipating Daiches' tripartite model, albeit with a more pessimistic mindset: too much time in Prague pubs perhaps), and this he literally maps out, in a borrowed car, in *Scottish Journey* (1935).[56] He agrees with London travel agents that the post-Clearance Highlands and Islands come out best as 'real' Scotland (because they are more 'Celtic', 'Gaelic', 'organic', 'natural', etc., etc.), but in any case, the nation is knackered. Only Orkney receives five stars, while the nation's largest city and its environs are, as for MacDiarmid, an urban hell. This may be, as Edwin Morgan suggests, an analogue of Muir's own Edenic 'fall' from Orkney, seen very much in those biblical terms, to his urban university days.[57] (Muir's *Essays on Literature and Society* are highly Christian, and Christianity seems to offer escape from an impending disaster.)[58] For Muir, the capital is acceptable as long as you avoid the Old Town and Leith Walk – Leith Walk always being in for it in Scottish literature.[59] Muir's Edinburgh would reappear as a parody of middle-class views of the 1930s Old Town in Spark's 1961 *The Prime of Miss Jean Brodie*. His separation of Edinburgh into different 'races' would receive a much more vicious answer in Irvine Welsh's colonial nightmare *Marabou Stork Nightmares* (1995), and his classism is exploded in *Trainspotting* (1993), where there is no longer any economic 'demand' for a station in which to spot trains from the Walk.

Similarly the New Town, although *newer*, is for Muir contradictorily more 'historic', for what are pretty clearly reasons of social class.[60] The New Town was, of course, built on the prosperity that 'rational', 'clear-sighted' Edinburgh *literati* and Glasgow commercialists had gained from

American tobacco investments which involved the packing of slaves into ships in conditions which drove them to madness and suicide.[61] Information on slavery, though, seems to be missing from all the 'historical' brochures provided by the Visit Scotland or Historic Scotland sites, which are full of crypto-racial 'Celtic' schmaltz: perhaps interested readers would like to let them know about this oversight, which they would doubtless be happy to amend; contact details are in the note here.[62] Nor is the 'economic base' of the Edinburgh *literati* mentioned by many of the most distinguished Enlightenment scholars, who link the idea of the 'Enlightenment' to that of the 'historical', whereas recent criticism seems to be leading to the conclusion that the Enlightenment was when a national Scottish history slipped its moorings.[63]

Alternatively: whose history is more historical? Why (and please ask an Edinburgh tour bus guide this question) does history occur in certain well-noted places and not in others? What is it that's happening in those other places if not history? History has been hijacked, and Scots hijacked it themselves, gave it away, then covered their tracks. *Was ist Aufklärung* indeed. The lack of willingness to look the Enlightenment's imperialist-classist place in this non-historicity in the eyeballs (Michael Fry's account doesn't count here, being a *celebration* of individual imperial 'successes')[64] is disastrous in a post-devolution, post-theory age. Blinded by the humanistic successes of the Enlightenment, we still seem to be struggling to get over its violence – yet Scottish literary thought has been urging us to do just that.

On the road, scunnered

The consequences of Muir's mobile anxiety over lost origins comes more into focus if we look at his *Scottish Journey* (1935) in relation not to J. B. Priestley's marshmallow-flavoured Anglo-British *English Journey* (1934), beloved of idiot prime ministers, to which book Muir's was nominally a 'reply'; Muir's journey might be better compared to George Orwell's much more specifically *English* (thus comparably un-British) journey, his Muir-like take on the modern, *Coming Up For Air* (1939).[65] Where for Muir, in unappetising fashion, central Scotland's pit bings are a 'substitute for nature', Orwell's George Bowling faces a very similar industrialisation of an England he thought was his – and Orwell, via the disaffection of Bowling, astutely recognises this as a phase in the economic rationalisation of capital – perhaps also begging questions about the role of English Romanticism.[66] Orwell's narrator, also in his forties, also alone in his slow-moving jalopy and world-weary, in need of a de-modernising, de-dissociating tonic, and revisiting unevenly remembered territory, views the loss of his England, in the Little England sense, ruined by empire, British standardisation and the tendency of industry to organise – or lay waste to – entire lives according to a twisted reading of Adam Smith's 'demand':

> [t]he very thought of going back to Lower Binfield had done me good already. You know the feeling I had. Coming up for air! . . .
>
> But where was Lower Binfield? Where was the town I used to know? It might have been anywhere. All I knew was that it was buried somewhere in that sea of bricks. Of the five or six factory chimneys that I could see, I couldn't even make a guess at which belonged to the brewery. Towards the eastern end of the town there were two enormous factories of glass and concrete. That accounts for the growth of the town, I thought . . .
>
> [n]early the whole of what used to be old Brewer's land had been swallowed up in the Council housing estate. The Mill Farm had vanished, the cow-pond where I caught my first fish had been drained and filled up and built over, so that I couldn't even say exactly where it used to stand. It was all houses, houses, little red cubes of houses all alike, with privet hedges and asphalt paths leading up to the front door. Beyond the Council Estate the town thinned out a bit, but the jerry-builders were doing their best. And there were little knots of houses dumped down here and there, wherever anybody had been able to buy a plot of land, and makeshift roads leading up to the houses, and empty lots with builders' boards, and bits of ruined fields covered with thistles and tin cans . . .
>
> . . . I'd come to Lower Binfield with a question in my mind. What's ahead of us? Is the game really up? Can we get back to the life we used to live, or is it gone for ever? Well, I'd had my answer. The old life's finished, and to go about looking for it is just waste of time.[67]

For Orwell, one of a tiny band of writers of his time to recognise England as a nation with no state,[68] the problem lies in the suddenly accelerated alienated labour built on the needs of British empire and then a war economy – a problem which would be critiqued in Scottish Situationism and play after the work ethic. Ugly suburbs have been thrown up during an edgy wait for the coming conflict – itself, of course, a result of an unworkable treaty following the previous world war, based in turn on a pure imperial rivalry in which Britain – and not his beloved Little England – took part.

In terms of the coming war, Muir certainly had four years' grace on Orwell – the 'friendly fire' is already exploding around Bowling's ears – but Muir has, like Orwell's Bowling, witnessed the relative failure of party political Nationalism between 1927 and 1934, when the Scottish National Party was turned into a heritage-based, anti-Catholic farce, giving itself no chance of recouping a national culture or addressing

Scotland's higher proportions of unemployment, far less imposing a presence on Westminster. It is possible that these failures added to the literary and political Nationalist MacDiarmid's creative breakdown in 1935, the year *Scottish Journey* appeared.

Orwell's Bowling's description above is matched uncannily (four years before) by Muir in the latter's description of new public housing, for example in Prestwick Road and Knightswood:

> The main road that now runs through both towns [Ayr and Prestwick], strung with houses all the way, is a glaring concrete waste, and the soil round about it has the angry inflamed look which one often finds in raw new suburbs . . .
> [t]hese suburbs [Knightswood] are no worse really than most of the suburbs that unevenly sprawl out of London on every side over the country; they have the same awkward intrusive air, as if they had pushed out farther than they intended, and were dismayed at finding themselves among fields.[69]

This Muir fits into the historiography of the 'manic' Jacobite collecting of Walter Scott's Abbotsford, which in turn fits too well into the classifying tradition from the Enlightenment, a periodisation which Murray Pittock has stretched forward the length of the nineteenth century.[70] In Muir's Scott's *The Heart of Midlothian*, Scotland reaches its most Anglicised, on the way to *Redgauntlet*, finally throwing in the towel of dissociation in 1824. Within the light of this 'convergence' or absorption we could read the second novel of Irvine Welsh – that illiterate hooligan of the chemical generation (etc., etc.) – its parodic colonial journey to the home ground of Heart of Midlothian football club.[71]

Nevertheless, Muir rightly notes that Scottish Christianity has tended to be more socialist and trade Union-oriented. However, it saw its aims compromised in a way to which there was no serious party-political alternative.[72] His problem in 1935 is that the poor are becoming a caste unto themselves rather than developing a class consciousness (though unlike Orwell, and despite translating Kafka, Muir was not a committed socialist anyway). This caste-creation he witnesses in the existence of pure, unabashed slums like Kilmarnock.[73] Similarly – with great insight and yet still somehow myopic to the class-fix and unionism involved in the process – Muir recognises the capital standardisation of central Scotland as a kind of 'second clearance' to follow the Highland Clearances for which the Enlightenment paved the way:

> At present, on a far bigger scale, a silent clearance is going on in industrial Scotland, a clearance not of human beings, but of what they depend upon for life.[74]

But it's in Glasgow that things get really nasty – ironically, the site of a language revival less than three decades later. In 1935 for Muir Glasgow speech is 'vile',[75] an inflammatory statement which provides a good marker to the beginning of the reverse eighteenth-century condition and the move towards the 1960s and 1980s Renaissances in which the dialectic between Glasgow speech and writing would re-emerge. After the post-Muir incursion into the literary of the language spoken by most people, in the terms of Deleuze and Guattari, '[c]ulture didn't belong to a particular elite anymore; it had been opened out'.[76] But in 1935 Scotland's high unemployment rate, economic stagnation and general industrial filth vindicate Muir's disdain. Surprisingly not making the socialist/existentialist connection, the slum is the kind of environment in which the dweller is 'always guilty' or 'always in danger', the kind of situation Muir has (partly) rendered into English from Kafka.[77] Glasgow's only saving grace is that unlike the mines, the site of the Second Clearances, the shipyards are clean[78] and could still be (and he we can be sure here that he isn't a socialist) revived by another war.[79]

Throughout the journey Muir retains the assumption that Glasgow was a clear beneficiary of Union: '[i]t was the Union with England that first started Glasgow on its road to prosperity'.[80] In the classic Whig-historiographical style latched onto by Unionist scholars on both sides of the border, Muir recalls pre-Union Glasgow's famines, depressions and various states of ignorance. Only reason – in the shape of what would become Daiches' Edinburgh *literati* – prevented starvation (and not, for example, slave labour).[81] Again, though, this classism is double-edged: *pace* G. E. Davie to come, Muir sees philosophy as an everyday activity among Scots of all classes, so that crucially, Union has always contained its own critique from the beginning, since, unlike commonsensical and traditionalist England, 'everyone [in Scotland], however illiterate, has a distant knowledge of, and respect for, logic'.[82]

Where Edinburgh is associated with rank, Glasgow is associated with equality; Edinburgh snobbery, Glasgow materialism.[83] The winner, of course, is not a member of this *faux* duality, but the Highlands. The analogy is for Muir a full-on racial one: Glaswegians are small, Highlanders sturdy – a thoroughly neo-kailyard and Anglo-Victorian trope.[84] Industrialisation thus, in a dubiously Darwinian argument, is simply a waste of good DNA.[85] Muir does note, though, that the loyal wee Glasgow Orangeman (*sic*) is fighting for a cause – the remains of empire – which also, ironically, enslaves him.[86]

His geopoetics of the Highlands nevertheless has two problems: firstly, actually getting there involves going through the ugliest parts of the country (Dundee is fingered as the worst, an ironic point since the publisher D. C. Thomson was around that time setting itself up as the archetypical chronicler of the neo-imperialist, Protestant Scottish experience);[87] and second, that Scottish resorts tend to allow English resorts, and even English education, to shift *en masse*, manners and all, up north, creating a culture clash in the vacuum created by the Clearances.[88] Muir also however sees sectarianism as more pronounced up north, and points out an interesting link between subdued light and Calvinism.[89] After an exposition of the Clearances in which he points out that crofters were turned into trespassers on their own land, he asserts that Highlanders are still 'easier to speak to', and more civil in general. The result, of course, is a solidification of the Enlightenment division between the Gaeltacht, the Lowlands and the Edinburgh *literati*, a problem to be given centre stage in literary criticism by Daiches' *Burns* (1950), and to lead on to *The Eighteenth-Century Experience*. In the face of this division, Muir gave up on a solution just after MacDiarmid had tried to create a dialectial whole: '[f]rom this indistinct and yet vivid image I tried to extract a picture of Scotland as an entity, but I did not succeed'.[90]

   This is the scunneration for which Muir is famous, and yet, in describing it, he achieves about the same as the dozens of doctoral students since, who have sought to 'problematise' Scotland by describing it as 'a land of many parts'. Tellingly, Eleanor Bell points out that 'what, at least at times, unites both writers [MacDiarmid and Muir] is the need for Scotland to be depicted as an organic community to escape from its political and cultural predicaments'.[91] This has for both, in retrospect, a Unionist tinge, that of the Leavises and New Criticism – the difference being that the latter already had a socially proven canon, effective at home (Anglo-Britain) and in empire, which merely needed to be refined (or, by F. R. Leavis's perverse logic, revamped). Scotland had, and in the 2000s still has, no such long-running and stable canon to be called upon – though some quarters are trying to develop one. What Muir is crying out for is a cultural solution, and, not surprisingly given the time (1935), he doesn't find it in party Nationalism. Viewed through the lens of his co-translations of Kafka, though, it is possible to read *Scottish Journey* as the problem of a single 'people' trapped in a land of slums, barbarism and division, like the over-surveillant antechambers of Czech boarding-houses, in which guilt is always already present. This landscape, literary- and geo-, would of course change with the Second World War. For literary thought, it would modernise rapidly in the early Welfare State.

Whose second life?

MacDiarmid's 'rediscovery' dates back to as early as his collection *A Kist of Whistles* in 1947, ostensibly 'New Poems', though mostly recycled earlier work.[92] The 'Second Scottish Renaissance', however, didn't really take hold until a group of poets, including T. S. Law, Alexander Scott and Sydney Goodsir Smith, had re-absorbed MacDiarmid's Synthetic Scots. The mid-period MacDiarmid seemed to have given up on lineation altogether, presenting facts towards a dialectic of information.[93] 'The Kind of Poetry I Want' is lineated with the subtlety of a Glasgow ned throwing bricks at derelict windows.[94] Yet the rebirth of Synthetic Scots, despite MacDiarmid himself now frequently writing in English, was perhaps never more influential than the time of the well-known survey *Hugh MacDiarmid: a Festschrift* (1962).[95] In his contribution to this volume, George Bruce describes MacDiarmid as 'the poet who now dominates the imagination in Scotland'.[96] So does the second public literary life of the 1960s belong to MacDiarmid? Was Synthetic Scots to be taught in schools instead of English by 2000?

Tom Hubbard shrewdly suggests the term 'reintegrated Scots', rather than Synthetic Scots or Lallans, to reaffirm a continuity with the single language MacDiarmid had attempted to recreate, rather than a written engagement with spoken language.[97] Hubbard also claims that Scots was now, in the face of English alternatives, a kind of cultural unconscious. This though, as in Muir, is disingenuous; for example, read through Deleuze, it means that Scots delivers blasts of guilt, or lack, to the conscious (English) mind at key moments, and has no higher aim.[98] If the topology conscious/unconscious is co-opted to serve capitalist 'desire' ('demand') – which Deleuze and Guattari's *Anti-Oedipus* argued it had – then the scrambling around for childlike babble which is Scots would merely play into the hands of a something missing held by some higher power. It would be an admission of loss, eighteenth-century style.

During the 'second Renaissance' the term Lallans – intended to point out those 'speakers' of a specific form of Lowland Scots – became *in toto* the title of a journal running from 1973 to the present – flying the flag for the southernmost area of the Muir/Daiches schema and more seriously attempting a recovery of the register of the border ballads. Gaelic's 'renaissance' was much slower; despite positive noises made by MacDiarmid, it has taken the more recent fame of Sorley Maclean to bring Gaelic literature back into serious consideration. (Maclean has been a Nobel Prize candidate: his importance in a language community this small is hard to overstate.) More noxiously though, during the Second

Renaissance, the tripartite cultural schema somehow got converted into the 'three languages of Scotland' model, a persistent but infuriating divvy-up considering the high levels of immigration to the UK from the 1950s to the present. Which of Scotland's 'three languages' is attributed to your neighbour in Pollokshields whose native language is Arabic? Scottish literary anthologies from about 1960–2000 used the pseudo-multiethnic 'three languages' model to ignore that neighbour, or make sure that she writes in Scots. Most immigrants after 1947 (India/ Pakistan) and 1962 (the Caribbean), perhaps unsurprisingly, settled in London.

Alastair Mackie's Second Renaissance *Sing a Sang o' Scotland* (1944) actually slightly pre-dates MacDiarmid's 'new' collection of poems (and the loss of India) and might be seen as the first work of the Second Renaissance; the most important successors in the tradition are usually seen as Robert Garioch, Sydney Goodsir Smith and Douglas Young. Garioch goes back, *pace* MacDiarmid, before Burns, to George Buchanan, to render into 'reintegrated Scots' Buchanan's Latin versions of *Jephthah The Baptist* (1959). For Hubbard, these versions, taken together with Douglas Young's *The Puddock* (1957) and *The Burdies* (1959), is demonstrative of the kind of Scottish humanism G. E. Davie would soon describe as a 'democratic intellectual' history.[99] Davie's tradition is indeed described by Hubbard as having been kept alive by artists of the 1940s and early 1950s who were left unpublished largely because they were working-class and left-wing and excluded from the business (thus accounting for the post-1935 hiatus).

Sydney Goodsir Smith, a makar who was most certainly not working-class, made important contributions with *The Deevil's Waltz* (1946), *Under the Eildon Tree* (1948) and the verse drama *The Wallace* (1960). But the two poets identified by Hubbard as being closest to MacDiarmid's ideal diction are T. S. Law and Tom Scott.[100] Scott took very seriously MacDiarmid's stricture to go 'back to Dunbar', writing a scholarly account of the poet (1966) which should be placed within the context of his own Scots poetry, for example, *Ode Til a New Jerusalem* (1956), *The Ship and ither Poems* (1963), *At the Shrine o the Unkent Sodger* (1968), *The Two* (1977) and *The Dirty Business* (1986). But perhaps Scott's most important work is *Brand the Builder* (1975), which pits the townsfolk of St. Andrews against the Reformers and Anglicisers, and could be seen to link the pre-Reformationist Muir to working-class novels of the 1990s. Some Second Renaissance poets (one thinks of Garioch's Edinburgh) took the dangerously un-MacDiarmid step of going urban. Both Muir's and MacDiarmid's Glasgow-phobia, we should remember, is despite Glasgow's position as Britain's most thoroughly socialist city, its becoming in the nineteenth century home to

Irish and Highland refugees from British *laissez-faire* policies, and its centrality to the old Labour Party.

For Law, following MacDiarmid's (and later, Edwin Morgan's) early Soviet revolutionary sympathies, the freedom of the people is dependent on the freedom of the poet. Law has published widely in magazines like *Lallans* and *Akros*, but what marks the post-war makars in general is that at collection-length they are often self-published or published by specific organs geared towards Scots work, suggesting a paradoxical lack of concern with the 'popular'. Synthetic Scots is certainly not what people spoke in the twentieth century. In a mode of compromise, two poets working in a mixture of English and Scots were Walter Perrie (*A Lamentation for the Children*, 1977 and Ian Bowman (*Orientations*, 1977). Described by Hubbard as 'trilingual' (again, one wearily assumes English, Scots and Gaelic, rather than Urdu, Chinese and Jamaican Creole) are the poets George Campbell Hay and William Neill, who meet in the anthology *Four Points of a Saltire* (1970).

At one point there seemed, then, a possible line of flight in which criticism saw crypto-Synthetic Scots and neo-MacDiarmid work as a progressive route out of Eng. Lit. For Maurice Lindsay in 1977, not only was the First Renaissance entirely successful, any attempt to write in anything but Synthetic Scots would lead to nothing more than an 'English-based, local Scots *patois*'.[101] Lindsay's anthology of six years earlier, for use in schools and thunderingly entitled *Voices of our Kind*, makes a point of emphasising Scots-writing poets ('us').[102] Alexander Scott's *Modern Scots Verse* (1978) is virtually dedicated to MacDiarmid's various periods, which are held in place by other Scots writers.[103] Alexander Scott's 1970 *Contemporary Scottish Verse* is tempered by being co-edited by Norman MacCaig, and the editors have taken a head-stagger by finishing with Kenneth White – a figure frowned upon in polite society until much later.[104]

If there is an adversarial Scots/English debate at this point, Edwin Morgan is an important player in progressive verse in both 'modes', after having came through a New Apocalyptic phase (which doesn't seem to have done him any harm poetically). His epochal and non-Synthetic Scots *The Second Life* appeared in 1968,[105] the year of the May Uprisings in Paris. Morgan and Ian Hamilton Finlay are among many attempting to give a different form of 'second life' (the phrase is Morgan's: the title is a trick question) to a Scotland limited by the tripartite linguistic model and an unwillingness to look outwards (abroad, or just out of the window, where brown people are talking). For Morgan, Scotland's confused linguistic situation is 'a blessing in disguise', multiplying possibilities.[106]

MacDiarmid's personal reputation continued to be pushed by the journal *Akros*, largely an organ of Second Scottish Renaissance poets. Although other Scottish modernisms made it look slightly antique on occasion, *Akros* remained a determined MacDiarmid/Renaissance vehicle, and is probably the best-known Scottish journal of the 1970s to deal purely with poetry. Biographical praise reached a peak in the special double number of *Akros* in 1970, which contains a vast and largely pictorial interview by Duncan Glen.[107] If MacDiarmid has missed the early hints of theory which were circulating in 1970, it is in large part because he has stuck to the idea that the figure of the poet guarantees the aesthetics. His supporters remained enthusiastic about the centrality of the author, as in Duncan Glen's *Hugh MacDiarmid and the Scottish Renaissance* (1964), which systematically accounts for the 1920s/ 1930s phenomenon by placing it both relative to the ethico-politics of Scots language and within a history 'from Stevenson to Spence'.[108] But in Glen's 1970 *Akros* interview MacDiarmid states, with a disingenuous support for New Criticism, that 'my man is Pound', and claims for himself a similar 'bardic' position in society.[109] The bard is the figure that 'the people' turn to when they lose faith in God; Hugh was therefore chosen over Christopher, since it denotes the poet's own divine wisdom.[110] (In *The Riverside Interview* Tom McGrath offers a corrective to the Poundian influence: 'I'm very cynical about MacDiarmid; I think he was looking for a great name to acknowledge and Pound filled that role'.)[111]

Meanwhile, Ian Hamilton Finlay's *Glasgow Beasts* (1962) refused the 'Synthetic Scots' model *tout court* and presented instead a bestiary of bachles accompanied by papercut pictures.[112] His stanzaic book *The Dancers Inherit the Party* appeared at the same time, and Finlay went on to produce hand-made poetry from around 1962 and sculpture, later hugely popular, from around 1966. Edwin Morgan's concrete poetry also became widely known from the early 1960s, consolidating his non-concrete work. In its MacDiarmid interview year of 1970, *Akros* also acceded to a 'Visual Number', publishing Morgan's important essay on concrete poetry, 'Into the Constellation'.[113]

By this time MacDiarmid's defensiveness towards the new critical modernism had developed into open warfare. When Edwin Morgan had reviewed *Glasgow Beasts* for *New Saltire* in 1961, he had asked 'Who will publish Scottish poetry?', commenting on the need for publishing reform within a system uneasy with experiment. One answer would come in the form of Finlay's influential and groundbreaking journal *Poor.Old.Tired.Horse* (1962–67), which continued the work of Alexander Trocchi's *Merlin* (1952–55) in forging links with American Beat writers and contemporary European poets, but there were many other, smaller answers. MacDiarmid's resistance to what he saw as a slip in standards spilled over during a now famous international writers' meeting at the Writers' Conference of the Edinburgh Festival in 1962, organised by the publisher John Calder, where MacDiarmid harangued as feckless and unpatriotic bohemians Trocchi, who collaborated in a pan-Scottish internationalist rebellion taking in R. D. Laing[114] and William Burroughs.[115] The 'beatnik' jibe would later be taken at face value by Morgan and given a comic-serious reply in 'The Beatnik in the Kailyaird' (1962),[116] suggesting a decisive split, and the attack on Finlay was intensified by MacDiarmid in *the ugly birds without wings* (1962).[117] Morgan's main point in his essay, nevertheless, is not MacDiarmid-bashing but that MacDiarmid has understandably over-reacted to the nostalgia of kailyard:

> In its excitement at having established a new literature – *A Drunk Man Looks at the Thistle*, *A Scots Quair*, *Under the Eildon Tree*, *Carotid Cornucopius*, *In Memoriam James Joyce* – the Scottish Renaissance has begun to loosen its hold on life . . . I am certain that Scottish literature is being held back, and young writers are slow to appear, not only because of publishing difficulties but also because of a prevailing intellectual mood of indifferentism and con-servatism, a desperate unwillingness to move out into the world with which every child at school now is becoming familiar . . .'[118]

For Morgan as early as 1970, this unwillingness to get into the world arises from a fear of rethinking what it might mean to be Scottish.[119] In the online journal *flashpoint*, Mark Scroggins quotes MacDiarmid in his *Letters* (1970) predictably attacking Ian Hamilton Finlay's *Glasgow Beasts*, and less predictably, still defending the Synthetic Scots experiment at all costs – with a now rather panicky turn in its radical élitism: '[Finlay's *Glasgow Beasts* is] not the kind of Scots in which high poetry can be written, and what can be done to it . . . is qualitatively little, if at all, above Kailyard level.'[120] On the contrary, for Morgan, 'Ian Finlay shows that the word Beat is not merely a journalistic gimmick',[121] but rather blends lyricism and constructivism.[122]

Morgan has spoken more diplomatically about the ambivalent osmotic influence of MacDiarmid, acknowledging his importance in terms much more qualified than those of the poets of the Second Renaissance. At times Morgan does share the project of going back through Scottish literature extensively and critically, and experimenting with 'vernacular' dialects. As Robert Crawford argues in a Morgan-dedicated issue of the journal *Chapman*, Morgan's work has in this sense acted as a unifier for post-Renaissance Scottish culture.[123] Unlike, for example, Ian Hamilton Finlay, Morgan has praised MacDiarmid's interdisciplinarity, in essays collected in *Crossing the Border*,[124] and has more generally been mindful of the voicelessness which preceded the 1920s. But a move now could be made towards the language heard all around: '[t]he MacDiarmid "renascence" of a general synthetic Scots fifty years ago can still be felt, and learned from, but the move should now be towards the honesty of actual speech'.[125] This kind of poetry he finds, for example, in Tom Leonard.[126]

Another critical moment came when an essay on David Hume by MacDiarmid was commissioned for *New Saltire*. After the journal's administrative committee rejected it as unsuitable for publication, Giles Gordon, later Scotland's most influential literary agent, resigned as co-editor and published the essay himself as a pamphlet.[127] One contention of this book is that looking Hume in the eyeballs has been as important for Scottish thinkers as, for example, those of Rousseau for French thinkers. Blocking such publications holds off post-Enlightenment criticism only momentarily – and even MacDiarmid was willing to take such a reading on, although Hume is predictably 'the greatest Scot ever'. Again there is a large conceptual debt to empire, and specifically to 'race'. The idea of creating a Synthetic Scots from archaic sources equates the Scot now with the Scot of the past, a solid link which we could only describe as ethnocentric (and can only ever describe as ethnocentric without statehood – thus Scotland *is de facto* racist, never mind the journalistic war of statistics).

Meanwhile Morgan was finding in Russian high modernism a rethinking of precisely those issues of continuous identity failing in the Anglo-American New Critical canon – with T. S. Eliot as ever a pivotal figure and Pound the ideologue-king of strong-ego – turning modernity into a lament appealing back to a lost great tradition:

> Ezra Pound was once, like Mayakovsky, extremely active in telling people to 'make it new', yet with the passage of time Pound's work seems more and more to be being sucked back into the late Victorian romanticism it tries to burst out of. Pound, of course, although he contributed to Wyndham Lewis's vorticist, sub-futurist magazine *Blast* in 1914–15, was no futurist, and Wyndham Lewis's description of him as 'demon pantechnicon driver, busy with the removal of old world into new quarters' is a telling pointer to the gulf between Pound's modernism and that of his Russian contemporaries.[128]

Thus,

> For example [Pasternak's and the later Neruda's poetry] is poetry with a sense of history, and it is suffused – ironic lesson to the West – with an awareness of the individual's place in history . . . a modernity which has 'come through' . . .[129]

Morgan has thus stressed the political potential of the imagery, which Eliot and others merely presented as the remnants of a damaging Industrial Revolution. His poetry fits into a descent from Mayakovsky and Russian, European and South American modernism, yet is fixed to the Scottish experience around him, especially that of Glasgow. As Rory Watson says: '[in *The Second Life*] Wordsworth's daffodils and Baudelaire's building sites rub shoulders with "yellow tower cranes", and Morgan can find the capacity for wonder and delight in them all'.[130]

This moral preference for Eastern European modernism over Anglo-American modernism is explored in Colin Nicholson's recent study of Morgan.[131] As well as being a 'Morgan survey', and stressing that Morgan's is a *re*reading of modernism, and not merely outdated modernism, as some critics persist in thinking, what we will be taking from Nicholson's study later is his relation of Morgan's translations to crucial moments of the Scottish labour movement. And although Morgan himself (as does Finlay) rejects restrictive political descriptions, we can see a strong seam of neo-Marxism running through his creative and critical work, one which holds speech and writing in a dialectic. It may have been in failing to recognise a new neo-Marxism in pursuit of nationalism at all costs that made the 1950s–1970s Second Scottish Renaissance forget the imperative of the dialectic altogether.

Notes

1. Kenneth White, *On Scottish Ground: Selected Essays* (Edinburgh: Polygon, 1998), p. 124; on the need to see Geddes in terms of *poetics*, see p. 135; on Geddes' attempts to persuade Mahatma Gandhi to reorganise the evolutionary sciences, see p. 143; on Renan's primacy in theory, see 'What is a Nation', in Homi Bhabha, ed., *Nation and Narration* (London: Routledge, 1990), pp. 8–22.
2. George Elder Davie, *The Democratic Intellect: Scotland and her Universities in the Nineteenth Century* (Edinburgh: Edinburgh University Press, 1961).
3. G. Gregory Smith, *Scottish Literature: Character and Influence* (London: Macmillan, 1919), p. 5.
4. Tom Nairn, *The Break-up of Britain: Crisis and Neo-Nationalism* (London: NLB, 1977).
5. C. M. Grieve, *Annals of the Five Senses* (Montrose: C. M. Grieve, 1923).
6. John Corbett, J. Derrick McClure and Jane Stuart-Smith, eds., *The Edinburgh Companion to Scots* (Edinburgh: Edinburgh University Press, 2003).
7. 'Ukania' is a sarcastic term used by Tom Nairn to describe the remnants of the UK in comparison to those of the Hapsburg empire, when it still imagined it was functioning as a discrete entity.

8. Eleanor Bell, *Questioning Scotland: Literature, Nationalism, Postmodernism* (Basingstoke: Palgrave, 2004), p. 26.
9. Edwin Muir, *Scott and Scotland: The Predicament of the Scottish Writer* (Edinburgh: Polygon, 1982 [1936]).
10. Ibid., p. 65.
11. Ibid., p. 62.
12. Michael Gardiner, *The Cultural Roots of British Devolution* (Edinburgh: Edinburgh University Press, 2004), p. 48.
13. Cf. Jacques Derrida, trans. Gayatri Chakravorty Spivak, *Of Grammatology* (Baltimore, MD: Johns Hopkins University Press, 1976), pp. 141–64.
14. Alexander Trocchi, 'Letter to Hugh MacDiarmid', 3 January 1964, repr. in Trocchi, ed. Andrew M. Scott, *Invisible Insurrection of a Million Minds: A Trocchi Reader* (Edinburgh: Polygon, 1991), p. 204.
15. Stephen Driver and Luke Martell, 'Blair and "Britishness"', in David Morley and Kevin Robins, eds., *British Cultural Studies* (Oxford: Oxford University Press, 2001), pp. 461–72: 463–4.
16. *Little Britain*, BBC TV, Series One, episode two (Tom Baker's voiceover).
17. Muir, *Scott and Scotland*, pp. 12–13, 25–6; there is, nevertheless, a strong tradition of showing the continuity of the line Voltaire–Burns–Scott–Stevenson–Renaissance, running from David Daiches' seminal 1950 study *Burns* to Alan Riach's *Representing Scotland in Literature, Popular Culture and Iconography: The Masks of the Modern Nation* (Basingstoke: Palgrave, 2005).
18. Muir, *Scott and Scotland*, p. 52.
19. Ibid., p. 6.
20. Oddly enough the mid-period MacDiarmid also leans towards the organic: see Edwin Morgan, 'Knowledge and Poetry in MacDiarmid's Later Work', in *Essays* (Manchester: Carcanet, 1974 [1962]), p. 209; more worryingly, Morgan discerns the trope of the colonial: *The Kind of Poetry I Want* is 'not so much an organism as a colony, a living and in one sense formless association of organisms which share a common experience', p. 212.
21. Ibid., p. 83.
22. Ibid., p. 100.
23. Ibid., p. 85.
24. Ibid., pp. 87, 91; Nairn, *The Break-up of Britain*.
25. Muir, *Scott and Scotland*, p. 89; Cairns Craig, *Out of History: Narrative Paradigms in Scottish and English Culture* (Edinburgh: Polygon, 1996).
26. Muir, *Scott and Scotland*, p. 7.
27. Ibid., p. 8.
28. Ibid., p. 41.
29. Ibid., p. 36.
30. Ibid., p. 21.
31. Ibid., p. 18.
32. Ibid., p. 28.
33. Robert Crawford, *Introduction to Crawford*, ed., *The Scottish Invention of English Literature* (Cambridge: Cambridge University Press, 1998), pp. 1, 2.
34. Ibid., p. 16.

35. Ibid., pp. 3, 6.
36. Ibid., pp. 13–16.
37. Muir, *Scott and Scotland*, p. 45.
38. David Daiches, *The Paradox of Scottish Culture: The Eighteenth-Century Experience* (London: Oxford University Press, 1964), pp. 19–20.
39. Ibid., p. 19; cf. David Daiches, *Robert Burns* (London: G. Bell and Sons, 1952 [1950]); here Daiches tellingly splits late eighteenth-century Scottish literature into three camps: the Anglophile (Anglo-British) Edinburgh *literati* who ran to English despite dissenters like the early, immediately post-Union Allan Ramsay (*The Paradox*, pp. 24–6), the untutored lowlands, and the Gaeltacht, which was noted by the *literati*, but largely ignored. Burns was a prime example of the *literati* failing to understand the lowlands on its own, largely anti-Unionist, terms.
40. Daiches, *The Paradox of Scottish Culture*, p. 35.
41. Ibid., p. 20.
42. Ibid., pp. 27, 35, cf. p. 73.
43. Ibid., pp. 71–3.
44. Ibid., p. 94.
45. Ibid., pp. 80, 81.
46. Ibid., p. 83; cf. p. 88.
47. Riach, *Representing Scotland*, pp. 53–72.
48. Edwin Muir, *Scottish Journey* (Edinburgh: Mainstream, 2004 [1935]) pp. 88–90.
49. Ibid., p. 33.
50. Ibid., p. 107.
51. Ibid., p. 48.
52. Ibid., p. 11.
53. Ibid., p. 55.
54. Ibid., p. 42.
55. Ibid., p. 111.
56. Muir, *Scottish Journey*.
57. Edwin Morgan, 'Edwin Muir', in Morgan, *Essays* (Manchester: Carcanet, 1974 [1963]), pp. 186–93: 188.
58. Ibid., pp. 189, 192; Edwin Muir, *Essays on Literature and Society* (London: Hogarth, 1965 [1949]).
59. Muir, *Scottish Journey*, pp. 5–39.
60. Ibid., pp. 6–7.
61. The most haunting description of slave transportation is perhaps to be found in Howard Zinn's *A People's History of America* (New York: Harper Collins, 2003 [1980]), pp. 23–38.
62. http://www.historic-scotland.gov.uk/index/contacts.htm; http://www.visitscotland.com/sitewide/contactus.
63. E.g. Alexander Broadie, *The Scottish Enlightenment: The Historical Age of the Historical Nation* (Edinburgh: Birlinn, 2001); cf. the older but highly influential Marinell Ash, *The Strange Death of Scottish History* (Edinburgh: Ramsay Head Press, 1980).
64. Michael Fry, *The Scottish Empire* (Edinburgh: Birlinn, 2001); cf. the compromise line taken by T. M. Devine in *Scotland's Empire, 1600–1815* (London: Allen Lane, 2003).

65. George Orwell, *Coming up for Air* (Harmondsworth: Penguin, 1984 [1939]).
66. Muir, *Scottish Journey*, p. 169.
67. Orwell, *Coming up for Air*, pp. 168, 177, 198, 223.
68. Cf. George Orwell, 'England, Your England', in *Inside the Whale and Other Essays* (Harmondsworth: Penguin, 1962 [1941]), pp. 63–90.
69. Muir, *Scottish Journey*, pp. 94, 164.
70. Ibid., p. 60; Murray G. H. Pittock, *A New History of Scotland* (Stroud: Sutton, 2003).
71. Walter Scott, eds. David Hewitt and Alison Lumsden, *Heart of Mid-Lothian* (Edinburgh: Edinburgh University Press, 2004 [1818]), Scott, eds. G. A. M. Wood and David Hewitt, *Redgauntlet* (London: Penguin, 2000 [1824]); Irvine Welsh, *Marabou Stork Nightmares* (London: Cape, 1995); cf. Muir, *Scott and Scotland*, pp. 92–9.
72. Muir, *Scottish Journey*, p. 54.
73. Ibid., pp. 95–7.
74. Ibid., p. 2.
75. Ibid., p. 117.
76. Gilles Deleuze and Felix Guattari, trans. Brian Massumi, *A Thousand Plateaus: Capitalism and Schizophrenia* (Minneapolis: University of Minnesota Press, 1987 [1980]), p. 103.
77. Muir, *Scottish Journey*, p. 121; cf. p. 137.
78. Ibid., p. 125.
79. Ibid., p. 128.
80. Ibid., p. 127.
81. Ibid., p. 134.
82. Ibid., pp. 151, 181.
83. Ibid., pp. 155–6.
84. Ibid., p. 156.
85. Ibid., p. 157.
86. Ibid., p. 162.
87. Ibid., p. 164.
88. Ibid., pp. 165, 207.
89. Ibid., pp. 194, 192.
90. Ibid., p. 225.
91. Bell, *Questioning Scotland*, p. 8.
92. Hugh MacDiarmid, *A Kist of Whistles: New Poems* (Glasgow: W. Maclellan, 1947).
93. See Edwin Morgan on MacDiarmid's *The Battle Continues*, 'MacDiarmid Embattled', in *Essays*, pp. 194–202: 198.
94. 'The Kind of Poetry I Want', in Michael Grieve and W. R. Aitken, eds., *Complete Poems Vol. II* (Manchester: Carcanet, 1994), pp. 1001–38; cf. Edwin Morgan, 'Poetry and Knowledge in MacDiarmid's Later Work', in *Essays* [1962], pp. 203–13: 205.
95. K. D. Duval and Sydney Goodsir Smith, eds., *Hugh MacDiarmid: a Festschrift* (Edinburgh: Duval, 1962).
96. George Bruce, 'Between Any Life and the Sun', in *Hugh MacDiarmid: a Festschrift*, pp. 57–72: 57.

97. Tom Hubbard, 'Reintegrated Scots: The Post-MacDiarmid Makars', in Cairns Craig, ed., *The History of Scottish Literature*, Vol. 4 (Aberdeen: Aberdeen University Press, 1987), pp. 179–93: 179.

98. Ibid., p. 179.

99. Ibid., p. 171.

100. Ibid., p. 184.

101. Maurice Lindsay, *History of Scottish Literature* (London: Robert Hale, 1977), p. 443.

102. Murice Lindsay, ed., *Voices of Our Kind* (Glasgow: Saltire Society, 1971); see also his *Scotland: An Anthology* (London: Robert Hale, 1974).

103. Alexander Scott, ed., *Modern Scots Verse* (Preston: Akros, 1978).

104. Norman MacCaig and Alexander Scott, eds., *Contemporary Scottish Verse* (London: Calder and Boyars, 1970).

105. Edwin Morgan, *The Second Life* (Edinburgh: Edinburgh University Press, 1968).

106. Edwin Morgan, 'Registering the Reality of Scotland', in Morgan, *Essays* (Manchester: Carcanet, 1974 [1971]), p. 156.

107. 'A Conversation – Hugh MacDiarmid and Duncan Glen', *Akros* V-13, April 1970, pp. 7–72.

108. Duncan Glen, *Hugh MacDiarmid and the Scottish Renaissance* (London: Chambers, 1964).

109. 'A Conversation – Hugh MacDiarmid and Duncan Glen', p. 43.

110. 'Hugh MacDiarmid and George Bruce: An Interview', p. 70.

111. Tom McGrath with Gavin Selerie, *The Riverside Interview* (London: Binnacle, 1983), p. 83. He goes on, 'In the TV film that was made about MacDiarmid you see him walking around, talking about what it means to be Scottish, and god it was frightening. He has a great austerity in him, with all that talk about rocks and barrenness. It's the legacy of puritanism', p. 103.

112. Ian Hamilton Finlay, 'Glasgow Beasts', in *The Dancers Inherit the Party, and Glasgow Beast, an a Burd* (Edinburgh: Polygon, 1996 [1962]); 'bachle' – working-class, especially middle-aged, male, Glaswegian.

113. Edwin Morgan, 'Into the Constellation', *Akros*, VI-18, March 1970, pp. 3–18.

114. [Laing's 'sigma'] participation was launched by Alexander Trocchi's brochure, 'The Invisible Insurrection of a Million Minds', to which Laing contributed.

115. Described by Andrew Murray Scott, 'Mr. MacDairmid and Mr. Trocchi: Where Extremists Meet', in *Chapman* 83, 1996, pp. 36–9, and by Edwin Morgan, 'The Fold-in Conference', in *Gambit*, Autumn 1962, repr. in *Edinburgh Review* 97, Spring 1997, pp. 94–102.

116. 1962 is usually set as Morgan's flowering, especially triggered by US Beat; see Colin Nicholson, *Edwin Morgan: Inventions of Modernity* (Manchester: Manchester University Press, 2002) p. 88.

117. Hugh MacDiarmid, *the ugly birds without wings* (Edinburgh: Allen Donaldson, 1962).

118. Edwin Morgan, 'The Beatnik in the Kailyaird', in *Essays* (Manchester: Carcanet, 1974 [1962]), pp. 166–76: 175, 168.

119. Morgan, 'The Beatnik in the Kailyaird', p. 176; cf. Morgan, 'Scottish Poetry in the 1960s', *Essays*, pp. 177–85: 178.

120. Hugh MacDiarmid, *Letters*, ed. Alan Bold (London: Hamish Hamilton, 1984), 687, 1970, quoted in Mark Scroggins, 'The Piety of Terror: Ian Hamilton Finlay, the Modernist Fragment, and the neo-classical sublime', flashpoint Web Issue 1, 1997: http://webdelsol.com/FLASHPOINT/ihfinlay.htm.

121. Morgan, 'The Beatnik in the Kailyaird', p. 176.

122. Morgan 'Scottish Poetry in the 1960s', pp. 184–5.

123. Crawford, 'Morgan's Critical Position', p. 36.

124. Edwin Morgan, 'MacDiarmid's Later Poetry', in Morgan, *Crossing the Border: Essays on Scottish Literature* (Manchester: Carcanet, 1990), pp. 188–204, 'MacDiarmid at Seventy-Five', in Morgan, *Crossing the Border*, pp. 205–12.

125. Edwin Morgan, 'Scottish Poetry in the 1960s', *Essays*, p. 178.

126. Ibid., p. 179.

127. Hugh MacDiarmid, *The Man of (almost) Independent Mind* (Edinburgh: G. Gordon, 1961).

128. Edwin Morgan, introduction to 'Wi The Haill Voice', *Collected Translations*, p. 111.

129. Morgan, *Collected Translations*, p. 29.

130. Roderick Watson, 'An Island in the City', p. 14.

131. Colin Nicholson, *Edwin Morgan: Inventions of Modernity* (Manchester: Manchester University Press, 2002), p. 88.

Chapter 3

Spark *contra* Spark

In a 1971 speech, 'The Desegregation of Art', perhaps known best by its quotation in various essays in Martin McQuillan's 2002 collection of Muriel Spark criticism, the Dame makes one of her most formalist and polemical statements.[1] Firstly, literature should be *worthwhile*, requiring 'the sacrifice of good things at the intelligent season'; this is then expanded to get at her target, the kind of art which pits oppressor against victim and lets the reader/viewer off the hook by identifying with the victim – realism.[2] A 'desegregation' would see culture play its proper part in sociopolitical life and 'the liberation of our minds from the comfortable cells of lofty sentiment in which they are confined and never really satisfied'.[3] Literature is to be judged by its effects, not its mimesis. mimicry?

Although often described (in the days before EasyJet) as the classic ex-pat writer, Spark's work as a whole has a Scottish ring, and carries within it a powerful critique of the Edinburgh morality of the *literati* of the eighteenth and nineteenth centuries. Ian Rankin finds some kind of reference to Scotland in every one of Spark's novels, while suggesting that 'Edinburgh to her means rationalism. Believing in a strong difference between right and wrong'.[4] And yet, as we have seen and as Spark was fully aware, the rationalism of the Edinburgh Enlightenment can be described in terms just as ambivalent as those of the French one. Rankin, a professional crime writer, has been one of a few who have so far pushed the early Spark's French connections, which are vital in this context.

 how is Edinburgh rationalist in Paris?

For Edinburgh's rationalism was as exclusive as it was 'universal'. Thus for the insider Spark herself in 1962, in what seems a paradoxical double movement, 'it was Edinburgh that bred within me the conditions of exile-dom'.[5] Edinburgh's blend of scepticism, moral enquiry, 'sense of civic superiority'[6] and ability to turn a blind eye to racial and class exploitation meant that its imperialists flourished within a British context. With this context in her sights Spark critiques the moral high-handedness which flirted with amoral pragmatism, cliquishness and, most brilliantly in *The Prime of Miss Jean Brodie*, fascism.

The critical novel: *The Comforters*

Until quite recently, it was common to see Muriel Spark as a skilled but fairly conservative practitioner of Eng. Lit. who thrived via the Scottish London diaspora. But a good place to start into a surprising account of literary thought from the 1960s is, I believe, her first five novels (1957–61), which scarcely fit this mould at all.

Though the connection has rarely overtly been made, *The Comforters* inaugurates a specifically Scottish, and Francophile, mode of narration which would travel through the prose of James Kelman to Alan Warner: the novel is autopoetic, or self-written, reaching both the reader and the characters 'in retrospect', with no sense of having been written at the time. Prose appears in third person as the actualisation of a future anterior (events will already have happened). In this case the heroine Caroline perceives the action of her world as she hears it tapped out on a typewriter, which both creates her and writes the story.[7] The typewriter goes so far as to reproduce tag clauses, cleverly reproducing Creative Writing 101 thuds ('she wondered'), and even hears and reproduces exclamation marks – to Caroline's distaste.[8] The typewriter inaugurates a Sparkian world of telepathy, which runs wormholes through any third-person omniscient narrator. Spark's narration inaugurates not an omniscience but a non-science – its action comes from nowhere.

This first novel has typically been described as a story of a heroine 'trapped within a novel'. Spark herself is not so direct: it is known that Caroline has had past psychiatric episodes – is this, we wonder, another? – and indeed she is definitively diagnosed by other characters as 'neurotic' in a way that would soon be given a social spin by Laing, Foucault, and Deleuze and Guattari – ' "You're mad", said the woman'.[9] Caroline feels *relieved* at this diagnosis (somewhat anticipating Janice Galloway's Joy Stone's trip to hospital),[10] since, although it doesn't represent a final verdict, it puts a name, or place, to her third-personhood and 'confirm[s] . . . her distress'.[11] In *The Comforters* what goes against the grain of the metropolitan Spark we have come to colloquially expect is her alliance with a fiction much more experimental than the Anglo-British novel of the time. Her affiliation with the French *nouveau roman* in this case may go so far, as Alain Robbe-Grillet's *The Erasers* (1964), published in 1953 as *Les Gommes*.[12] In this novel similarly, the story is auto-written by an outside presence which also turns out to be autopoetic – here, a virtual detective trying to solve a murder – and Rankin's interest in possible *nouveau roman* connections where many literary critics have missed them, puts an entirely different spin on the pile-them-high king of Scottish crime fiction. Robbe-Grillet's detective is *ironically* equated with the all-seeing eye of the reader, while the characters themselves 'suspect' authorial intervention:

> Motionless in front of the mirror, the manager watches himself laughing; he tries as hard as he can not to see the others that are swarming across the room, the jubilant troupe, the wild legion of minor heartaches, the refuse of fifty years of badly digested existence. Their racket has become intolerable, the horrible concert of brays and yelps and all at once, in the silence that has suddenly fallen again, a young woman's clear laugh.
> 'Go to hell!'
> The manager has turned around, wrenched from the nightmare by his own cry. No one is there, of course, neither Pauline nor the others.[13]

The *nouveau roman* connection here, as well as unmooring Spark from her default Anglo-British critical home, suggests a post-Enlightenment criticism of vision: here, *the reader* is the detective who has to 'solve' the murder, and does so with an ironically clinical eye which negates any idea of vision as the fount of ethical perception. Rankin points to this Robbe-Grillet–Spark theoretical alignment; his unfinished doctoral research at Edinburgh University was on Spark, with a rare ear open to the *nouveau roman*. In *The Erasers*, packed with what we would later be called metafiction, the figure of detective is inseparable from that of reader. Its characters attempt to hide 'their' secrets from 'us'; the reader is aware of having too much influence, of in a sense making the novel, or at least making Caroline make it. Rankin writes:

> From early in her career, she [Spark] was aware of the theories and writings of authors such as Alain Robbe-Grillet and Samuel Beckett, recalling in a 1971 interview that 'in the early 1950s, there was no Robbe-Grillet, and scarcely anyone had heard of Beckett. Hardly anyone was trying to write novels with all the compression and obliqueness I was aiming at'.[14]

And, 'as early as 1961, Spark was championing Alain Robbe-Grillet, at a time when only two of his novels were available in English translations'.[15] Whether Spark had *Les Gommes* in mind while writing *The Erasers* is uncertain, but there is a sizeable area of conceptual overlap (and obvious similarities of title), as well as Rankin's implication that Spark was motivated to go straight to the French version. (Spark had, of course, spooked for European intelligence during a war played out largely in France, and her language skills were doubtless good enough to read Robbe-Grillet before he came into translation.) In any case, '[l]ike Beckett, Robbe-Grillet and others, Spark attempts to define for herself the conception of reality which a writer brings to the modern world' (and here Beckett and Robbe-Grillet, two figures central to Scottish literary thought, are bracketed together within the space of four pages).[16] Rankin here also cites as autopoetic later novels including *The Public Image* and *The Driver's Seat*, in which, like *The Comforters'* Caroline, the main character tries to outwit her writers, and 'Lise, the apparent victim, actually spends her last day on earth searching for someone to kill her' (an idea pinched by Martin Amis for *London Fields*, where Nicola Six is known as 'the murderee' from the outset).[17]

We know also that Caroline has spiritual problems in being accepted as a believing *converted* Catholic, and, more subtly and most importantly, that her belief-system, as far as we make it so, is 'right': the story *is* being written about her. She is, in a theoretical sense, ahead of its time, a woman 'made of' writing, and this is the main 'story' of the book. This critically engaged fiction (let's drop the annoying word 'meta-fiction') was hardly in the ascendant in Anglo-British fiction, even among Spark's champions like Graham Greene. The point is that Spark, while appearing as the perfect Scotto-British literary guardian of Eng. Lit., supposedly the inheritor of the mantle of the *literati*, seems to have slyly domesticated the *nouveau roman*, which often eschewed author-controlled story in favour of autopoesis, pursued yet further in Alain Robbe-Grillet's *In the Labyrinth*, published in the same year as *The Comforters*. *The Comforters* is a novel which, if we must separate out types of writing, puts its own criticism centre stage; it throws open the question of what, to anticipate the terminology of Barthes and Foucault, the place of the author really is. The fact that this question is asked *in a novel* makes it especially critical, since the story must somehow enact its own answer, even if only by default. And the question of the author is pointedly asked by *both* the character and the person behind the name on the book jacket, and even, in some strangely prurient sense, by the reader:

> Was the author disembodied? – She didn't know. If so, how could he use a typewriter? How could she overhear him? How could one author chant in chorus? – That she didn't know, that she didn't know. Was the author human or a spirit, and if so –
>
>   'How can I answer these questions? I've only just begun to ask them myself. The author obviously exists in a different dimension from ours. That will make the investigation difficult.'[18]

One neat biographical answer to these problems is that Spark, former president of the Poetry Society and famously wary of joined-up lines, took up Caroline's hallucinations as a procedural method of making the writing of her first novel easier to get through; the novel 'writes itself'. And – need we invoke Derrida? – writing *does* always precede the written work. Here the work of the typewriter comes before the action/voices,[19] to the extent that Caroline (biographically, we might say, Spark *contra* Spark) determines, like Lise, to outwit her own omniscient narration by acting unexpectedly, in a character/author battle taking place within the *act* of writing, in the sound of the typewriter's tap-tap-tap:

> 'I've just jerked up to the fact', she said, 'that our day is doing just what the voices said it would. Now, we chatted about Eleanor. Then about ourselves. All right. We've frittered the day. The narrative says we went by car; all right, we must go by train. You do see that, don't you, Laurence? It's a matter of asserting free will.'[20]

This character free will is underscored by comments made by Spark in the journal *Twentieth Century* in 1961 to the effect that 'the narrative part – first or third person – belongs to a character as well'.[21] In an interview with Frank Kermode two years later, ('Seven English [*sic*] Novelists') she strikes out with a high formalism which undercuts any realistic reading of characters – recalling the agenda of the *nouveau roman*: 'I don't claim that my novels are the truth [i.e. not Tolstoy] – I claim that they are fiction, out of which a kind of truth emerges'.[22] She even motions towards Deleuze in rejecting the idea of 'three-dimensional' characters which are bound to (interpellated) ideas of the unconscious: 'I think the best thing is to be conscious of everything that one writes, and let the unconscious take care of itself.'[23]

Caroline then turns out to be an author-character making strong statements against the authorial use of realism to fix the way we see the world. Early on Caroline realises that the 'novel' and all its characters are a fiction;[24] she realises also that the wild tales of Satanism and diamond smuggling within it are too fantastic to be 'real', yet, with what would become a typically Sparkian twist, we are never quite sure whether the diamond smuggling and Satanism are to be taken seriously 'within' the story. Caroline's interpellated madness arises, a psychoanalytic critic of old might have said, from a 'neurosis'; alternatively, she is unable to stop questioning her objective status as character – '*Tap-tap* [sound of the typewriter]. *It was Caroline herself who introduced the story the question of Mrs. Hogg's bosom.*' (And how coincidental is that name? Names are rarely picked at random in the early Spark. Has the story been 'mothered' by Hogg? This would certainly tally with Spark's post-Calvinist thematics.)[25]

The 'coming' of the invisible 'comforters' also prefigures the novel to 'come', and indeed the sexuality of the marriage 'to come'. The comforters' coming in the form of a textual/sexual promise haunts the whole novel and is introduced by the first incomprehensible tap-tap-tap, itself an erotic image lost on those of us who have always slid our hands across a computer keyboard.[26] The haunting of her 'self' by herself in the novel is confirmed for Caroline when she finds that she is having a great influence even when she believes herself to be 'absent', in hospital.[27] Herself a student of the novel, she even senses the end of the narrative 'coming' (on around p. 170 of around 200 pages); her fiancé, however, takes this to mean the end of the book Caroline is writing, rather than the one in which she is featuring:

> 'Naturally, I look forward to the end of the book', she said, 'in a manner of speaking to get some peace'.
> 'I meant', said Laurence with a burst of irritation, 'of course, the book that you are writing, not the "book" in which you think you are participating'.[28]

The author–character equation is made overt early on by the fact that Caroline is writing a book about 'the novel', which she eventually finishes, then decides to start writing 'a novel', so conflating the two 'genres'. Having realised that writing writes her, she goes on to writing herself:

> Caroline had finished her book about novels. Now she announced she was going away on a long holiday. She was going to write a novel . . .
> 'What is the novel to be about?'
> Caroline answered, 'Characters in a novel.'
> Edwin himself had said, 'Make it a straight old-fashioned story, no modern mystifications. End with the death of the villain and the marriage of the heroine.'
> Caroline laughed and said, 'Yes, it would end that way.'[29]

Of course, we know that this novel will always already have been written, as it were, before and beyond intention as well as with it, and not simply by 'the author'. The author is no longer the sole site of literary art, and an individual becomes a relay for narrative flows.

Moreover, since, despite the efforts of the Humean *literati* of the late eighteenth century and their later disciples, Scots had been excluded from the canon of Eng. Lit. *as Scots*, English Literature was *de facto* seen as 'English', meaning that Caroline's 'writing' of herself 'by' a name on a book-jacket that we readily associate with a Scot can be understood as a device of the 'voice' of someone who cannot speak. Strangest of all to a London audience, Spark's precedent is the funny foreign one of the *nouveau roman* (this being the time of Kingsley Amis and 'the

Movement's famous xenophobia). And, in what we will come to understand as readable in the Scottish context as an anti-imperial move,
Caroline has *chosen* to become a Catholic – on some level of consciousness rejecting an imperialist rationale predicated since the eighteenth
century on Hanoverian Protestantism. The British empire, for which Spark
had spied before she passed on the mantle of haunting to Caroline's comforters, had only a decade before lost its most important colony and was
now shakily reliant on the conjunction of a remaining war consensus,
monarchy and imperial Protestantism, the target of her next novel.

A Scottish postcolonialism: *Robinson*

J. M. Coetzee's *Foe* (1986) is often rightly praised for its attempt to
rewrite Daniel Defoe's Eng. Lit. classic *Robinson Crusoe* (1719) from the
point of view of the island's native. There was a lot at stake in Defoe's
tale for Scots: firstly and most obviously, the story is based on the pseudo-
imperial 'adventures' of Alexander Selkirk. More crucially, *Robinson
Crusoe* is the work of an author who was perhaps the single most important English literary pro-Union pamphleteer around 1706–7, and the
novel was published only a dozen years after the enactment of Union
itself. Pre-dating Coetzee by almost two decades, Spark's novel also
pulled this particular rug from under the imperial Eng. Lit. canon, not
only from the obvious aspects of right to territory and command, but
more importantly from the related themes of sectarianism and gender.

Robinson opens by letting the reader know, like Defoe, that the hero
has been stranded 'by misadventure' and that what is to follow is stuck
together from memory – again, autopoesis.[30] This narrator is pointedly
not the owner of the island and is always kept at arm's length from its
workings. Like Crusoe's native servant Friday, she is known merely by the
month of her birth, January, or at times, in an echo of Joseph Conrad's
seminally postcolonial *Heart of Darkness*, the surname Marlow. (The
forename may also be a grim word-play on imperial-explorers-in-the-
tropics: for the benefit of far-away readers, never attempt tourism in
Scotland in January.) Velma Bourgeois Richmond has pointed out that,
while retaining *The Comforters'* autopoetic first-person narrator as inves-
tigator, the novel's characters all have anti-realistic, analogous names:
Marlow is a Conradian who asks too many questions, Jimmie acts as a
narrative crowbar and Waterford as a bridge between people.[31]

January – our access to the main story is afterwards, through her
autopoetic notebook – remains a step behind the island's ruler
and Protestant work ethic-inspired inventor-of-systems, Robinson –

a postcolonial strategy also later used by Coetzee's *Foe*, which similarly reverses the paradigm in attempting to account for the strange death of Friday's history at the hands of Defoe.[32] The use of postcolonial writing strategies so early, doubtless driven by the thinly veiled anger of the earlier, Rhodesian *Spark*,[33] gives the lie, as do so many Scottish novels, to the 1990s non-argument about whether Scottish literature is fit to engage with postcolonialism: Scottish literature has been engaging with it for decades.

Robinson, as in Defoe, is the *de facto* owner of this island; his name is also the name of the island, which is itself in the shape of a man, of himself,[34] a total geopolitics which allows the refugees differential access to only some of the island's secrets.[35] From the beginning, he insists that January keep a journal,[36] perhaps meant as a guard against disorientation (or orientation), but again triggering the autopoetic technique we have seen used to extremes in *The Comforters*, since the novel is recreated retrospectively from fragments of the journal. Robinson himself lives in a colonial-style building, and January is again already a writer, one who could never resist a story[37] – and the physical object of the journal-book shows that this story was not resisted – whereas Robinson has vulgar tastes in books, which he never seems to read.[38] Significantly, he has the whole set of *The Golden Bough*, placing him as a classic Scotto-British encyclopaedist and proud inheritor of an Enlightenment/ imperial/Eng. Lit. tradition.[39] Meanwhile January's autobiography has to remain secret, in the unknown, and at the beginning unwritten, though only in its pages lies hope for the future – for the novel and for their rescue.

What follows between Robinson and January is a masque of the kind of platonic (that is, proto-Enlightenment) education which we will see savaged in *The Prime of Miss Jean Brodie*. Robinson sees January as 'the female problem', and his own place as 'leading her on'.[40] He assumes the position of leader rather than teacher, bringing out what is already there (*e-duco*),[41] since for Robinson there must be an absolute moral knowledge that we all share (except that, as January reminds us, some versions of 'we' are female, non-property-owning, strangers to our own 'homes', and at least temporarily without property – the Deleuzian Hume's prerequisite for rational discourse). Of course, in Robinson's platonic education, this leads to predestined forms of 'discovery'; for example, in a shadow-plot, Robinson's helper, Miguel, lays himself open to the mysticism of the fraudulent refugee, Tom Wells.[42] Robinson himself strategically withholds vital information from January about the island, which is mysteriously full of caves and short cuts leading to other parts of the 'body politic': he blocks her lines of flight through her own intellectual environment.[43] The novel is in a very serious sense a parody of the Jean Brodie type of platonic e-ducation or leading, embodied by the mysteries of the island known only to Robinson. Strategic imperialist that he is, Robinson partitions the island and divides and rules, playing his unexpected guests against one another. His sovereignty is predicated on the textuality of the woman we have seen in *The Comforters*: while encouraging January to write a journal, he is later able to confiscate this account of the story, and January has to struggle to maintain her own historiography of the adventure.[44]

The parodic sectarian-imperial element here inheres in the way Robinson is continually portrayed, despite his own 'protestations', as a merely nominal Catholic and merely nominal republican, having deserted during the Spanish Civil War – a crucial point when related to Defoe's new Hanoverian monarchy. Spark will take this further in *The Prime of Miss Jean Brodie*, in which one of the Brodie set is killed fighting in Spain *for Franco*, whereas common knowledge says that concerned Brits fought for the republican side (and not for nothing is Irvine Welsh's psychopathic Leith-dweller, Francis Begbie, known by the name Franco).[45] Indeed there are pre-shocks of *Miss Jean Brodie* when, in one of a number of flashbacks to pre-crash life (Spark's control of flashbacks and flashforwards in these first five novels is exemplary), January likens Robinson to her erstwhile suitor, Ian Brodie:

> During these first weeks on the island I was increasingly struck by similarities between Robinson and Ian Brodie . . .
> when Robinson showed his anxiety to keep authority on his island, to know what was going on between us, to prevent our quarrelling or behaving other than impersonally, and to prevent our making friends with Miguel, and most of all, to detect any possibility of a love affair between Jimmie and me, I was reminded of Ian Brodie, and noticed very much the shape of Robinson's head [also the shape of the head of the island]. I was reminded of instances of Ian Brodie's extraordinary urge to ferret into my private life, and in particular of a morning towards the end of the Easter holidays when I said to my son Brian, 'Let's get out of this'.[46]

While the Protestant work ethic and drive for individual betterment, as concretised in the 1707 Union of Governments and Defoe's *Crusoe*, was subsequently used to summon up enthusiasm for the possibilities empire held for lads o' 'pairts – or even for lost boys or spies – Spark's parodic Robinson is a Catholic, but a Catholic of the most dubious hue. He disapproves of the conversion to Catholicism of Miguel, and confiscates January's rosary. Unlike Defoe's Crusoe, for whom Providence is rarely far away, Robinson seems to have no sense of a higher purpose, limply acceding to God's ability to 'dispose'.[47] Moreover, the crypto-Calvinist

Robinson has a rabid mistrust of all Catholic idols, an 'anti-Marian fervour'.[48] January's rosary ends up pinned onto, and punned onto, the goat named Rosie, which is about to be slaughtered:

> Robinson said quickly, 'If you mean the rosary, I do not want the boy to see it.'
> Miguel looked interested. 'Show me Rosie.'[49]

Here January's perception of Robinson relates back temporally, and forward intertextually – to Brodie's (Ian's, though it may as well be Miss Jean's) spleen over the 'mob hysteria' of Catholicism. Robinson becomes paranoic about his 'son' Miguel, when January makes him his own rosary.[50] This neo-eighteenth-century story of Protestant Imperialism comes to a parodic head when January defends her own rosary against Robinson, who is revealed as a spiritually empty and pragmatic coloniser in contradistinction to Crusoe's Providence, which would always provide for the individual in far-flung reaches:

> I [January] replied, 'I chucked the antinomian pose when I was twenty. There's no such thing as private morality.'
> 'Not for you. But for me, living on an island – I have a system.'[51]

From here on the plot takes a typically Sparkian turn into genre-fiction-in-sixth-gear – one of Spark's distinguishing qualities is her ability to shift between literary fiction and genre convention – when Robinson goes missing, prompting a frenzied whodunnit, as for most of the second half of the novel Robinson is absent. This even enforces a temporary doubt within January *herself* over her own innocence in the affair, and the perception of a generalised *lack* on the island, of the kind prone to psychoanalysis, and rejected by Spark, and later by Foucault, Deleuze and Guattari. There is a wonderful moment when Jimmie, ostensibly due to imperfect grammar, utters a sentence about lack which itself lacks an object:

> On our return late that afternoon Tom Wells said:
>   'Been through all the caves?'
> Jimmie said, 'Yes, but they lack.'
> 'Lack what?'
> 'Robinson,' said Jimmie.
> 'Naturally,' said Wells.[52]

The caves themselves are labyrinthine and only fully known to Robinson – a rhizomic sub-structure – which one man – one capitalist, detached from his system of capitalism – attempts to possess, rendering them all the more empty. Conversely, when January is negotiating the caves, her echo seems to be perceived prior to and to be greater than her 'self'.[53] As in *The Comforters*, this self is eclipsed by the excess of writing, or the writing's supplementarity, in the classically Derridean figure of the echo.[54] Significantly, January is also without a source of *light* in the tunnel, lacking, unlike Robinson, the visual metaphor which oversaw the bringing of Enlightenment to unknown lands.[55] All that is left for January is mimicry, as she begins play-acting at being others.[56] In the end her journal, which, as we know, will become a novel, is her only weapon against Wells in establishing an account of what happened on the island.[57]

After the dénouement of the mystery (which was nevertheless not very mysterious: Spark was merely zipping in and out of the generic form), we get a wider picture of Robinson the individual, systematic survivalist ('[w]hen Jimmie told him of our long search he assumed the air of a triumphant schoolmistress'[58] – again taking us forward in Spark's *oeuvre*), versus January, for whom meaning is only comprehensible within community. A clear postcolonial description emerges of the impulse that sent out individual Scots to create an empire, while, at the time of writing, in a high-Welfare Statist Britain, a specifically Scottish community had increasingly become an oddity at home. Neither the Britishness of imperialism nor the Britishness of the over-extended war consensus makes any sense – '[w]hen I think of Robinson now, I think of him as a selfish but well-meaning eccentric'.[59]

Border ballads: *Peckham Rye*

Muriel Spark was scarcely the first writer to use a Scottish character to throw a spanner in the works of English society: this had been going on in the novel since the mid-eighteenth century, often to the (self-)degradation of Scots, who coveted English airs. But she was probably the first to use the critical novel to have a Scot as both actor in, and despoiler of, a local working-class English community whose civic standards were well-established and respectable.

That community was Peckham, which has since, of course, become famous as the site of the BBC sitcom *Only Fools and Horses* (and, to foreign students, as the place you go through to get to Goldsmith's College).[60] In 2005 *Only Fools and Horses* was voted the favourite-ever sitcom of the 'British public' in an online BBC poll.[61] Both the prime developer of the medium of television, John Logie Baird, and the first premier of the BBC, John Reith – a strong unionist and proponent of 'educative television' not only in SE but also in Received Pronunciation

(RP) – were Scots;[62] Scots are heavily implicated in the popularity of virtual Peckham, the irony being that the comically un-RP dialogue of the sitcom is made to contrast with 'correct English'. Yet since the poll was conducted online, voters were more liable to have been the type of Reithian middle-class property owners who peopled Edinburgh's Historic New Town than Peckham itself.

In the novel, the Peckham incomer Dougal Douglas, who is only in the most tendentious way a lad o' pairts or even a 'Scot on the make', blends in instantly with his new London surroundings, yet is also instantly seen as 'disgusting', 'different' in some disturbing way which can't be pinned down, and, worst of all, 'full of ideas'.[63] Almost from the start, via Douglas, Spark's tone is determinedly poetic, starting with a description of Peckham's 'broad lyrical acres'.[64] Alan Bold is undoubtedly right when he points out that this Scottishness shows in Spark's underwiring Peckham speech with a balladic rhythm, both an echo and a subversion of the Daniel Defoe/Walter Scott truism about Unionist Scots in London behaving as good Britons:

> the ballad technique can also be recast in prose by writers who plunge rapidly into the action, who use conversational contrasts to advance the narrative, and who habitually allude to other-worldly phenomena. *The Ballad of Peckham Rye* develops these devices and Spark draws the reader into her design by opening on an exchange that could be read as a quatrain with identical rhymes:
> 'Get away from here, you dirty swine,' she said.
> 'There's a dirty swine in every man,' he said.
> 'Showing your face round here again,' she said.
> 'Now, Mavis, now, Mavis,' he said.[65]

We should remember that the origins of the fiercely nationalistic Hugh MacDiarmid, spokesman for the first Renaissance and his nation, were less than ten miles from the English border, ballad country, and that for Edwin Muir on his journey, the borders remained the *least* Anglicised region since they remained a frontier region requiring cultural defence:

> The Border formed a rampart against English invasion for centuries, and it is still the part of Scotland which is least Anglicised . . .
> When one enters Dryburgh Abbey [in Melrose, in the borders] one leaves this curious country and is back in ordinary time again.[66]

For Muir border ballads had a 'superhuman passion' which was able to fully define Scottishness. Spark's ballads are here seen, in Edwin Morgan's words, 'crossing the border', and are displaced into a community of 1960s Del-boys, triggering some form of personal fiction in every character: Humphrey's technicalities, Druce's euphemisms, spurious and over-practised social roles, and the general pantomime of the classes-within-classes within an over-unionised factory.[67] (Spark's greatest moment in irony towards the modernising-vulgarising impulse of the Welfare State is perhaps her short story 'You Should Have Seen the Mess', in which a teenage girl slips down the social ladder by failing to appreciate anything but the modern, the clean and the efficient.)[68]

Throughout the novel, Spark carefully limits her iterative marks to 'I said' or other staccato phrases so that the balladic feel is maintained for long stretches, even as it is interspersed with the lyricisms and peculiarities of Douglas. As Bold notes, the most significant aspect of this is not pure literary flourish, nor even the truism that 'Spark's prose is highly poetic', but that she inserts a specifically Scottish form, the one that Walter Scott determinedly tried to hold on to and that therefore became an arena within which the question of the continuation of Scots as a literary language was contested. What Muir saw as Scotland's most prominent cultural form is here insinuated into a working-class London area where Dougal Douglas's foreign accent prompts others to ask if he has just arrived from Ireland (as reversed in the figure of Neil Jordan's IRA deserter in *The Crying Game*).[69]

Douglas, fresh out of an Edinburgh University which, although it was central to the development of Eng. Lit. in the eighteenth century, has now dropped any latent obsession with prescriptive grammar, can choose his phrasing with high precision to suit the occasion (he indulges in 'style-drifting', to use the sociolinguistic term). He incorporates the playful, the lyrical, the absurd, the SE and the Scots. The only characters really worried about the correctness of their own English in the novel are the English themselves, in a reversal of Smith's and Beattie's obsession with the removal of those Scotticisms which might have proved an impediment to advancement in Enlightenment society and empire. Dixie in particular, the perpetual saver, self-improver and *engagée*, is continually 'correcting' her family and friends' native English:

'My own American Dad pays my keep,' Dixie said.
'He thinks he do, but it don't go far.'
'Does. Doesn't,' Dixie said.[70]

Although Dougal is dextrous with SE, his speech is peppered with overt Scotticisms – 'wee', 'rare', 'greet', 'fey', 'aye', 'blether'. Used to style-drifting, he also picks up Peckhamisms quickly.[71] If there is any snobbery about Peckham, it is in the reverse-classism of the residually British residents, especially Dougal's boss's wife, Mrs Willis – again neatly ironising ambitious Scots' desire to 'escape into Britain' as they helped solidify it as a cultural entity in the late eighteenth century.[72] On this occasion, the aspiration comes from the other side of the border.

Dougal has come to State-happy Peckham in part because of industry's need to create a form of 'leisure' which can then be separated from work to increase overall efficiency – the kind of packaging of life attacked by movements surrounding Situationism in Scotland and France. The post-war attempt to manage the entire person, work and play, finds its classic account in Nikolas Rose's Foucauldian *Governing the Soul*, and has more recently been critiqued from a twenty-first-century perspective by Pat Kane.[73] Dougal's boss personifies this new neo-utilitarian form of leisure, using the terms 'attractive' and 'useful' interchangeably.[74] Dougal, though, is post-Enlightenment in his refusal to share, or even acknowledge, the same goal of industrial efficiency arising from the division of labour and leisure. Even during his interview he fails to understand his boss's ambitions for an 'arts man', answering in ludic and punning language (his humped back gives him 'only a hunch').[75] He is already making other plans for his 'research time', under-defined by a boss who remains none the wiser and lacks any knowledge of disciplines other than his own.

One of Spark's master-strokes during these early pages is to compare Dougal's approach with over-specialised English education, four years before G. E. Davie's *The Democratic Intellect*. Before Dougal's arrival, the boss had tried a Cambridge graduate whose interests were firmly fixed in a utilitarian, neo-Enlightenment time-and-motion maximisation of efficiency. This distinction also coincides perfectly with the 'theoretical' issue of Scottish personalism (John Macmurray, H. J. Paton, the early R. D. Laing), which prioritised action, resistance and change, over the Oxbridge approach of logical positivism (A. J. Ayer, Bertrand Russell, Ludwig Wittgenstein), which concerned itself with the 'truth' of propositions. Dougal would later have a dream about this Cambridge graduate, gifting him 'an absurd lyricism';[76] for Oxbridge graduates there is no hiding from the psychosocial sphere, not even in others' dreams.

The generalist is also used to deflect Dougal's friend Humphrey Place, a solid union man (of an era when unions were pillars of the work/leisure dichotomy), and whose fiancée, Dixie, is obsessively putting money away. Dougal's poeticism is played against Humphrey's old-left politics:

> 'It is right and proper,' Dougal said, 'that you should be called a refrigerator engineer. It brings lyricism to the concept.'
> 'I don't trouble myself about that,' Humphrey said. 'But what you call a job makes a difference to the Unions. My dad doesn't see that.'[77]

Dixie describes her own regime of saving as 'tiring' – an image we will find again in James Kelman, and one that can be related to Deleuze and Guattari's idea of perpetual 'debt' – and before them, to Laing, and before him again, to Wilhelm Reich. *Contra* Reich and Laing, Dixie remains infuriatingly celibate until marriage, drawing a moralistic, Deleuzian link between sexual and monetary debt. When Humphrey does become frisky, Dixie assumes that this is down to Douglas, who she thinks must be anti-marriage and anti-family *per se* – again flagging up the contemporary ambivalence over the family in Laing in the year of *The Divided Self*.

Humphrey's vulgar Marxist obsession with social class is, then, constantly undercut by Douglas's *non sequiturs*; eventually Humphrey's 'jobs and prospects' model is crushed entirely, leading in part to the novel's 'dénouement', of which, typically, we are told at the outset. (In Alasdair Gray's *1982: Janine*, Jock McLeish's father will perform a similar function in his unshakeable straw man faith in the Welfare State.)[78] When Douglas does invoke a work ethic, it is with deep irony, to account for his own flâneuristic behaviour, his being 'out and about' and yielding no results in a monetary form that the boss can understand. He is even simultaneously hired by a rival company. Added to his fiscal promiscuity, Dougal's rhetorical skill gets him in trouble by being seductive of the 'wrong' type of women.[79]

Dougal is thus led to manipulate the Scotland/Britain relationship: one by one Dougal reels out the images (for, in the spectral sense, 'images' are what they are) which promoted Scots' centrality to the empire; he even retells the 'nothing under the kilt' *Carry On* soldierly yarn, despite the fact that the reader knows that his hunch got him off national service.[80] His punning is also disturbingly visual: he is able to 'shape-shift', like a Calvinist devil, using 'only a hunch'.[81] He even resorts to overt mimicry of his new-found enemy, Trevor Lomax, to general mirth.[82] Spark reminds us that, in a broadly consensual-Unionist Britain, both the English and the Scots were stuck with stateless nations, and a pragmatic industrialism within Britain. Dougal's new boss, a Scottish industrialist of neo-Calvinist ilk, unaware that Dougal is already 'employed', simply mirrors Dougal's first boss in his reforming utilitarianism; we find that the fellow-Scots' Druce and Dougal's idea of the word 'vision' is comically different; Druce's has to do with company loyalty, while Dougal's ties in both a much more democratic-intellectual sense of community and the danger of surveillance. 'Vision' is playfully thrown back at the boss in a literal reading:

> 'Mr. Douglas,' said Mr. Weedin, 'I want to ask you a personal question. What do you mean exactly by vision?'

'Vision?' Douglas said.

'Yes, vision, that's what I said.'

'Do you speak literally as concerning optics, or figuratively, as it might be with regard to an enlargement of the total perceptive capacity?'[83]

The Del-boy aspect to the situation is that neither of Dougal's bosses knows that he is being duped, and the employee-researcher is able simply to reverse his name on either side of the Rye, to become Doug to his friends, or, most absurdly of all, to hyphenate his name.[84] Ironically, both bosses, while finally failing to understand what he's talking about, think that they share with Doug a code of industriousness, steadiness and seriousness.[85] The Scottish work ethic has had its chips, but only someone the age of a recent graduate, and from a Scotland which is decreasingly 'British', realises this.

Another vital function of Dougal/Douglas, as well as answering his two bosses in what we could seriously call a Derridean manner – taking the bosses' work/leisure dichotomy and vexingly digging out its supplementarity – is to create a generic disturbance, to upset the writerliness of what seems to have been *already* written down according to negotiated rules. This post-generic impulse takes two twists in the story: firstly, Dougal adapts real-life episodes to the biography of an elderly actress which he has been asked to write, and again, in a strongly formalist move, Spark has Dougal chastised only for writing which the actress feels represents her badly, not for actual untruths.[86] Secondly, Dougal's notes on this biography are so cryptic that Trevor and his gang, and eventually the police, take it as a secret code and Dougal as some kind of agent (to Trevor, one open to blackmail; to the police, one open to suspicion).[87] The term 'agent' also has resounding significance for Scottish thought; as over the Anglo-British 'subject', the former is characterised by action within a shifting psychosocial landscape; the latter confirms its position by reference to known relations and specific problem-solving. 'Agent', moreover, takes on metaphysical overtones in the novel, in which Dougal is suspected of being a 'real-life' devil, overactive and, in part due to real or imagined 'horns' in his head, inducing fear and paranoia.[88]

Just as in *Robinson*, the end of Dougal's adventure involves a passage through darkness as he tunnels through a half-made underground pipe to escape the jealous Trevor Lomax. He finally eludes Trevor only by using, in Derridean fashion, 'haunted' bones as a weapon.[89] Dougal Douglas is that most common mixer in the early Spark, the Scot working through a 'Calvinist' history, real or imagined, on foreign soil and only allowing him/herself to be seen-and-named in the most spectral and ludic fashion – here accepting salaries from two competing companies as a largely spurious 'consultant' merely by reversing his name. This is a wilfully displaced Scot, one who is, in Willy Maley's terms, 'de-picted' by Spark[90] – rejecting the bogus ties of 'race' to stir things up in a nation which has not yet grasped the cultural differences between 'nation' and 'state' at all. In Spark's 1960, de-picted Scots are waking up to this difference between their placement and their agency, and proactively putting it to playful and political use.

Memento Vivere

Spark's fourth novel and one of her best-known, *Memento Mori*, centres on a group of old people who all receive the same phone message which tells them only 'remember you must die'. The reader is encouraged via Godfrey – the husband of a successful and now elderly novelist – to regard this message as threatening. We might equally describe the content of the phone calls as a kindness, since, to the extent that 'you must die' is thinkable, 'you are now alive' must be true. We are invited to think death, the impossible which only throws back images of life. This Sparkian irony is fanned out across various characters' reactions, and their reactions define their attitudes in the Macmurray sense of making a choice by declining all other possibilities in the full knowledge that these possibilities cannot return, and so form history. Some use the message as a reminder to *act*, while others are frozen into *activity* and the reminder of life is squandered.

Dame Lettie, deeply disturbed and no longer as sharp as she was, misses the death sentence's supplement, its being predicated on life, and the phone calls cause her to give over her remaining time to struggling not to think the impossible:

> 'Can you not ignore it, Dame Lettie?'
> 'No, I cannot. I have tried, but it troubles me deeply. It *is* a troublesome remark.'
> 'Perhaps you might obey it', said Miss Taylor.
> 'What's that you say?'
> 'You might, perhaps, try to remember that you must die.'[91]

The three characters who find the death sentence least 'troublesome' are Charmian,[92] the aged artist who is at peace with her coming death and who, via a charming slice of karma, has her novels come back into print during the course of the story, the policeman engaged to 'solve' the 'mystery' – another explosion of generic crime fiction since there is nothing to solve – and the gerontologist Alec Warner (one who warns), who feels that his *raison d'être* dies with the 'death' of his notes in an accident, but maintains that the promise of death is a proof of existence: ' "[t]his grave-yard is a kind of evidence", he said, "that other people exist".'[93] Some of the book's keenest irony comes with the demand by the less thoughtful characters that the policeman Mortimer 'solve' the mystery of death; Mortimer opens the files to all involved, and there is little agreement as to the nature of the voice which utters the generalised death sentence.[94] Nor should there be, since the warning is the mere neutral statement of a limit. The mystery is magnificently unmysterious – all must die, the ultimate autopoesis – and the ageing policeman fully agrees that there is an alternative logic working within what is lazily perceived to be a threat:

> 'Without an ever-present sense of death life is insipid . . .' [said Mortimer] . . . 'I consider,' said Janet Sidebottome, 'that what Mr. Mortimer was saying just now about resigning ourselves to death is most uplifting and consoling. The religious point of view is too easily forgotten these days, and I thank you, Mr. Mortimer.'[95]

This is the double-bind in 'remembering death', since to do so one has to conjure up an unthinkable future, never quite coming yet always *a-venir*.[96] No crime has been committed by the phone calls, unless it is the crime of being human itself, which could be 'solved' only by a metaphysical presence, an absurd narrative omniscience: ' "[t]he trouble with these people", he said, "they think that the C.I.D. are God, understanding all mysteries and all knowledge. Whereas we are only policemen." '[97] At the non-conclusion of the non-investigation, Charmian, who has little idea what the fuss is all about, merely declares that she has enjoyed the car-ride to Mortimer's and the day out among friends, rendering benevolent the voice which reminds everyone that death is what all this pleasure is *not*, or not yet: ' "I for one like Henry Mortimer, and I thoroughly enjoyed the drive".'[98] Charmian's memory is, as always in Spark's key characters, highly novelistic in its ordering of events (to the frustration of the other characters); yet it is also more certain – she is less troubled by whether something has 'really' happened than by its effects (in 'her' narrative and Spark's).[99]

Even more ironic are the constant battles between the would-be benefactors of the wills of the yet older 'grannies' in hospital, and of those found in the keenly read obituary columns. In a sense the grannies, though alive, have allowed themselves to be reduced to bare *will* itself – as is attested by their tendency to use up most of their remaining life discussing who has died. Much of the plot centres on the claim on the estate of the recently deceased Lisa Brooke, whose helper, Mrs Pettigrew, plots for Brooke's money throughout, as she will later plot for Charmian's.

Pettigrew hatches schemes to solicit Charmian's undisclosed signature, failing to realise that the exchange of signatures implies her own death in the closure of her future, the settling of her own *will*.[100] Will is subject only to the limit of the will of God: '[i]f this is God's will then it is mine'.[101] The behaviour of contesting wills is all form and no content.

Lettie thus expresses her anger via threats to change her will, gambling her remaining *will* itself without realising.[102] Action reasserts itself through the determination of inaction. The fact that *will* exists only in the form of joyless money takes the same logic as the novel's leitmotif, 'remember you must die': the spectre of poverty is so great that it can cause each character to miss the present, in the sense understood by postcolonialism, a time at which experience is not split – in this case between a future already spoken for, the abstract power conferred by signing the will, and a past during which one has been destined to struggle to keep up with *will*.

Even the grannies' *mauvaise foi* obsession with the recently deceased, however, receives a true *memento mori* as the ward takes in a new batch of the super-old, the seniles, who are unable to do much for themselves.[103] Each new batch causes shock and thanks to God (there – temporarily – but for the grace of), another comparative activity which blocks action. But it turns out that, hidden within the talk of the Maud Long Ward (the 'maudlin word'?), is the insight that the order 'remember that you must die' would represent a real summoning up of the unthinkable.[104] The irony of the novel, again humorously posing as crime fiction, largely inheres in the fact that the death sentence is not a crime, it is a promise,[105] and, as with all promises, it merely pushes action into the future: the goal, the *telos*, of each character is their own extinction.[106] When the grannies check the obituary columns keenly each day, they go through minor stages of mourning, inflected by wry Sparkian dialogue, via which process they are more able than the doctors to affirm their selves.[107] This holds true only so long as they don't get locked in a battle of *wills* or frozen by a death sentence.

Towards the end of the novel – between the breakdown of the 'police investigation' and the list of obituaries which will end the book – there is another wander into genre crime nearly as absurd as that of *Robinson*, in which the right to pronounce the identity of the one behind the death sentence and the battle of wills brings almost all of the characters into suspicion. The eventual 'conclusion' and the bathetic loss of the big prize to one who has already lost his mind are shown to be almost unnecessary, since it has by now become clear that the message, whatever form its voice takes, is a telephonic and telepathic – that is, from somewhere else, reading, as in *The Matrix* (1999) – [108] telephonic communication as virtual transportation, metaphor. Endings are virtually transported from beyond anything fixed in the writing of the text itself, and within the writing of a narrator which is ironically *too* omniscient to be omniscient. This also accounts for the irony of the inevitable autopoesis of the story as the death sentence is used as a refrain in a mock-Georgian poem by a churlish elderly gentleman – pointing 'back' to *The Comforters* and 'forward' to the child-like absorption of generic yarns in *The Prime of Miss Jean Brodie*.[109]

Telepathy here is narratively enabled by the way the ages of the protagonists allow dialogue that is at times chaotic and seemingly senseless, wherein lies the inevitability and impossibility of death.[110] The telephone merely ironises the omniscient narrator in showing how its impossibility is a 'segregated' form of telepathy:

> Dame Lettie thought, She is jealous of anyone else's having to do with Charmian.
>   Perhaps I am, thought Miss Taylor who could read Dame Lettie's idea.[111]

In the maudlin word, telepathy is rampant in a sense that makes a nonsense of – or rather, takes fully at its word – the idea of an omniscient narrator letting the reader in on various details as they unfold in a traditional Eng. Lit. style narrative.[112] The telephone call, whose content is always already known to all, yet is always the limit of all possibilities, is merely an image of this telepathy. There is (again recalling the *nouveau roman*) no story to be unfolded; we are in the realm of pure form, with no goodies or baddies, merely the impetus to action, which some of the characters take up more readily than others.

But this argument has not itself come to me entirely telepathically; in fact, it has been suggested via the thousand-year-old technology of the book. A merciful move away from the Spark-as-Eng. Lit. tradition towards seeing Spark as specifically Scottish and critically proactive came with the 2002 book *Theorizing Muriel Spark*: edited by, wouldn't it be, a Scot. This book showcases a wide range of readings of Spark's *oeuvre* which diverge sharply from views of Spark as Eng. Lit. slim-volume-monger, and contains at least two contributions which should change the tone of Spark studies altogether – those of Willy Maley and Nicholas Royle (from whose essay this chapter sub-title has been purloined, just as Royle himself purloined Spark's *Memento Mori* as the title of his chapter). Appropriately both essays appear in the 'Deconstruction' section. The novel opens itself up to productive deconstruction in its anti-realism, or as Royle puts it,

> [the death-listing] final section of *Memento Mori* operates as a kind of memento, a kind of warning or foreshadowing of – and hinting towards – the eerie structure of *The Prime of Miss Jean Brodie* (1961). In this novel, too,

notions of age, in particular youth and prime, are subjected to strange displacements. The final section of *Memento Mori* performs a time-skip and lets us know, in a comically but disquietingly cursory manner, how and when the various remaining characters in the story died. In *The Prime of Miss Jean Brodie* these death-divulging time-skips punctuate the narrative throughout . . .

The Prime of Miss Jean Brodie is another *memento mori*, at once about the concept (if it is one) of 'memento mori', and itself a *memento mori*. The earlier novel rings and resonates across it.[113]

'Prime', as in 'Enlightenment'

It is in the hirsute gait of Miss Jean Brodie that we find Spark's most post-Enlightenment, most theoretical, statement. This is Spark's only novel so far set in Scotland, but this fact, as Ian Rankin reminds us, should not blind us into thinking that there is no specifically Scottish thinking being worked out through the whole of Spark's work. *The Prime*, though, takes Edinburgh Enlightenment thinking by the jugular, unfolding as a struggle of individual betterment against barbarism, set in an Edinburgh in which the Enlightenment is building up to its logical climax via the last gasps of empire, 'free trade' and 'race': the 1930s seen from the narrative stance of the Welfare Statist late 1950s.

Only half-consciously does Miss Brodie take on the fact that the idea of the great individual over decision-by-committee, the legacy of that same Enlightenment which built Edinburgh New Town to celebrate the city's achievements and separated its thinkers into sterile, single apartments, was born from aspiring eighteenth-century thought stuck in the eighteenth-century condition. Her self-styled 'Scottish and European' is clearly a nonsense: Jean Brodie shows just how British Edinburgh can be. Edinburgh is perhaps, Scottish Parliamentary pantomimes notwithstanding, the most British city left today (since Leeds, for example, doesn't have much consciousness of a difference between British and English). Spark uses extremely subtle touches to let the reader into this historiography and its violent legacy. As Alan Riach says,

It is possible to imagine Muriel Spark's world written by someone else without a sense of humour but it is, most essentially, that combining of deadly seriousness with murderous laughter that is so entirely characteristic of that world. It is the most unmistakable quality in *The Prime of Miss Jean Brodie* or *The Ballad of Peckham Rye*.[114]

As is made explicit in the novel, Brodie sees her own creation of a small clique of 'great individuals' (she is a fan of Thomas Carlyle, the Scot famous for his 'Great Men' view of history, who went to enormous lengths to Anglicise himself and wheedle his way into the Eng. Lit. canon), as a complement to the cliques formed in the image of Mussolini and, later, towards her downfall, Hitler. From the crucial first ten pages of the novel we learn that what is special and heroic about Miss Brodie and her set is that they are anti-curriculum, have no 'team spirit' and understand that fame and heroism require pragmatic distinction.[115] This form of betterment, of course, is the direct inheritor of the eighteenth-century condition, which buried any national culture available to the nineteenth century. Miss Brodie's own experiences are ranked in import-ance before the standard histories, as in the comic episode in which text-books are used as camouflage against the invasion of the headmistress.[116] And again the key to moulding a society from great individuals lies in the Enlightenment analogue of the visual: ' "[w]here there is no vision," Miss Brodie had assured them, "the people perish . . ."'[117]

This is solidly platonic and has the quality of a leading-out (*e-duco*) mentality, as in the moment (often taken as merely humorous) when Brodie asks 'who is the greatest Italian painter?' and then replies to her pupil's answer, ' "[t]hat is incorrect. The answer is Giotto. He is my favourite".'[118] This is funny, but there is also a serious destruction of absolutes taking place here, and these platonic absolutes are as much the target of the critical-ironic Spark as they were of the critical-ironic Derrida with whom she roughly shares a time-frame. Miss Brodie's job as she sees it, as was Plato's, is to lead her pupils towards the truth, which, as absolute, has always and will always be there. This is a work of constant progress *towards*, and we can discern Adam Smith's stadial theory of history as underpinning Miss Brodie's ideas of movement both through stages of indoctrination and from youth to prime. Thus David Lodge has pointed out thematic similarities to *Jane Eyre*, where *The Prime* is a warped *bildungsroman* – whether that prime be the prime of individuals or of nations/races, as in Mussolini's *fascisti*, growing from the heroism of ancient Rome.[119]

As Lodge points out, in Eng. Lit. the omniscient narrator lost favour when Nietzsche took a grip over Hegel.[120] If Spark's novels are a guide, this happened in Scotland before England, where the omniscient narrator remained omnipresent during the early 1960s, suggesting that Scotland chimed with Foucauldian and Derridean thought sooner than has gener-ally been appreciated. And all of this hints at what is to come: the *exclu-sion* (rather than the centrality, as is often assumed) of Spark from Eng. Lit. leads to forms of narration which show close similarities to the free indirect speech and interplay of persons in James Kelman. Lodge notes that the narration of *The Prime of Miss Jean Brodie* makes the film version (1969) far too flat and monocular.[121] Flash-forwards are certainly difficult in film, making the novel's interplay of points of view impossible, missing the thematic point of ironising Edinburgh *literati* progress, and reducing a philosophical address to a tale of a bossy teacher.

Returning to a device of *Robinson*, another character has to step forward to deal with what is now a full-blown fascistic (neo-Enlightenment) megalomania, this character being Sandy Stranger – the only real *stranger* in the Brodie set. Again, Sandy's actions, like January's, are to rescue a spirituality from Brodie's secular, self-made, fascistic, religion.[122] The realisation that her teacher has elected herself as a Calvinistic conduit of Providence – and a supporter of Hitler – is what leads Sandy to 'betray' Brodie, again undoing the sect which the teacher has built up around herself.[123] It is in this sense and this sense only that Spark uses the omniscient narrator, to show, frequently to brilliantly comic effect, the abuses of omniscience.[124]

Notes

1. Muriel Spark, 'The Desegregation of Art', *Proceedings of the American Academy of Arts and Letters*, second series, 1971, excerpted in Joseph Hynes, ed., *Critical Essays on Muriel Spark* (New York: Hall, 1992), pp. 33–7; ed. Martin McQuillan, *Theorizing Muriel Spark* (Basingstoke: Palgrave, 2002).
2. Spark, 'The Desegregation of Art', pp. 34–5.
3. Ibid., p. 36.
4. Ian Rankin, 'The Deliberate Cunning of Muriel Spark', in Gavin Wallace and Randall Stevenson, eds., *The Scottish Novel since the Seventies: New Visions, Old Dreams* (Edinburgh: Edinburgh University Press, 1993), pp. 41–53: 51.
5. Muriel Spark, 'Edinburgh-born', *New Statesman* 64, 10 August 1962, p. 180, repr. in Hynes, *Critical Essays*, pp. 21–23: 21.
6. Ibid., p. 22.
7. Muriel Spark, *The Comforters* (London: St. Martin's Press, 1957), pp. 42 *et passim*.
8. Ibid., p. 150.
9. Ibid., p. 46; cf. R. D. Laing, *The Divided Self: A Study of Sanity and Madness* (London: Tavistock, 1960); cf. David Cooper, *Psychiatry and Anti-Psychiatry* (London: Tavistock, 1967); Gilles Deleuze and Felix Guattari, trans. Robert Hurley, Mark Seem and Helen R. Lane, *Anti-Oedipus: Capitalism and Schizophrenia* (Minneapolis: University of Minnesota Press, 1983 [1972]).
10. Janice Galloway, *The Trick is to Keep Breathing* (Edinburgh: Polygon, 1989).
11. On neurosis see e.g. Spark, *The Comforters*, p. 78; quotation is from p. 54; Joy Stone is from Galloway, *The Trick is to Keep Breathing*.

12. The case is strengthened by Alexander Trocchi's mid-1950s interest in contemporary French writing, which travelled back to Scotland, and the publisher John Calder's championing of the *nouveau roman*; John Fletcher and John Calder, eds., *The Nouveau Roman Reader* (London: John Calder, 1986).

13. Alain Robbe-Grillet, trans. Richard Howard, *The Erasers* (London: Calder and Boyars, 1966 [1953]), p. 7.

14. Rankin, 'The Deliberate Cunning of Muriel Spark', p. 42.

15. Ibid., p. 43.

16. Ibid., p. 46.

17. Ibid., p. 43; Martin Amis, *London Fields* (London: Cape, 1989).

18. Spark, *The Comforters*, p. 95.

19. Ibid., pp. 53, 56.

20. Ibid., p. 97.

21. Muriel Spark, 'My Conversion', *Twentieth Century* 170, Autumn 1961, pp. 58–63, excerpted in Hynes, *Critical Essays*, pp. 24–8; p. 27.

22. Frank Kermode, 'Interviews with Seven English Novelists', *Partisan Review* 30, 1, Spring 1963, excerpted as 'Muriel Spark's House of Fiction', in Hynes, *Critical Essays*, pp. 29–32: 30; Kermode's orthography.

23. Ibid., p. 31.

24. Spark, *The Comforters*, pp. 69, 76.

25. Ibid., p. 139.

26. See Jacques Derrida, trans. Catherine Porter, 'Psyché: Inventions of the Other', in Lindsay Waters and Wlad Godzich, eds., *Reading de Man Reading* (Minneapolis: University of Minnesota Press, 1989), pp. 25–65.

27. Ibid., p. 137.

28. Ibid., p. 170.

29. Ibid., p. 202.

30. Muriel Spark, *Robinson* (Harmondsworth: Penguin, 1964 [1958]), p. 7.

31. Velma Bourgeois Richmond, 'On Robinson', in *Muriel Spark* (New York: Ungar, 1984) excerpted in Hynes, *Critical Essays*, pp. 104–8: 105.

32. J. M. Coetzee, *Foe* (London: Penguin, 1987 [1986]).

33. See, for example, 'The Seraph and the Zambesi', said to have inaugurated her prose career, with its bird that cries 'go 'way', in *All the Stories of Muriel Spark* (New York: New Directions, 2000 [1987]), pp. 232–73.

34. Spark, *Robinson*, p. 83.

35. Ibid., p. 17.

36. For example, ibid., p. 50.

37. Ibid., p. 93

38. Ibid., pp. 19, 23–4.

39. Ibid., pp. 124.

40. Ibid., pp. 30, 20.

41. Cf. Gilles Deleuze, trans. Daniel W. Smith and Michael A. Greco, 'Plato, the Greeks', *Essays Critical and Clinical* (Minneapolis: University of Minnesota Press, 1997 [1993]), pp. 136–7.

42. For example Spark, *Robinson*, pp. 55–6.

43. Ibid., p. 37; cf. Gilles Deleuze and Felix Guattari, trans. Brian Massumi, *A Thousand Plateaus: Capitalism and Schizophrenia* (Minneapolis: University of Minnesota Press (1987 [1980]), pp. 203–5, 510.

44. Spark, *Robinson*, pp. 64, 59.

45. Spark, *The Prime of Miss Jean Brodie*, p. 133; Irvine Welsh, *Trainspotting* (London: Minerva, 1993).

46. Spark, *Robinson*, pp. 80–1; see also, for example, pp. 90, 165.

47. Ibid., pp. 51, 75.

48. Ibid., p. 80.

49. Ibid., p. 89.

50. Ibid., p. 129; see also p. 135.

51. Ibid., p. 161.

52. Ibid., p. 115.

53. Ibid., pp. 111, 113, 120, 155–6.

54. Cf. Jacques Derrida, trans. Samuel Weber and Jeffrey Mehlman, 'Signature Event Context', in *Limited Inc.* (Evanston, IL: Northwestern University Press, 1988), pp. 1–23.

55. Spark, *Robinson*, p. 153.

56. Ibid., pp. 116 *et passim*.

57. Ibid., p. 149, see also p. 152.

58. Ibid., p. 163.

59. Ibid., p. 162.

60. *Only Fools and Horses*, BBC TV, 1981–2001.

61. http://www.bbc.co.uk/sitcom/winner.shtml. Consulted 2005.

62. See Michael Gardiner, 'Endless Enlightenment: Eye-Operated Technology and the Political Economy of Vision', *Reconstruction* 4.1: http://www.reconstruction.ws/041/gardiner.htm.

63. Muriel Spark, *The Ballad of Peckham Rye* (New York: New Directions, 1999 [1960]), pp. 25, 8.

64. Ibid., p. 9.

65. Alan Bold, *Muriel Spark* (London: Methuen, 1986), p. 53; see also Peter Kemp, 'On *The Ballad of Peckham Rye*', in Hynes, *Critical Essays on Muriel Spark*, pp. 114–22: 120; cf. Linda Colley, *Britons: Forging The Nation 1707–1837* (London: Pimlico, 2003 [1992]).

66. Edwin Muir, *Scottish Journey* (Edinburgh: Mainstream, 2004 [1935]), pp. 45, 50.

67. Spark, *The Ballad of Peckham Rye*, p. 76; Kemp, 'On *The Ballad of Peckham Rye*', pp. 115, 119, 122.

68. Muriel Spark, 'You Should Have Seen the Mess', in *All the Stories of Muriel Spark*, pp. 141–6.

69. Spark, *The Ballad of Peckham Rye*, pp. 19, 63; Neil Jordan, dir. *The Crying Game* (British Screen et al., 1992).

70. Spark, *The Ballad of Peckham Rye*, p. 38.

71. Ibid., p. 60.

72. Ibid., p. 118.

73. Nikolas Rose, *Governing the Soul: The Shaping of the Private Self* (London: Routledge, 1990); Pat Kane, *The Play Ethic: A Manifesto for a Different Way of Living* (London: Macmillan, 2004).

74. Spark, *The Ballad of Peckham Rye*, p. 83.

75. Ibid., p. 15.

76. Ibid., p. 50.

77. Ibid., p. 26.

78. Alasdair Gray, *1982 Janine* (London: Cape, 1984); cf. Duncan Petrie, *Contemporary Scottish Fictions: Film, Television, and the Novel* (Edinburgh: Edinburgh University Press, 2004), p. 47.

79. Spark, *The Ballad of Peckham Rye*, p. 37.

80. Ibid., p. 39.

81. Ibid., p. 65.

82. Ibid., p. 110.

83. Ibid., p. 72; see also p. 64, and cf. Dougal's comic-flirtatious use of 'visions' to distract Merle, p. 99.

84. Ibid., pp. 68, 70, 75.

85. Ibid., pp. 119–21.

86. Ibid., p. 76; Kemp 'On *The Ballad of Peckham Rye*', p. 114.

87. For Trevor, see Spark, *The Ballad of Peckham Rye*, pp. 97, 134; for the police, p. 114; for Douglas *as* police, p. 125; cf. Merle's confusion of the police report and biography, p. 129.

88. Ibid., pp. 81, 102, 135.

89. Ibid., pp. 138–9.

90. Willy Maley, 'Not to Deconstruct? Righting and Deference in *Not to Disturb*', in McQuillan, ed. *Theorizing Muriel Spark*, pp. 170–88: 181.

91. Spark, *Memento Mori* (New York: W. W. Norton, 2000 [1959]), p. 39.

92. Ibid., pp. 128, 147.

93. Ibid., p. 72.

94. Ibid., pp. 149–52.

95. Ibid., p. 153.

96. Cf. Jacques Derrida, 'This is not an Oral Footnote', in Stephen A. Barney, ed., *Annotation and its Texts* (Oxford: Oxford University Press, 1991), pp. 192–205.

97. Spark, *Memento Mori*, p. 155, cf. p. 169.

98. Ibid., p. 159.

99. Ibid., pp. 76–80.

100. Jacques Derrida, trans. Barbara Harlow, *Spurs: Nietzsche's Styles* (Chicago: University of Chicago Press, 1979), p. 127; Derrida, trans. Thomas Dutoit, *Aporias: Dying – Awaiting (One Another at) the 'Limits of Truth'* (Stanford, CA: Stanford University Press, 1993), p. 74.

101. Spark, *Memento Mori*, p. 17.

102. Ibid., p. 104.

103. Ibid., p. 172.

104. Ibid., p. 176.

105. See Jacques Derrida, trans. Tina Kendall and Shari Benstock, 'Ulysses Gramophone: Hear Say Yes in Joyce', in Attridge, *Acts of Literature* (London: Routledge, 1992) pp. 256–309: pp. 277–83, pp. 300–5.

106. Cf. Jacques Derrida, trans. Samuel Weber, 'Afterword: Toward an Ethic of Discussion', in *Limited Inc.* (Evanston, IL: Northwestern University Press, 1988), pp. 111–60.

107. Cf. Jacques Derrida, trans. Peggy Kamuf, '*Istrice 2: Ich Bünn all hier*', in *Points . . . Interviews* (Stanford, CA: Stanford University Press, 2005), pp. 300–26.

108. Andy and Larry Wachowski, dirs., *The Matrix*, Groucho II et al., 1999; cf. Oshii Mamoru, dir., *Kokaku Kidotai* [*Ghost in the Shell*], Bandai et al., 1995.

109. Spark, *Memento Mori*, p. 198.

110. For example, ibid., pp. 30, 106.

111. Ibid., p. 40.

112. Cf. Jacques Derrida, trans. Peggy Kamuf, *Given Time: 1. Counterfeit Money* (Chicago: Chicago University Press, 1992), p. 153.

113. Nicholas Royle, 'Memento Vivere', in McQuillan, ed., *Theorizing Muriel Spark*, pp. 189–203: 199–200.

114. Alan Riach, *Representing Scotland in Literature, Popular Culture, and Iconography: The Masks of the Modern Nation* (Basingstoke: Palgrave, 2005), p. 241.

115. Spark, *The Prime of Miss Jean Brodie*, p. 2.

116. Ibid., pp. 5, 9.

117. Ibid., p. 4.

118. Ibid., p. 8.

119. David Lodge, 'The Uses and Abuses of Omniscience: Method and Meaning in Muriel Spark's *The Prime of Miss Jean Brodie*', from *The Novelist at the Crossroads and Other Essays on Fiction and Criticism* (London: Routledge, 1971), pp. 119–44, repr. in Hynes, *Critical Essays*, pp. 151–73: 162.

120. Ibid., p. 153.

121. Ronald Neame, dir., *The Prime of Miss Jean Brodie*, Twentieth Century Fox 1969; Lodge, 'The Uses and Abuses of Omniscience', p. 157.

122. Lodge, 'The Uses and Abuses of Omniscience', pp. 160, 165.

123. Ibid., pp. 165–8.

124. Ibid., pp. 166–7.

Chapter 4

Les Évènements Écossais

The Situation

Alexander Trocchi edited the journal *Merlin* from Paris from the surprisingly early year of 1952. It went on to become the first organ to promote Samuel Beckett to an Anglophone audience and to publish Eugene Ionesco in English, and maintained an extraordinary cast of writers throughout its three-year tenure. On a research scholarship to Paris, Trocchi had become involved with the movement of Lettrism, a socially proactive alternative to Surrealism, which was seen as having been fossilised by Maurice Nadeau's *History of Surrealism* (in French, 1945).[1] The Lettrists, and later, more significantly, their heirs the Situationists, drew no distinction between literary and political acts, but rather attempted to turn everyday events, via the *dérive*, into politico-cultural happenings. Trocchi became a key connector within the movement, and his apparent lack of novelistic output belies his productivity as an editor and activist.

Trocchi began a creative relationship with Guy Debord in 1955, but Situationism's importance in Scotland would take until the early 1960s to sink in. This is slightly ironic: in Edwin Morgan's reading, Sartre and Camus are obvious continental precedents for Trocchi, indeed Sartre is the glue from which the Situationists were trying to unstick themselves, but equally, Trocchi is an obvious descendant of James Hogg, the critical writer on Scotland's 'Calvinist inheritance', Puritanism and the Protestant ethics of the Enlightenment.[2]

By September 1960, the Situationist International (SI) were producing a pamphlet for the Trocchi drugs trial in London, entitled *Hands Off Alexander Trocchi*, 'who is beyond all doubt England's [sic] most intelligent creative artist today'.[3] As with Kenneth White later, there was a slight puzzlement in France over why Trocchi was not more widely read in his native land. Trocchi was a thoroughgoing practitioner of the *dérive* (junkies had to be resourceful anyway), but he was also an editor aware of his position in publishing history, and perhaps picked up on how Debord-style Situationism's perpetually jittery sense of contemporariness tended to lose its sense of literary-historical placement altogether, so that even Alain Robbe-Grillet, the avant-gardist of five years earlier (he who prefigures the early Spark) comes in for abuse simply for being five years early. This kind of stuff almost leads one to wonder whether there were any French artists *not* claiming to be avant-grade. History in Debord's Situationism seems to have closed down to a series of Althusserian sections equally readable as slices of the whole ideology. But when 1960s Scottish radicals came to Althusser, they were more inclined to see an ongoing dialectic of ideology and resistance than frozen totalities; Scots aimed more at a place in *a* history and to read precursors on their own terms, however flawed they seemed. If this is right, it separates Trocchi from Debord, and the former, *de facto*, would have a longer-lasting cultural currency. If historical precedent was to be run down by French Situationism, it may even be that Scots grasped the postcolonial context of 1968 more directly than French Situationists, since they recognised the Algerian War of Independence as *still* being central, as they would see other decolonisations in the Anglophone world as part of their own ambivalent inheritance (and 1968 itself saw a decolonisation of parts of the Caribbean).

The time of the rise of Situationism, the early 1960s, was also crucial to the Scottish cultural imagination, most dramatically seen in factional shenanigans at the 1962 Book Festival, but also reflected, more fundamentally, in the way people lived: the vast majority of Glasgow rehousing took place between 1958 and 1965. The convergence of the tower and the literary is important not only for the changes wrought in the Glasgow novel from the beginning of the 1960s, but also, as we have seen in Chapter 1, for the tower's 'plagiarism' of physical resistance to the earth, as the personal is rendered systematic and subjective. Situationism similarly saw overdetermined urban space as its raw material, the *dérive* its 'text': they perceived space not as a Humean projection into a visual field of associations (horizontal or vertical), but as pure social product, the output of institutions: an 'abstract space homogenises the conflicts that produce capitalist space'.[4] In part chiming with a very early Virilio, they claim that 'everything that was directly lived has moved away into a representation', and 'abstract space homogenises the conflicts that produce capitalist space'.[5] 'Capitalist space', for Deleuze and for radical Scots, was now revealed as the space of Humean universalism, once projected wishfully onto the empire and concretised in both Edinburgh New Town and later in the more abrupt and system-built version of the Welfare State's tower block.[6] (In a wonderful turn of irony, Gregor

Fisher, later the Glasgow everyman punter Rab C. Nesbitt, joins the highly English Winston Smith (John Hurt) in studiously ignoring an expected lift malfunction in Victory Mansions under the watch of a Party telescreen, in Michael Radford's film version of *Nineteen Eighty-Four* [1984].)[7]

For the Situationists, proactively inhabiting urban space *was* literary experiment – with the caveat that the habit of wandering around the streets was not to be merely Baudelairean flâneurism, since it sought to suspend and challenge social class, to recognise the city as a 'war zone' between experience and image (*pace* Virilio), rather than maintaining class at a decadent remove.[8] ('Warlike' in Latin, we should bear in mind from here on, is *polemic*.) The idea of the city as image requiring a proactive response was not lost on those Glaswegian thinkers – Trocchi included – who were seeing their home city rationalised in terms of the tower. There is a whole history of Scottish Situationism and Scottish pro-1968 thought buried under the official one which states that a few poets took drugs and thought up crazy schemes condemning education and promoting schizophrenia. This is also the time of Alan Spence and William McIlvanney, when Glasgow speech broke into prose literature, albeit not yet with the assurance of Alasdair Gray and James Kelman.

The anti-spectacular movements of the Situationist *dérive* in urban space, then, begin to unravel a whole range of pro- and neo-Enlightenment *Scottish* technological 'advances', in the stadial sense of the term advance, including the very pavement itself (tarmacadam) – the making official of the path – street culture – the train, developed by James Watt and linking Edinburgh and the suddenly remote London, and John Logie Baird's pure spectacle of television, which has since morphed into new forms of auto-interaction.[9] These advances would be rolled back, returned to earth in what Kenneth White later called geopoetics, his 'Jargon Papers' being published at exactly the time when Glaswegians were being moved to out-of-town estates, and resonating with Trocchi's stress of play over state-controlled 'leisure'.

Trocchi's 'Invisible Insurrection of a Million Minds' can now be read as an important point of crossover; it appeared in *New Saltire* in 1963, a journal which printed radical and international (meaning, from abroad) literature. Trocchi's publishing career by this time was well underway, but, like White, he either stuck to publishing outside Scotland, and tended to dry up while there, or found little favour there. White, who had started by studying Surrealism, which – although quickly derided by Situationism – he aptly saw in terms of opening up 'fields',[10] returned to Glasgow in 1963 and started the Jargon Group, whose first paper was appropriated for Trocchi's Sigma Portfolio. White found that distributing Sigma material while lecturing at Glasgow University put him in disfavour, and returned to France. At this point Trocchi and White both saw Glasgow as educating dysfunctionally. In an address in 1989 – precisely bisecting the inter-referendum dates – White spoke of 'abandoning a sinking ship' which had been leaking since 1745, and of a Scottish tendency to 'mistake ruts for roots'; later he would describe a Spenglerian decline in Glasgow between 1954 and 1967.[11] Since then, in a sign of the times, Glasgow has become one of Scotland's most proactive universities.

Split into parts and ignoring the generic borders of the poetic and the prosaic, White's 'Travels in the Drifting Dawn' begins with a fictional meeting with Trocchi ('Joe'), probably describing White's first meeting with Trocchi in real life.[12] (Trocchi was highly unusual in being a non-American writer to have a commonly used Beat pseudonym.) Despite the sense of passing through – the later White is sometimes associated with Deleuzian lines of flight in contradistinction to Trocchi's heroin-bound plans for safe environments – and despite White's having become a French citizen, the prose of the meeting is full of Scotticisms. As always, walks become travels through conceptual and literary landscapes; here Leith Walk (again) acts as Hyde to middle-class Edinburgh's Jekyll and carries its own ghosts.

From 1961, White's missives from Gourgounel, France, begin to feed into his ideas on geopoetics, a movement concretised in the *Insitut international de géopoétique* from 1989, and a poetic formalising of the relationship between perception and the physical environment. He participated in the events of Paris 1968 – themselves based on a movement of ideas to which Scots had contributed. Nevertheless, as Michel Duclos points out, afterwards in Pau, White set to digesting a number of French thinkers, including Deleuze and Guattari, in order to contextualise what had happened in 1968.[13] Deleuze would be one of the panel judging White's doctoral thesis on nomadism in 1979. A slightly curt and late-added mention is to be found in Deleuze and Guattari's *A Thousand Plateaus*:

> Kenneth White recently (1970) stressed this dissymmetrical complementarity between a race-tribe (the Celts, who feel they are Celts) and a milieu-space (the Orient, the Gobi desert . . .). White demonstrates that this strange composite, the marriage of the Celt and the Orient, inspires a properly nomad thought that sweeps up English literature and constitutes American literature.[14]

From the mid-1960s, France was in general more welcoming to White as a theorist than was Scotland (helping to explain why we persistently see May 1968 as purely French, and perhaps balancing the fact that Trocchi is now undergoing such a high-profile rediscovery in Scotland).

In 1985 he was awarded the *Grand Prix de rayonnement français de l'Académie française* for his work as a whole; at around the same time, conversely, he was writing for a Francophone audience on Scotland in an academic/traveller vein, the closest volume entitled simply *Écosse*.[15]

The interest shown by figures like Trocchi and White came at a critical time in French history and added to a general assault on what had been taken for granted by the eighteenth-century *literati*: not only France dealing with its post-colonial legacy in theory, but also Great Britain dealing with its own legacy. The breakdown of the British empire with Scotland at its centre would become a form of postcolonialism outwith recognised Postcolonial Studies (perhaps because Scotland was never fully coloniser or colonised, which leaves many critics uncertain as to where to find their victim) – while the Scottish literature and criticism which appeared in anthologies in Scotland itself was still largely Second Renaissance.

'The Invisible Insurrection of a Million Minds' would become the first paper of Trocchi's Sigma Portfolio, which ran from 1963 and assumed, half a decade before the *évènements*, manifesto-like and interventionist tones which showed full interest in writing's effects and none in its typology. In this first paper Trocchi argues for the need for a cultural revolution based on broadly Situationist lines, a revolution which must be total (thus suturing the eighteenth-century split of voice and environment) in order to avoid reconfinement and reabsorption into the academy: not a Leninist *coup d'état* but a *coup du monde*.[16] Or as Debord had it, there was a need for a move from a 'romantic-revolutionary' stance to 'an organisation of professional revolutionaries in culture'.[17]

As a move towards an experiential *coup du monde*, Trocchi's Sigma Project imagines a spin-off general cultural advisory service, a zany idea for its time perhaps (though not to R. D. Laing and radical poets like Edwin Morgan, Ian Hamilton Finlay and Tom McGrath), but one which seems entirely reasonable in the 2000s in the light of Pat Kane's *The Play Ethic*, which can be seen as re-reading Trocchi-ite Scottish Situationism within the polemic zone of the digital divide. Trocchi agrees with Debord in stressing that a revolution should be 'culture-led', rather than the result of any wishful change of government.[18] Indeed, if intelligence – which, in his definition, entails knowledge of freedom – becomes self-conscious, politicians will be sidestepped:

> cultural revolt must seize the grids of expression and the powerhouses of the mind. Intelligence must become self-conscious, realize its own power, and, on a global scale, transcending functions that are no longer appropriate, dare to exercise it. History will not overthrow national governments: it will outflank them.[19]

In November 1962 Trocchi formally joined the Situationist International (SI) but resigned in 1964 when the SI refused to participate in his fledgling Sigma Project.[20] Which of the two projects is more pioneering – or even which has more relevance to the cultural politics of May 1968 – is debatable. In any case the Sigma Project, like the anti-university, remained successful in Amsterdam through the early 1970s. In paper number one, in what we would now see as strikingly Deleuzian language, Trocchi states that in place of an unchanging human nature (or a universal state of sympathy, as in Hume), we should accept the process of becoming: '[w]e must reject the conventional fiction of "unchanging human nature". There is in fact no such permanence anywhere. There is only *becoming*.'[21]

For the Trocchi of the early 1960s, as for Guy Debord before him, and the Deleuze and Guattari of *A Thousand Plateaus* after him, insurrection can only occur spontaneously and *en masse*, in a cultural figure whose function is:

> modifying, correcting, polluting, deflecting, corrupting, eroding, outflanking . . . inspiring what we might call the *invisible insurrection*. It will come on the mass of men, if it comes at all, not as something they have voted for, struck for, fought for, but like the changing seasons; they will find themselves in and stimulated by the *situation* consciously at last to recreate it within and without as their own.[22]

Since problems of redistribution of wealth were not, for Trocchi, being solved by the United Nations, and the two superpowers were at stalemate, 'this world' of perceptions (again, like Virilio on virtual 'plagiarism') was a site of literary polemic. This prefigures the movement of the lines of flight which in *A Thousand Plateaus* move through received concepts to prevent them being frozen into 'opinion'. Thus (and here we can read in a Nietzschean turn, which would become central to 1968 thinking) if we witness 'the end of the world' in a Situationist revolution, it will merely be the end of the world as it has been commodified to be seen: '*Si nous ne voulons pas assister au spectacle de la fin du monde, il nous faut travailler à la fin du monde du spectacle.*'[23]

At this point 'The Invisible Insurrection' takes an intriguing turn: Trocchi cites Lloyd George's virtual admission of defeat after the 1919 disturbances and the threat of a General Strike – disturbances which were centred in Glasgow – where the prime minister gives as his only defence the idea that the strikers would precipitate a constitutional crisis which would leave a vacuum needing to be filled by another governmental body. Lloyd George assumes that the Leninists were, in Deleuzian terms, 'state-happy' – perhaps correctly, as it turned out.[24] Situationism was a different case, and Trocchi's answer to Lloyd George, as would be the answer of Deleuze, Guattari and Foucault to the lurch towards the Stalinism of the French Communist Party after May 1968, would be that if such a vacuum opened up, it would be filled by hitherto unknown political structures rather than substitute states: anticipating both Deleuze and Derrida, for Trocchi the fact that such structures could not yet be described was the very proof of their usefulness.

The opened-out politics of Trocchi and his sympathisers also anticipates the 'DIY Culture' (the phrase is the title of a collection of 1990s clubculture essays, almost inevitably edited by a Scot)[25] of direct action, becoming an actor *despite* 'politics', finding Hakim Bey's Temporary Autonomous Zone in clubculture terms, or even an online hotspot, as in Pat Kane's 'netizens'.[26] Party politics is largely subordinate to literary experiment – and, on occasion, drugs. Trocchi and his associates, including Laing – unfairly, given that Laing's most significant attempts to join politics to everyday experience were in the late 1960s when he was assumed to have gone a trip too far[27] – came towards the turn of the decade to be seen by many in Scotland as drug-addled liabilities, while Guy Debord had (ironically, like André Breton's Surrealism) purged the SI until it was almost too small to organise in May 1968.

But Laing was a serious cat: man, he was a *doctor*. Of *medicine*. He's fondly discussed in The Hitch-hiker's Guide to 1968, Deleuze and Guattari's *Anti-Oedipus* (with the caveat that his use of 'relief' implies that there is a disease in the first place).[28] If by no other route, one would like to think, via the passage of European thought through theory, could be lain to rest Laing's inane reception in the Anglophone world, in accounts such as Elaine Showalter's *The Female Malady* and Peter Sedgwick's *Psycho Politics*.[29]

Merlin and friends

The cash plea which dominated the editorial of *Merlin* I-1 was followed in the next number by a fuller exposition of the magazine's aims, which were, as we would expect, formalist and anti-genre: '[m]ost of the traditional categories are merely distinctions, hallowed by antiquity, which have been allowed to harden, and which, in the hands of unscience, have become an inquisitorial rack to which the flesh of contemporary writing is to be twisted'.[30] This generic hardening is, in Trocchi's post-Enlightenment terms, 'utilitarian' – literature serving another purpose. Already in 1952 *Merlin* was out to subvert any motives served by generic division and logical correctness – 'suspension of categories leads to immediacy of experience'.[31] And, in a tone of poetic artifice presaged by the young Scot Veronica Forrest-Thomson and by American postmodernists, '[t]he poetic experience *is*. But it is also more or less formalized, and thus it has a technical aspect and thus there are problems of poetry.'[32]

Forrest-Thomson, writing in 1978, and almost always overlooked by Scottish literary historians, is hugely formalist, concentrating on poetry's inner workings, the 'play of formal features and structure of relations internal to a poem', avoiding 'external naturalisation' via 'internal naturalisation'.[33] In Kristevan vein, 'linguistic categories are subsumed and altered by rules specific to poetry'.[34] Forrest-Thomson's method of close reading nevertheless dangerously skirts New Criticism, except in that it refuses any naturalist expansion to the world (as in the way New Criticism's canon remained implicitly imperial). She concentrates on the '*formal* creation of meaning, e.g. reversal of feet, changes in formal pattern'.[35] This is explicated through a highly complicated vision of the 'image-complex', 'the node where we can discover which of the multitude of thematic, semantic, rhythmical, and formal, patterns is important and how it is to be related to the others'.[36] Forrest-Thomson then calls, in a way reminiscent of the studied over-density of J. H. Prynne, but also looking forward to Marjorie Perloff, for an increase in poetic artifice as such, blocking any naturalistic reading: '[t]he reader must work through these initial thematic fictions before trying to naturalise'.[37] Her context is an avoidance of the poetry of the Movement, 'stranded on the beach of the already-known world'.[38] Her formalism is impeccable, but is sometimes uncomfortably close to Wittgensteinian logical positivism in a 1970s Cambridge where his echoes were still rumbling through radical poetics; Trocchi had been more vocal about separating poetic language and the *a priori* statement, however buried in artifice (an obvious separation, until we look at the Movement, which loves statement-poems). For Trocchi, 'what is demanded is that [the poet] should recognise for once and all that it is poetry that he [*sic*] is writing, that he is dealing with what is emotionally significant and not necessarily with propositions which are true or false'.[39]

By the first number of the second volume *Merlin*'s contents had expanded to include a mix of Eluard, Sartre, Genet and Miller, while still aiming to 'publish . . . young rebels who can't get published at home'.[40] It is two numbers later, in II-3, that its most substantial editorial appears, in effect an article by Trocchi split into two. This probably helped give *Merlin* its reputation as non-partisan; the point, though, is less about partisanship in literature (any decent magazine is 'partisan') than about aesthetic absolutism. Faced with nuclear destruction and totalitarianism, a non-binaristic, non-'political' way of thinking politics had become necessary (thus the lead into Lettrism and Situationism). The relative and the contingent are spread out from cultural experience rather than beginning from the statement. This is an attack on Anglo-British logical positivism very similar to the one John Macmurray was making in his Gifford Lectures (which became the books *The Self as Agent* and *Persons in Relation*) at almost exactly the same time.

This long editorial also sees political deadlock as a partner to aesthetic absolutism, and the evangelical wing of New Criticism as being in partnership with mainstream American poetry. T. S. Eliot's laying down of absolute aesthetic standards is particularly suspect here – not merely because he has aesthetic standards, but because he doesn't realise that these standards are absolute. For Trocchi, as if deconstructing the *cultural* pronouncements of Hume, the ability to see that there is a supplementary belief tagged on to absolutes is a requisite for all reading:

> Absolutism arises when empirical verification is treated lightly because propositions so verified can never be more than probable and when *a priori* <knowledge> is mistakenly treated as though it had factual content, i.e. when it is thought to be synthetic and not analytic or tautological. This confusion leads to the claim that it is possible to frame valid propositions that are neither empirically verifiable nor tautological; specifically, <metaphysical propositions>, whose validity is capable of being apprehended intuitively.[41]

Since Eliot's work sets a specific period as benefactor of definite standards (the period just before Union, as if England were unconsciously coming to realise itself, as in Muir's nostalgia),[42] any relativism which draws away from Anglican tradition merely denotes the horror of the modern and engenders moral panic:

> Absolutism, the systematic passion, seems to be excited by the subjective perception of chaos in <the moral world> and from a fear of the growing complexity of the universe of modern science which, in its methods, posits the relativity of truth and threatens the so-called <ultimate truths>.[43]

This threat (the word is even more apt today, and its sources even more vague – 'general', Virilio might say) is used as an excuse for faith in a truth beyond poetry itself, yet delimiting poetry – and it was logical positivism's truths that worried Scottish generalist thinkers like Laing, Alistair MacIntyre and John Macquarrie, and even Christian personalists like Macmurray and H. J. Paton. In Eliotic New Criticism there are two levels of measurement, one of science and one of theology,[44] and the diagnosis of disassociated loss of faith has arisen as the theological standard has slipped away. This reading was, of course, familiar north of the border, and is one reason why Eliot is often likened to Edwin Muir: '[i]n the cultural sphere the disease manifested itself in the 17th century, in the phenomenon which, after Mr. Eliot, has come to be known as the <dissociation of sensibility>'.[45] The relativism of science was thus for Trocchi in danger of being overtaken by a contentless metaphysics, leading to totalitarianism. In an argument anticipating Virilio, Trocchi warns that science, when it concerns itself with questions of truth, contains within itself the means of self-destruction (the 'accident'), exemplifying Heisenberg's uncertainty principle as a point where relativism gives way to pseudo-scientific belief. An increasingly co-opted science is at the mercy of a 'messianic drive' in culture and foreign policy', revealed in the way that Eliot sees nothing odd in considering in *The Observer* in 1947 the atomic bombing of the Soviet Union ('Russia').[46] Thus for Trocchi, Eliot's absolutism reveals him as a 'closet totalitarian' (though for most readers today, Eliot's already been outed from the closet and is holding hands in a circle with a rainbow alliance of other totalitarian headcases).[47]

Trocchi argues thus that European literature has a duty to get in the way and raises the heretical suggestion that the New Critical US is not, after all, 'God's country'.[48] He calls for a 'literature without risk' and, ironically, for a closer reading of texts on their own merit, which was what New Criticism, at least in its versions which drew on Practical Criticism, put on the table.[49] (In this sense Forrest-Thomson offers a useful corrective: the problem is not with the close-reading process or its dealings with artifice, but in its assuming a stable relationship between the literary work and its naturalisation in 'the world'.) Since, as Trocchi notes, the still current US national standard is of a war economy – high defence expenditure and low domestic purchasing power[50] – areas of free expression have closed down post-war and market forces have spread into previously sacred fields such as literature. Inevitably mainstream writers in the US have become more market-led and, by implication, more absolutism-led. This absolutism represents 'a prosperity which threatens to end in annihilation',[51] and, since Stalinism works along the same principles, literature risks a state of 'absolute-choice', which is no choice at all.[52] This is Virilio's scientific 'accident', and can only be perceived retrospectively via the written word – thus the need to reclaim freedom in the process of writing one's self outwith the given boundaries. By issue III-1, now proactively seeking the opinions 'of historians, of sociologists, of philosophers, of psychologists',[53] *Merlin*'s recipe for the reclamation of supplementarity over the duality of absolutism sounds even stronger: persons always have the opportunity to 'analyse their own attitudes, to suspend their responses, to think critically, and then, in the historical context, to *act*'.[54] This final italicisation is telling, given that, in Glasgow at around the same time, Macmurray was carefully differentiating between the subject's activity – performed without proper reference to another person – and the agent's action.

Sigma: the care of the self

Trocchi's Sigma Portfolio is a collection of 30-odd loose papers, with no overall structural organisation. Paper Four, 'a communication from the sexistential maniac',[55] entitled (after similar Situationist titles) 'Potlatch', sets out Sigma's stall by explaining the limitations of surrealism and Dada, and the flux of the agent, or a break from the (Protestant) work ethic as it has been organised, Peckham-style, in contradistinction to enforced leisure – 'what is written seriously (at play, as you will see)'[56] – and of state control over literature – '[a] state is an existential absurdity'.[57] It also however sweeps away Hume as continental philosophy as 'French' theory did Rousseau/Kant, by announcing that institutions, those corner-stones of Humean communication, have become irrelevant for meaning-ful exchange.[58] Here, almost a decade before *Anti-Oedipus* and two decades before the formalisation of Postcolonial Theory which stressed the recovery of the present from the colonial time-lag, Trocchi declares: '[w]e are concerned with the *present* and only by the way with a future ideal state (process) of society, the articulation of whose functions is forcedly *terra incognita*'.[59] The negotiation of what kind of state we are headed towards is, of course, precisely the 'state (process)' which Scotland has been undergoing since.

The same theme of occupying the present – overcoming the time-lag – begins *Sigma*'s next paper, 'General Informations'; quoted here is Debord's idea that all must change at once or nothing at all, an idea asso-ciated with R. D. Laing and (the avowedly revolutionary-Marxist) David Cooper.[60] Here, *pace* Situationism, and striking a chord which will res-onate through Scottish literary thought, Trocchi plots to get rid of the 'conventionally passive audience', the producer/consumer split which was undermined in theory in general.[61] As Debord had said of the de-authorising *dérive*, 'the collective task we have set ourselves is the creation of a new cultural *theater of operations*, placed hypothetically at the level of an eventual general construction of its surroundings through the prepa-ration, depending on circumstances, of the terms of the environment/behavior dialectic'.[62]

The fifth Sigma paper announces that Lawrence Ferlinghetti – perhaps the most underrated of the Beat poets – intends to use his City Lights bookshop as a clearing-house for Sigma publications.[63] A chemical agenda is also hinted at via another Laing collaborator (and Scot) Aaron

Esterson, who, in no lesser organ than *The Lancet*, has stated that '[c]ertain hallucinatory properties of drugs make them central and urgently relevant to any imaginative enquiry into the mystery of the human mind'.[64] Laing returns with the typically zany suggestion that children start their chemical careers with marijuana instead of alcohol or nicotine, drugs which are more purely destructive.[65]

The sixth paper is a well-known piece by Laing himself, entitled (returning to the politics of time) 'The Present Situation'. Here Laing declares himself, in collaboration with William Burroughs and Trocchi, to be working on a book on drugs and the creative process – a book which never appeared, presumably because they were always too caned.[66] But herein a specifically Scottish philosophy kicks in, with proto-Deleuzian undertones: Laing's hope, exactly like Macmurray's and that of person-alist philosophy in general, is to provide the circumstances for an authen-tic meeting between persons: 'we need concepts which indicate both the interaction and inter-experience of two persons'.[67] But psychotherapy (for Macmurray, science in general) can *intensify* alienation, and it is in this sense that an analyst's own schizophrenic tendencies, raised above her diagnostic ambitions, can become *productive*. (In terms of poetics, the use of schizophrenic speech would later influence the American L=A=N=G=U=A=G=E poets.)[68] Laing finds no use for a Freudian conscious/unconscious split, since, again as in Macmurray, the interper-sonal is the only unit of consciousness.[69] Laing, though, also delves into existentialism, ending with the wonderfully poetic sentence '[e]xistence is a flame which constantly melts and recasts our theories'.[70]

The seventh paper is an unpaginated piece of agitprop given away at the Edinburgh Festival Fringe in 1964 as a riposte to the Scottish *Daily Express*'s consternation over drugs and obscenities. The newspaper notes that '[t]he pride of the City of Edinburgh is a terrible thing', appropriate since the Edinburgh morality which took hold among the eighteenth-century *literati* is indeed what is being eroded, more deliberately than the *Express* thinks.[71] This paper is also in part a thanks to Jim Haynes, founder of the Traverse theatre and all-round literary activist, who pushed for a poetry festival apparently against the wishes of the Festival authorities.

A number of subsequent papers are lists of interested parties (contain-ing some unexpected names), roundups and mission statements; Paper 16, a more ambitious 'Letter to Universities', outlines the Sigma Project as a whole and urges them to take up some of Sigma's practices (despite threatening them at the same time with the anti-competition of an anti-university).[72] Paper 18, by Trocchi and Philip Green, recycles a 1960 piece entitled 'Cultural Engineering: Manifesto Situationiste', asserting that by now the invisible insurrection is already happening, that the 'compulsory leisure' of automation is already being undermined, and being undermined by a less spectacle-led play: '[t]hus freed of all economic responsibility, man will have at his disposal a new *plus-value*, incalculable in monetary terms, a *plus-value* not computable according to the accounting of salaried work . . . *PLAY-VALUE*'.[73] This Situationist call to *homo ludens* over the worker would again be heard four decades later in the face of New Labour's flimsy calls for social responsibility as the Welfare state is abandoned.

Matching the intransigence of dualistic trade unions (showing how well Spark's Humphrey was depicted), the possibility of nuclear annihilation in absolutist dichotomy, about which Trocchi has been worrying since *Merlin*, is here culturally recognised in the protestors at atomic bases and folk songwriters; since most of western Scotland had become a major target; instead of the work/leisure complex, 'we should do well to explore the creative possibilities of the leisure situation now and adapt our findings to the education of future generations'.[74] The pairing of '[f]orced labour, passive leisure'[75] must be transcended, but, given the success of the idea of compulsory and controlled leisure, we are 'rich' in pseudo-games which render the real experimenter a criminal (here the writers also point up the banning of Trocchi's *Cain's Book*). This is a similar argument to Spark's on 'desegregation', since an easy realism can act as a salve for liberal consciences, detracting from the mechanics of the politics of everyday life – why is a certain character on TV presented from the same angle, what expectations does it trigger in us, and can we ever escape the pallid pleasures of these expectations' fulfilment? Again the literary is, as in White's reading of Patrick Geddes, a synecdoche for a whole environment, 'along with a dynamic and globally orchestrated town-planning'.[76] And Trocchi loudly reminds us of the Franco-Scottish context within which this Situationist struggle is being carried out, in the extraordinary statement that '[o]ur "1715" would, we feel certain, be followed by a successful "45" '.[77]

Paper 21 is a slightly obscure piece by Michael McClure, notable for its assertion, common to Trocchi and White, that *logos* is dependent on *eros*, and that, in a new twist, eros-as-revolt should be seen primarily as an asexual division, an escape of part of the self from the self.[78] Emphasis on the positive nature of desire *as such*, pointing towards Deleuze and Guattari, also means that 'Wilhelm Reich is the creator of true romance and a golden medievalist' – and gives rise to the classic Reichian statement that '[a] "political" revolution is a revolt of men against a love-structure that has gone bad'. The erotic is unstoppable in its 'desires and flights' – a phrase which strongly looks forward to *A Thousand Plateaus*.[79] The statement that '[e]ach action fulfils a vital use or need' (rather than 'demand'-begging activity) does indeed point forwards, but also backward to the Macmurray who defines history as a series of human choices which are active in rejecting the unchosen. The immediate context for this foray is the French Enlightenment – a '[r]evolt of a group is an agreement not a contract' – but is also linked to the Scottish personalist stress on the tactile: '[o]nly meeting life gives solidity to the body-image and causes it to conform to the exact shape and verity of the body'.[80]

The next paper returns to the ludic, and tickles the reader in Derridean fashion with statements which seem to deny the self-obvious – '*sigma* does not exist', yet '[o]ur "renaissance" (*internationale*) is under weigh'. (Is MacDiarmid's 'second life' in danger here?) It also outlines a strategy of sorts for linking subsidiaries to a general holding company. This paper also contains, apparently, the first suggestion that the Sigma Portfolio as a whole be created.[81] By Paper 23 Trocchi had discovered Kenneth White's 'Jargon Paper One', already delivered in Glasgow in 1964, published as a pamphlet with a cover price of 3d, and leading with the powerfully anti-generic comment '[p]oetry, philosophy, it doesn't matter what you call it. The best writing is both.'[82] (The gravity of this is in the reuniting of the separated generic disciplines around which, for example, 'good English' was allowed to grow as a correlate to Eng. Lit.) White lays out the guts of what will become geopoetics, a linking of the person to lines of travel across the earth: ' "I", too much alive to be a humanist. Poetry is always more than merely human. My own predilection is for a pre-humanist or post-humanist world where what is alive in me is in contact with what is forceful and alive in the universe' (note the use of the term 'post-humanist' in 1964).[83] Here as elsewhere, White joins Coleridge's 'joyance' to Tao and Zen in terms of humanity's need to feel out the earth in travel, even though this is bound to render one's own previous assumptions 'slippery'[84] – thus the ironic name of the 'Jargon' group. (Look up 'jargon' in the dictionary and it says 'jargon': an inanely pejorative word meaning any set of terms specific to any activity; yet 'jargon' was frequently used seriously and pejoratively by those who decried theory in the UK in the 1980s–1990s). What White calls for, like a Laing feeling out the lie of the land, is an 'existential intelligence'.[85]

From Paper 24 onwards the emphasis is on individual poets' work (and, in Paper 25, a novelist, Neil Hallawell); papers 26 and 27 are contributions by Robert Creeley (Scots of the era seem to have slipped Creeley into their publications remarkably casually, despite the stature he would have in twentieth-century poetry.) Paper 28 shows another high-powered collaboration in promoting The Castilia Foundation, led by Timothy Leary, with other ex-Harvard associates, inviting people to take acid in a peaceful environment over a weekend for a modest sum – snacks included – and doubtless a few of the left-field Scots of the era took up the challenge to become inner cosmonauts. Other of the Sigma papers are sporadic and either showcase a writer or stress the need for individual consciousness-raising (through shock, if need be) before the formation of contingent communities.[86] When all the papers are seen together rather than excerpted, as they so far have been, they represent a remarkably prescient and challenging collection.

Far out

Trocchi's loose alliances aimed, then, at an evolutionary-environmental change in the tradition of Geddes as well as that of Debord, much of which can also be found in Macmurray, whose most mature work is contemporaneous with Debord's.[87] Acknowledging the need for mutual recognition, this thread of thought also precedes Virilio in seeing culture as a result of city planning (and ultimately of polemics),[88] defining the university, ideally an integral part of the city, in the more environmental sense of civilisation, rather then a place for specific training. This prioritises the university's position in its surroundings (and for Trocchi and Laing there would be no border at all), and involves a new city planning, at exactly the time when Glasgow's slums were being decanted into out-of-town estates like Castlemilk, which the state would subsequently deny infrastructure.[89]

Trocchi's preferred location, like Laing's, was a country house with plenty of space and amenities, in its own grounds yet near a big city – the kind of place where students and lecturers can stay in touch yet wander round on drugs without being freaked out.[90] Participants were described by Trocchi as 'astronauts of inner space' and also as, in oddly Deleuzian terms, 'dream machines'.[91] A new university would require, in the wording of Michel Foucault, a new art of living, or a recreation of the 'community-as-art-of-living'.[92] The creation of an 'anti-university' (perhaps not the best choice of terms, though the experiment was successful for a time, and still has a strong analogue in the Free University in Amsterdam) was not, for Trocchi, something which should cause surprise to the Scottish public: he cites a long Scottish tradition of secession of universities from other universities (after Trocchi, Dundee would leave St. Andrews, and so on).[93]

Trocchi again takes a Situationist line in insisting that any writing for economic ends should be described by participants as business, rather than as art fit for education – an opinion he shared with the pioneering publisher John Calder, whose patience seems to have been tried only by

Trocchi's being too dependent on heroin and too willing to hide behind his Sigma and anti-university projects to write a novel to follow *Cain's Book*.[94] And for Trocchi, if writing is business, he imagines a counter-duty to follow the ideas of Walter Benjamin in attributing to an original artwork an 'anti-aura', even an 'infection', sensing an unhealthiness in the claim to literary ownership – a feature which recurs in Scottish literary thought from the 1960s. He also stresses the lack of any barrier not only between town and gown but also between the teacher/performer and student, whether in the G. E. Davie sense of peer participation in the university, or in the theatrical sense – a challenge which would be taken up by dramatists like Tom McGrath. (McGrath has nevertheless rightly noted that what post-war Scottish literature has lacked is a popular theatre: how many of us have seen, for example, the drama of James Kelman?)[95] Trocchi also claims, pre-Davie, that universities as they stand are too exam-centred and that exams are damaging to free thought, an idea dating back to the pre-Union traditions of the ancient Scottish universities.[96]

The space of the perfect university, set up for both outer-environmental and inner-psychological exploration, was laid out by Trocchi in detail:

> The original building will stand deep within its own grounds, preferably on a river-bank. It should be large enough for a pilot-group (of astronauts of inner space) to situate itself, orgasm and genius, and their tools and dream-machines and amazing apparatus and appurtenances . . .[97]

Trocchi thus also perceives his cosmic cultural launch-pad *as* a form of city planning – '*l'art integral ne pouvait pas se réaliser qu'au niveau de l'urbanisme*'.[98] The city, the *polis*, becomes the attempt to make the polemic self-conscious and free of the deprivations of nomadism.[99] Trocchi, as would Tom McGrath,[100] sees some signs of this liberty in the Black Mountain educational experiment's 'free play of productivity',[101] some of whose poets would go on to form a relationship with Ian Hamilton Finlay's cutting-edge journal *Poor.Old.Tired.Horse*. The university would be self-funding, proactively internationalist at a peer-driven level (as opposed to the 'student exchanges' we have now), and rhizomic, student-to-student, rather than top-down.[102] Finally, he insists, such a far-out space must be redefined as *polis* itself, since the overdetermination of privatised spaces has meant that 'the world is awfully near the brink of disaster'.[103] We are waiting for an 'accident' which cannot be predicted but which we have a duty to work against, in the mode of Scottish personalist philosophy – stressing mutual recognition – rather than being driven by an absolutist model of self-interest.

Self-consciousness in this tradition, or rather the care of the self, is meaningless unless it is mutual (thus the Bond-like name Sigma, meaning 'all'). It is in this spirit that Trocchi calls for pockets of situation-making, by which he means spontaneous 'happenings' which have direct 'political' significance.[104] Again, the ideal learning culture has no separate teacher and student (or artist and audience), and Trocchi, taking the Scottish tradition at its word, calls for the abolition of examinations entirely.[105] Again, it is worth noting that G. E. Davie's pioneering book of about the same time claims that Scottish classes have to a much greater degree been 'peer-examined' than their southern counterparts.[106]

Trocchi's new university would thus be, and here he picks up on a classic postcolonial image, a 'shadow-university', centred in 'shadow-towns',[107] in the *polis* and yet way out, in the *polis*'s unimaginable future. Indeed, the university, as in a reversal of Virilio's war-based analysis, would become a blueprint for the settlement itself. This resonates with Davie, when he stresses, with some historical justification, the peaceful and mutually regarding relationship between town and gown in the ancient Scottish universities.[108] Trocchi's universe-ities would even be 'dream towns', recalling the later Wilhelm Reich, whose harvesting of positive sexual energy ('orgone') was central to his project of psychic liberation (and that of William Burroughs, who owned his own ongone box, and who was singled out with Trocchi for a lambasting by Hugh MacDiarmid in 1962). That a junkie should come up with 'dream towns' is perhaps not in itself so surprising, but Trocchi did what he could to find his own Temporary Autonomous Zones and experimentally inhabit them, rather than using them as a mere escape from the social. If we again turn to the terms of *Anti-Oedipus*, Trocchi sought to replicate junkie-like effects using the body-without-organs on the plane of continuity.[109] Much of *Cain's Book*, the tale of escaping The Man for long enough to get high, and for so long seen in the shadow of *The Naked Lunch*,[110] is about the quest for what is felt as a real freedom, a freedom of the kind which the ideal university might have provided. Sigma's anti-university did have a degree of success in 1968, and attracted well-known names. And although heroin is the last drug in the world to lead to concrete creativity, we might also reflect that Irvine Welsh's *Trainspotting*'s Renton is much more lucid when he is *on* junk than when he his struggling to come off it. Whether on or off drugs, indeed whether inside or outside their specified disciplines, the anti-university was conceived as a safe space to explore, where other universities, even in the 1960s, were increasingly perceived as diploma-factories.

Cainspotting

Cain's Book is not an overt influence on *Trainspotting*, any more than *Trainspotting* is a sequel to *Cain's Book*. To assume so would be to downplay both the Beat feel of *Cain's Book*, its early working-through of the narrative of the junkie as a way of life, and the intellectualism of Welsh's post-Thatcher dystopia. The themes of *Trainspotting* range from sectarianism to gender (forget the film: it drops everything of importance), and the novel was published after fourteen years of Conservative government during which the figure of the junkie assumed a permanent seat at the bottom of the social ladder in a system which had reinstated the 'deserving poor'. *Trainspotting*'s key themes have been bent towards heavy sarcasm; the book either borrows from Thatcherite opportunism or critiques it, depending on whose account you read. In any case, its characters neither 'reflect' nor 'deny' the facts of Thatcherism; they merely seek to survive within them. Nevertheless, where in 1993 it could have been said that *Trainspotting* catalogued Thatcher's running down the Welfare State with no alternative and was thus 'cynical'; with hindsight, and given the drift of my previous chapters, we can see that the Welfare State itself has itself been a vehicle of social engineering since the days of the early Muriel Spark – used to great effect by New Labour – and Welsh's critique has more affinity with *The Ballad of Peckham Rye* than most would assume.

In a sense the roots of the Spark–Trocchi era of disaffection lie in the way that the induction of the Welfare State was, forming a continuum with the Second World War, Scotland's most Anglo-British moment of the twentieth century. Since Scotland had had by the time of *Trainspotting* almost three decades of state government moving in generally the other direction, governments which, since 1979 at least, it didn't want, it's not surprising that next to Trocchi's early intellectual energy and care for the self, Welsh is easy to portray as intellectually lazy (though Renton is highly self-aware).[111] Thus, when Welsh made enough money he repaired to Amsterdam to write back to an impossible situation in which people couldn't yet imagine (unlike Paris 1968) having real power for themselves, manoeuvred first by a candid monetarism and then by a polyvocal state management still committed to enforced leisure.

It would have been nice, though, if some comparison with Trocchi had been made when the film of *Trainspotting* was released in 1996.[112] The film dropped the novel's key themes of sectarianism, Enlightenment and colonialism for a 'stylish' Britpop for the under-fifteens, and the subsequent literary rediscovery of Trocchi resulted in the single most tedious text ever written by Trocchi, *Young Adam*, becoming another

Ewan McGregor vehicle (in 2004).[113] (Despite the undoubted confidence of Scottish literature in the 2000s, when we find the clean-cut Ewan 'Alec Guinness' McGregor cast as every Scottish Literary Heroin Addict, we know that something's up.) *Cain's Book*, though, is extraordinary, like Trocchi's journal *Merlin*, in its ability to soak up foreign literary cultures; in this case, despite frequent Scottish clues, the prose and the themes are close to the William S. Burroughs of *Naked Lunch*. And yet.

In an article in the influential American journal *Kulchur* in 1962 (coincidentally, before an article by Gael Turnbull), the poet and critic Ed Dorn compares *Cain's Book* to Burroughs's *The Naked Lunch*, considering the former to be a much more mature and challenging work. Both books take a diary format and concern the procurement of junk, but Trocchi's use of the first person is for Dorn highly dextrous and points to the effects on the self, whereas 'Burroughs is a genius, but not intellectually vigorous – for instance, he makes less sense about dope than Trocchi does'.[114] Since Trocchi understands the limitations of his self and his narration, he 'never makes the mistake of turning against the best interest of his subjective universe'.[115] Dorn conversely sees *The Naked Lunch* as a series of small incidents carried on around the leitmotif of junk, as reportage, '[t]raditional American journal writing . . . entertainment'.[116] With his experience, we might say, of the Welfare State and of Situationism, Trocchi is not given to such whimsy, and sees junk (and this does indeed point forward to *Trainspotting*) as a proactive, pleasure-seeking, anti-work form of action. He recognises, as had the Muriel Spark who had come through the same Welfare State, that '[u]nemployment is not the same as leisure', and that in bringing this object called heroin into play he is 'using a drug which has a life only in terms of a man'.[117] Trocchi's 'I', Dorn goes on, belongs to the tradition of Dostoievsky – where a person is seen in 'a single stem of commitment'[118] – whereas Burroughs repeats small episodes without giving much idea of how these will affect persons, thus becoming preachy, jokey or 'boring' (and the criticism of *The Naked Lunch* gets a lot stiffer: 'a vortex of horseshit perpetrated for one irrelevant reason or another').[119]

Dorn interestingly also perceives in Burroughs the kind of abandonment to the virtual which we have seen critiqued in Virilio, in contradistinction to Trocchi, who struggles to keep a grounded person behind his actions: '[t]he Burroughs prose is of little value unless a general abandonment of the earth is forthcoming (which might appear to be the case)'.[120] Burroughs, compared to *Cain's Book*, throws forth a series of inconsequential missives into the bitstream: 'those "endless" fragments in the stream of what is called reality'.[121] Trocchi's 'I' is an actor, a person who feels and has feelings thrust on him; Burroughs's narrator remains safe in a 'self-satisfied containment in isolation'.[122] Trocchi thus, on an intellectual rather than a stylish plane (and we don't need semaphore to draw an analogy to Welsh's *Trainspotting* versus Boyle's), is behind some of what we now understand to be Beat writing, and thus, via the Franco-American connections made in the days way before french fries became patriot fries, the lead-up to May 1968. For Dorn,

> Trocchi should be given money, grants, whatever, because he is the primary aesthetician of habit. The National Science Foundation could do no better than support him. Trocchi at least has the decency not to preach. He's not a man called Peter. I find the "appreciation" of dope in *C's. B* of a deeper order than in *T.N.L.* Trocchi's precise *will* is a superior conveyor than Burroughs' mere autonomy of needle.[123]

In a comment which recalls the 'dead baby' episode in *Trainspotting*, Trocchi's conversion of the work ethic to the junk ethic is seen as a personal choice and an acceptance of responsibility: 'Trocchi is simply saying no matter what happens I will have the shit cooking, which strikes me as utterly sensible and clear.'[124] Thus, in an appropriately nauseating phraseology, the travelling Scot is placed at the intellectual centre of his actions, for others to 'arise' from/through: 'Trocchi continues to write as a man with the conscious range of a mind which has grasped what it is capable of. It seems to me this process is both older, and will be, newer, than the locally modern, i.e., upset stomachs, throw up Burroughs.'[125]

Burroughs's fast-paced prose of traversing the city like a ghost to meet untrustworthy acquaintances known only by pseudonyms certainly bears similarities to the Edinburgh housing estates of *Trainspotting*, but Trocchi apparently belongs on the shelf with those American post-war classics which have long been seen as subcultural – cover out rather than spine out. And again, *Cain's Book*, as in the tradition we have seen used by Spark, is autopoetic and seen in book form only 'by accident'; this was the format followed in Trocchi's early pornographic novels, of which *Helen and Desire* has been the most popularly rediscovered and reprinted.[126] There is a spiritual aspect to this: Tom McGrath has noted that while a vein of mysticism (religious or non-religious spirituality) has been a recurrent thread in Scottish literature, so has heroin.[127] Heroin addiction, damaging though it doubtless was to Trocchi's career, shows a classic ad-diction, as in the Latin *dicere*, a desire to make one's own actions re-iterable, to remain and have effect.[128]

Trocchi's point in *Cain's Book* is that the junkie is a flag of convenience for societal ills, a necessary underclass set to inhabit the shadows (and Welsh broadly concurs, though the film contrarily stresses economic 'choice' – a word used once ironically in the novel but in the film repeated mantra-like by Ewan McGregor wearing an expression like a Jehovah's Witness). Trocchi also tellingly, in the context of turn-of-the-60s New York, likens the junkie to the black as 'scapegoat'.[129] If blacks were scapegoats during the grim American battles for civil rights, then Trocchi had seen something similar, with Algerians in Paris. As is logged in the Sigma Portfolio, and as is adhered to by other literary figures of the time like R. D. Laing and Tom McGrath and Sigma's Leary-ites, psychoactive drugs may or may not be 'mind-expanding', but the idea of the state denying experimentation is recognised as a direct political move against which a self sets itself up. Or as in Welsh's Renton's sarcastic comment about being 'classic liberals' on the freedom of drugs, Trocchi not only stresses the need for *personal* control over the drug (and the painstaking account of doses and psychic effects in sections of *Cain's Book* sometimes resemble Thomas De Quincey's opium diary);[130] more forcefully, Trocchi notes the pleasures of heroin and public ignorance over its use, as have a continuum of Scottish writers and film-makers up to Welsh.[131] Falling foul of these pleasures, as Trocchi shows that all junkies *know* they will at some point, is represented as a personal responsibility rather than an abstract moral judgement.

This thinking, fairly obvious so far, takes a Situationist turn when Trocchi suggests that heroin is an excuse for the surveillance of an under-class, and a further Laingian turn in that hospitals, in pushing state-licensed drugs over unlicensed ones against the wishes of the user, *increase* schizoid tendencies.[132] Being a junkie has become a punishment, putting the user on the front line for monitoring. As in Foucault, the difference between the state-controlled drug and the personally controlled one is the clinic: the medical profession's monopoly on drugs is a *cultural* one.[133] And again as in Laing, and before him Wilhelm Reich, expressed through-out his long relationship with the Scottish educator A. S. Neill,[134] the clinic equates art and sexuality (as in the withholding of both), which are recovered together with the responsible self.[135]

And as the Reich/Neill correspondence suggests, the literary revolution, pivoting around positive, post-Freudian ideas as in those with which Laing would precede Deleuze and Guattari, was also a sexual one. It is well known that the freewheeling Jim Haynes was running a bookshop in Edinburgh in 1962 when he co-founded the Traverse Theatre, now one of Edinburgh's most prestigious venues. Less well known is his long-running 'sexpaper', *Suck*, and the spin-off discussions it engendered, such as an interest in group sexual activity.[136] Kenneth White has asserted that *logos* derives from *eros*, which is to be understood not in relation to spe-cific persons, but to an overall unity.[137] White has also, in an argument usually associated with Laing, linked the writer with the lunatic, since the irruption of both is something that society, via institutions such as the clinic, seeks to shut away.[138]

Cain's Book also speaks to Scottish critical theory in terms of the loss of any extensive sense of time and space which is engendered by heroin – a counter to the desire to expand throughout empire among the eighteenth-century Humean *literati*. A basic of Irvine Welsh's narration in which days go by in unspecified addicts' flats, heroin's loss of extensive space can be linked to a loss of faith in the configuring of space and time in terms of expanding Union and scientific thought. More generally, postcolonial theory tells us that the placement of colonies as atemporal 'outsides' depended on the centrality of London, Glasgow and Edinburgh as 'insides'. Cliché though it might be, *Trainspotting* did boldly go into the estates that about one per cent of tourists in Edinburgh come across, and this does represent a destabilising move. Colonial culture is 'late' in relation to the correctly functioning metropolitan 'insides' – the colonial time-lag – as it has been since the days when the seeing-knowing Scottish Enlightenment was enabled by the slave trade, to the First Renaissance's general contention that Scotland should try to remain at the centre of empire. In Trocchi, the insides are thrown up, vomited out. When time and space become disoriented, the confidence of British imperial centrality, itself largely a Scottish invention, no longer holds.

1962 and All that

Slightly Trocchi's junior, and apparently somewhat in his awe, the poet and playwright Tom McGrath came to fame reading beside Ginsberg and Ferlinghetti at the Royal Albert Hall in 1965. After becoming features editor of *Peace News*, he founded *International Times*, which ran between 1966 and 1967, and, after some success in the jazz world, became the first director of the Third Eye Centre, an important gallery space in Glasgow, from 1974 to 1977. His introduction to the American Beats who were to influence his whole aesthetic through and beyond 1968 came via Trocchi, whom he apparently ran into in a Glasgow street, and who then introduced him to writers who were fast becoming superstars – most importantly for McGrath, Charles Olson.[139] Like Trocchi and Situationism, McGrath would come to champion the simultaneity of thinking and writing, precociously taking as his model not the Ezra Pound of Olson, or, nominally at least, of MacDiarmid, but the Gertrude Stein who would later be primary to the American L=A=N=G=U=A=G=E poets: 'Gertrude Stein insists that the act of writing and the act of thinking are simultaneous in the present'.[140] In other words, '[y]ou just move through it and you know you're moving through it, in a particular set of circumstances. The act of writing the poem is a unified response to your surroundings':[141] So '[w]hat [McGrath] was drawn to was Olson's more positive view of a "human universe", an open environment where people could move across the ocean, remain literally in touch with things, and *make* their reality'.[142] Here 'in touch' is as important as ever, and the divergence from MacDiarmid's Pound's Olson vital: what McGrath finds important in Olson is physicality – the way that feeling (in the sense of both tactility and instinct) comes before meaning.[143]

McGrath never contributed to Sigma, despite a distinguished career which has culminated in his ploughing a lonely but vital furrow along the boardwalks of literary Scottish theatre. But the thirty-some Sigma papers from 1963 to 1968 collated by Trocchi and supported by the likes of McGrath are central to the debate in defining an aesthetic up to and through debates on devolution. For many at the time, Trocchi was already eclipsing MacDiarmid's efforts, and today, despite ongoing con-firmations of MacDiarmid's radicalism, and his virtual 1970s hegemony in anthologies, Trocchi and White have now been undergoing more than a decade of reappraisal. In contradistinction to some of MacDiarmid's later positions which were confusedly crypto-Stalinist, Sigma is neo-Marxist and clear, delineating value from money: 'the confusion of value with money has infected everything'.[144] This is value for the other and not (as in Stalinism) value for the state, and could have easily come from the pen of R. D. Laing, a Sigma contributor and spokesman for a Scottish counter-culture which would continue to pitch value against monetarism during the Thatcherism of the 1980s, leading to the *Claim of Right* (1988), when devolution and independence hit the negotiating table.[145]

While Scots were involved with, and central to, the aesthetics of the French events of May 1968, in Scotland itself the effects were more muted. The obvious retort is that Paris 1968 was driven by the context of the Algerian War of Independence; yet since the end of the Second World War Britain had also had its own troubles with colonies from India to Northern Ireland. The year 1968 was enough to frighten the French republic, and Gavin Bowd has noted a concomitant early 1970s move to the right in French politics as a reaction, after which the left began to stink of Stalinism and Maoism.[146] In Scotland, this was blurred by the position that the nation held in the UK: the results actually pointed to a movement away from the British empire, but there was no party political structure through which to articulate this (and the SNP don't count: after 1968 they pressed on with ethnic pride and a faintly ridiculous argument about 'our' North Sea oil; even at the opening of Holyrood in 2005, they were still quoting MacDiarmid on memorial glasses).

According to Edwin Morgan, the five Scottish recipients of Trocchi's Sigma Portfolios were Morgan himself, Hugh MacDiarmid, Tom McGrath, Kenneth White and Ian Hamilton Finlay.[147] This is an interesting combination which shows not only a will to form alliances amongst the last three, but also a will towards a compromise with MacDiarmid, as is backed up by Trocchi's letters. A compromise was, however, not reached, ultimately to the detriment of MacDiarmid, since in the intervening decades, the centrality of Trocchi to European thought has been reassessed at the same time as MacDiarmid's inflexibility, long defended as radicalism. Experiment with Synthetic Scots had come to be viewed with great suspicion by the group which had formed around Trocchi–Laing–White–McGrath. MacDiarmid's resistance to a non-Synthetic Scots voice speaking for the country he had come to see as his own spilled over during the Writers' Conference of the Edinburgh Festival in 1962, where his main targets were Trocchi, Laing,[148] and Burroughs.[149] A 1964 letter of Trocchi's suggests that in 1962 MacDiarmid denounced the changes taking place in the most aggressive terms:

> whatever Mr MacDiarmid's views are now (and I heartily hope they have changed), in August 1962 he was indignantly denouncing such writers as Burroughs and myself as 'vermin' who should never have been invited to the conference . . . [150]

Trocchi thereafter describes MacDiarmid as wielding the 'long rifle of John Knox': in other words, whatever MacDiarmid states his own nationalist politics to be, his defence of Synthetic Scots as tradition shows him to be Calvinistic and neo-Reformation.[151] In a letter of later that month, Trocchi took the analogy further to say that '[t]hen, as now, his terms of abuse were those of a rabid nationalistic moralist'.[152] Further letters show, with important repercussions for pre-1968 activity, that Trocchi felt that the *literary* side of the festival had been smothered by the Edinburgh establishment.[153]

In an extraordinary article first published in the radical Scottish journal *Gambit* in 1962 and reproduced in an *Edinburgh Review* of 1997, Edwin Morgan concurs, in an unusually partisan account of the rammy between Trocchi's crowd and MacDiarmid's, in a mixed voice which, as well as getting across the personal severity of the argument, tends to describe MacDiarmid as, in Deleuzian terms, state-happy, endorsing socialist central control at any cost:

> *Hugh MacDiarmid* no whisky no Russians I am ONLY truly committed writer present McEwan vault personal national commitment not commitment

self not-self not commitment but I am committed I am a COMMUNIST [MacDiarmid rejoined the party in 1957 despite the Soviet occupation of Hungary] why am I a communist I am a communist what I tell you three times is true culture removed stranglehold capital ruin flourish people should will flourish panels of perseverance some say I am not a real communist fierce proud loud telegram Alexei Surkov congratulations my 70th birthday fierce so I AM a Survok credentials that's why fierce communist fighter flourish presbyterian people's republic. (Old Stalinist Surkov telegram should keep very quiet, no column of humour there, man!)[154]

Morgan has, *contra* Synthetic Scots, described his *Newspoems* (1965–71) as a kind of disorienting (and humorous) counter-advertising, which would imply a strong allegiance to Situationism.[155] In 1989 he took to parody in creating a Synthetic Scots poem in which as few words as possible had been 'contaminated' by English, and which was therefore incomprehensible.[156] Morgan also suggests that poetic forms are primarily emotional, and secondarily linguistic – an analogue of Macmurray's thinking – in answer to a questionnaire from an *English* university, traditionally more concerned with analytical questions of diction.[157] The Scottish adoption of anti-author-itarian ideas, to which Morgan was essential, can be seen continuing through the August 1989 'Festival of Plagiarism' in Glasgow,[158] and further to the famous neo-Situationist wheeze of the band KLF (Kopyright Liberation Foundation), when they burned (or did they?) a million pounds.

Part of the fallout of the 1962 squabbles was the endangerment of the hugely important American connections formed by Trocchi and Finlay around the turn of the decade. This is ironic given MacDiarmid's detemination to tie himself to Pound, while the American correspondents of Finlay were generally viewed as Pound's authentic re-thinkers via Olson and projectivist and objectivist verse. A wide range of Scottish poets continued to be influenced by the Finlay/objectivist/Black Mountain nexus – Tom McGrath, Douglas Oliver, Thomas Clark – but anthologists tended to see this influence as being something which either didn't happen in Scotland, or happened deep underground.

Alec Finlay and Ross Birley, in their fascinating short overview of Scottish counter-culture, *Justified Sinners*, point up a number of lines of participation which continued from the fall-out of '62, but have not been much documented, for example staged public performances by Edinburgh Arts Summer School in the early 1970s, the continuation of the journal *Scottish International*, direct challenges to the funding establishment as in 'Get Arts' (1970), and the exhibition 'Between Poetry and Painting' at the ICA in 1965, which involved key Scottish underground figures on a British stage for the first time, and the participation of figures

like Joseph Beuys, Buckminster Fuller and Jimmy Boyle. Beuys in particular would prove a powerful radical voice to add to Scottish literary
thought and remained influential throughout the 1970s and 1980s.[159] A
slow cultural build-up was taking place which would not yet be matched
by anything overtly 'political' in the way we usually understand it, but
rather came from 'below', from cultural identifications, from a Derridean
impossible future. In a sign of the times after the first, failed, devolution
referendum, Tom Nairn's famous phrase about Scotland being free when
the last minister was strangled with the last *Sunday Post* was used as a
front cover for *Radical Scotland* in 1983.

Another strain of cultural 'sinning', connected to the *évènements* via
pacifism and protest, is the 'revival' of the folk song. The songs which
were painstakingly collected by Hamish Henderson throughout his life
question the idea of a break and 'revival' in folk music at all, which, as
he demonstrates, shows a strong continuity. When he charted the rise of
folk song clubs, for example those surrounding Edinburgh University, at
the end of the 1950s, Henderson also saw himself as heir to an early twentieth-century phase of folk-art collecting, doubtless itself heir to a Scott-
inspired underground of collecting.[160] Thus, in a counter-Muir argument,
if Scots prose and poetry were arrested in dissociation, ballad-makers
continued to keep the leid literary until the tripartite model of post-Union
Scotland no longer held.[161] Moreover, the 'revival' of folk can also be
applied to a purely written culture: '[t]he search for surviving balladry has
gone hand in hand with investigation of the folk-tale'.[162] In a way this is
also a return to an older geopoetics, an attempt to capture folk song in a
living form (as opposed to MacDiarmid's archaic language). Henderson
saw Scots move underground in song and spent a lifetime collecting songs
to prove it. Similarly, the Franco-Scottish habit of pamphleteering or creating books independently of large publishers, recalling of course the
times of the Union, also characterises the Scottish *évènements*, and would
return in the 1990s, notably with Alec Finlay's pocketbooks, but also the
counter-entrepreneurial early 1990s responses to Thatcherism in the
shape of the Clocktower Press's ten booklets between 1990 and 1996, and
Rebel Inc.'s output from 1992.

Building the Hacienda

In his important small book on Trocchi and White, Gavin Bowd identifies a number of areas of importance for the two writers which also
overlap with key concerns here. Firstly, they were both more concerned
with the reformation of urban space than with revolution in its older

Marxist sense; as the Sigma Portfolio goes on, the desire for zoned environments, as in Laing, becomes increasingly important, amplified by the famous slogan (of Chtcheglov) 'the Hacienda must be built' (thus, via the neo-Situationist-cum-entrepreneur Tony Parsons, the naming of the turn of the 1990s club in Manchester).[163] Secondly, Situationism, and Sigma, were based on small conjoined sects rather than a central ordering committee.[164] Thirdly, there is a commitment to self-publish – avoiding large concerns – and to publish in unusual places (for example, White and Burroughs were to collaborate on a piece for the London Underground) – a tradition kept alive in Scottish publishing and illustrated by recent Scottish small press successes.[165] Fourthly, unlike Maoists and older Marxists, these writers sought to distance themselves from the Stalinist nightmare which had undermined the modernising moment of the 1910s, rather encouraging the kind of individualism which is linked to the cosmos yet keeps questioning the bogus universal.[166] Fifthly, both Trocchi and White disdained genre – *Cain's Book*, while packaged as a novel, is semi-autobiographical and, like Burroughs, includes long, wandering sections of non-fiction. White's output has, by himself and others, been split into criticism, creative prose and poetic way-books, but he is perhaps simply that figure who is easier to accept in France than in the UK as a writer. Finally, and touching on a point to which this book will finally return, the usual suspects (Trocchi, White, Laing) all stress the importance of play to well-being, even at the expense of seeming to disdain hard labour, and seemingly going against their 'Calvinist inheritance'. For the Situationist Trocchi the question was 'how could the undirected, wasteful activity of play coexist with the end-oriented activity of politics?' For all three, as for Deleuze and Guattari, capitalist forces were co-opting people into unnecessary labour designed to keep them not-quite-satisfied.[167]

Although Bowd contrasts White's 'flight' with Sigma's interest in the static space, he also notes that May 1968 was beneficial to the reputations of both, since both were already pro-Nietzsche and both were already geared towards thinking through the nomadic.[168] In 1983 White took the chair of twentieth-century poetics at the Sorbonne; he founded the *Institut International de Géopoétique*, which is much larger than most people in Scotland imagine, in 1989. White has probably been the most determined scholar of intellectual crossovers between Scotland and France. One stress is that, unlike over-specialised Anglo-Britain, France resembles the Scottish democratic intellectual ideal in that 'in France . . . the *general* cultural question was always posed'.[169] Franco-Scottish crossovers in the modernist era date from Geddes who was influenced by the wonderfully named Le Play, to the First Renaissance whose sons might have regarded Le Play as one of the 'vermin' of 1962. Famously, it was Denis Seurat who helped break MacDiarmid in the *Revue Anglo-américaine* in 1925, translated him and identified a 'Scottish Renaissance group'.[170] White has also written 'Sur Ernest Renan' – a figure hailed by Anglophone postcolonialists as seminal figure to nation-theory – though the essay is not mentioned by any of them. He moreover unpacks the French influences of the James Frazer who was so central to modernism.[171]

The play between Le Play and Geddes is clearly one of White's starting-points for a Franco-Scottish Alliance (one largely ignored by Second Renaissance accounts of the First Renaissance), and when he talks of the university being like the universe and vice versa, the idea of the world as a *de facto* centre for learning resonates with Geddes.[172] Perhaps a parallel might more easily be drawn between these two figures if we drop for a second Bowd's distinction between inner and outer nomadism in Trocchi and White, and bear in mind the 'lines of flight' of *A Thousand Plateaus*: 'what geopoetics is saying is that at the centre of every live culture there is a poetics, and that the most necessary poetics comes from contact with the earth, following out world lines'.[173]

In White's *Une Stratégie paradoxale* (1998), he recaps some of his past strategies, reprinting Jargon Papers One and Two in a first section tellingly entitled *La Revolution culturelle à Glasgow*, and describing '[c]e groupe que nous avons formé ici à Glasgow'.[174] The second paper, which did not fall into Sigma hands, stresses again the close link between culture and politics.[175] As he puts it in a later essay, '[c]ependant, l'expression la plus authentique de ce mouvement politique . . . reste culturelle'.[176] In 1968ist vein but also as a corrective to Hume, culture is in danger of becoming a commodity when it lacks an existential body.[177] As with Trocchi, this demands a complete change in the human, 'créer un changement fondamental dans la psyche humaine',[178] a 'fundament' which would become the earth itself in geopoetics.[179] In other words, as well as Situationism's removing itself from the slide of history which had become merely the history of the spectacle – here identified with Hegelian influence[180] – the cultural revolution is to be Taoist, not Maoist.[181] And while Laing, Trocchi, McGrath and their Beat co-conspirators were struggling to get eastern, it is perhaps White who shows the strongest desire to engage with specific instances of eastern thought.[182] Like Trocchi and Laing, White also precedes Deleuze and Guattari in recovering action guided by unguilty desire [désir]: 'on pourrait appeler la substitution du moi créatur au moi habituel. Car tous les créaturs créent a partir de leur désir . . .'[183] He repeats the call for a non-utilitarian university '[c]ontre l'usine à diplomes' more fully in the essay 'Vers Une Université Créatrice'.[184]

Here, as in Trocchi and Laing, is some of the strongest evidence that theory was being carried out by Scots, even if it wasn't being given that name. Like other Scots, White participated in May 1968, often thought of as a purely French affair (or, slightly more accurately, as a Franco-Algerian affair). A special number of the literary journal *Chapman* was dedicated to White's work, perhaps surprisingly, before that of either Edwin Morgan or Ian Hamilton Finlay. In 'Mai 68; Une Analyse',[185] White describes the rebellions in which he took part as anti-progress (that is, anti-capitalist), anti-culture – where culture implies a solitary author and a fixed audience – and, in the sense of Trocchi's warnings on absolutism, anti-political.[186] He describes the events as a warning about the sickness of civilisation in both Marx and Freud (via Fourier), where in *Anti-Oedipus* Deleuze and Guattari would explain the events more strongly as having arisen from a rejection of *lack* in Freud and *demand* in Marx:

> Sans tenter ici une *synopsis* (retour aux texts eux-mêmes!) du freudisme ou du marxisme, il suffira pour justifier, à supposer que cela soit nécessaire, un mouvement anti-civilisation, de renvoyer à l'aliénation de l'être humain tel que l'analyse Marx (*passim*) et à la déformation de l'être humain analysé par Freud (en particulier dans *Malaise dans la Civilisation*), Marx et Freud se rencontrant pour ainsi dire dans Fourier et sa critique de la civilisation (et les plans qu'il imagine pour remplacer celle-ci par ce qu'il appelle 'l'Harmonie').[187]

In a *Verse* interview with David Kinloch, White maintains a Situationist mistrust for the strong canon (one which goes deep into Anglo-British constitutionalism): 'I have no respect for tradition as such.'[188] This attitude marks him out from the Eng. Lit. habit of relying on precedent, even in New Criticism's identification of texts as good on what Forrest-Thomson (and Muriel Spark) would call a bad naturalisation, and has set him apart from habits of canon-forming. Thus he has in turn remained relatively un-canonical in Scotland. As Stuart Kelly says,

> David McCordick's 1000 page anthology *Scottish Literature in the Twentieth Century* omits mention of White altogether. So too does the *Penguin Anthology of Scottish Poetry*, edited by Mick Imlah and Robert Crawford . . . He was also unrepresented in the volume's predecessor, edited by Tom Scott, or the Oxford anthology edited by Scott. White does not appear in the Penguin book of poetry written after 1945, edited by Simon Armitage and Robert Crawford . . .[189]

The years leading up to Paris 1968 and their fall-out provide a rich seam of Scottish theory. One writer who regularly appeared in the anthologies was also one who nevertheless subversively introduced many of the ideas outlined in this chapter, and for whom 1968 was also a flag-ship year. He would also speak to subsequent events in literary politics: for Paris 1968 read Glasgow 1972, or Westminster 1979. It is to this poet and critic that we turn in the next chapter.

Notes

1. Maurice Nadeau, *The History of Surrealism*, trans. Richard Howard (Harmondsworth: Penguin, 1973 [1945]).
2. Edwin Morgan, 'Alexander Trocchi: A Survey', in *Crossing the Border: Essays on Scottish Literature* (Manchester: Carcanet, 1990), pp. 300–11: 308; see also the artwork of Douglas Gordon, particularly *Confessions of a Justified Sinner*, in Gordon, *Kidnapping* (Eindhoven: Stedlijk Van Abbesmuseum, 1998), pp. 76–7.
3. Gavin Bowd, '*The Outsiders*': *Alexander Trocchi and Kenneth White* (Kirkcaldy: Akros, 1998), p. 9.
4. Tom McDonough, 'Situationist Space', in *October* 67, Winter 1994, pp. 59–77, repr. in McDonough, ed., *Guy Debord and the Situationist International: Texts and Documents* (Boston: MIT Press, 2002), pp. 241–65: 250, 249.
5. Ibid., p. 252.
6. Ibid., pp. 254, 249.
7. Michael Radford, dir., *Nineteen Eighty-Four*, Virgin et al., 1984.
8. McDonough, 'Situationist Space', pp. 253, 255, 259.
9. On interactive TV, see my 'Endless Enlightenment: Eye-Operated Technology and the Political Economy of Vision', *Reconstruction* 4.1, January 2004, http://www.reconstruction.ws/041/gardiner.htm; Paul Virilio, trans., *The Art of the Motor*, excerpted as 'The Data Coup d'État', in Steve Redhead, ed., *The Paul Virilio Reader* (Edinburgh: Edinburgh University Press, 2004), pp. 165–74.
10. Michele Duclos, 'Kenneth White et la France', in Richard Price and David Kinloch, eds., *La Nouvelle Alliance: Influences francophone sur la littéra-ture écossaise moderne* (Grenoble: Ellug, 2000), pp. 115–45: 132.
11. Kenneth White, *On Scottish Ground: Selected Essays* (Edinburgh: Polygon, 1998), pp. 86, 87.
12. 'Underground London', in Kenneth White, *Travels in the Drifting Dawn* (London: Penguin, 1990), pp. 11–20.
13. Duclos, 'Kenneth White et la France', p. 137; for Derrida, May 1968 rep-resented the 'univocity of the real', affirming the possibility of an unknown but future-oriented politics; he is nevertheless sceptical about the idea of a completely 'free' speech; quoted in the introduction to Paul Patton and John Protevi, eds., *Between Deleuze and Derrida* (London: Continuum, 2003), pp. 1–14: 7–8.
14. Gilles Deleuze and Felix Guattari, trans. Brian Massumi, *A Thousand Plateaus: Capitalism and Schizophrenia* (Minneapolis: University of Minnesota Press, 1987 [1980]), p. 379; on motive and dating, unpub-lished correspondence with Kenneth White, 26 October 2005.

15. Kenneth White, *Écosse* (Paris: Arthaud, 1984).
16. Trocchi, 'Invisible Insurrection of a Million Minds', in Andrew M. Scott, ed., *Invisible Insurrection of a Million Minds A Trocchi Reader* (Edinburgh: Polygon, 1991), pp. 177–91: 177.
17. Guy Debord, 'Theses on Cultural Revolution', originally in *Internationale situationiste* 1, June 1958, pp. 20–1, repr. in McDonough, ed., *Guy Debord and the Situationist International*, pp. 61–5: 62.
18. Ibid., p. 62.
19. Trocchi, 'Invisible Insurrection of a Million Minds', p. 178.
20. Bowd, '*The Outsiders*', p. 9.
21. Ibid., cf. Trocchi, 'Invisible Insurrection of a Million Minds', p. 182.
22. Trocchi, 'Invisible Insurrection of a Million Minds', p. 179.
23. Ibid., p. 182.
24. Ibid., p. 183.
25. George McKay, *DIY Culture: Part and Protest in Nineties Britain* (London: Verso, 1998).
26. See Hakim Bey, *T.A.Z.: The Temporary Autonomous Zone, Ontological Anarchy, Poetic Terrorism* (New York: Autonomedia, 1991); Pat Kane, *The Play Ethic: A Manifesto for a New Way of Living* (London: Macmillan, 2004).
27. See R. D. Laing, *The Politics of Experience and the Bird of Paradise* (Harmondsworth: Penguin, 1967).
28. Gilles Deleuze and Felix Guattari, trans. Robert Hurley, Mark Seem and Helen R. Lane, *Anti-Oedipus: Capitalism and Schizophrenia* (Minneapolis: University of Minnesota Press, 1983 [1972]), p. 360.
29. Ibid., pp. 84, 95, 124, 131, 135, 362; Elaine Showalter, *The Female Malady: Women, Madness, and English Culture* (London: Virago, 1987), pp. 220–47; Peter Sedgewick, *Psycho Politics* (London: Pluto, 1982); as a first counter-measure of sympathy, see Zbigniew Kotowicz, *R. D. Laing and the Paths of Anti-Psychiatry* (London: Routledge, 1997); a recent guide placing him within a longer history of Scottish ideas is Gavin Miller, *R. D. Laing* (Edinburgh: Edinburgh Review Introductions, 2004).
30. *Merlin* I-1, 1952, p. 55.
31. Ibid., p. 56.
32. Veronica Forrest-Thomson, *Poetic Artifice: A Theory of Twentieth-Century Poetry* (Manchester: Manchester University Press, 1978), p. 56.
33. Ibid., pp. xi, xii.
34. Ibid., p. 2.
35. Ibid., p. 9.
36. Ibid., p. 16.
37. Ibid, p. 25.
38. Ibid, p. 59.
39. Ibid., p. 57.
40. *Merlin* II-1, 1953, p. 3.
41. Ibid., editorial article, pp. 141–3 and 209–27: 141–2; orthography is as in the original.
42. Compare my likening of elements of the Scottish Renaissance to Eliotic New Criticism in *The Cultural Roots of British Devolution* (Edinburgh: Edinburgh University Press, 2004), pp. 29–38.

43. *Merlin* II-3, p. 209.
44. Ibid., p. 209.
45. Ibid., p. 209.
46. Ibid., pp. 217, 213.
47. Ibid., p. 216.
48. Ibid., p. 218.
49. Ibid., p. 220.
50. Cf. Howard Zinn, *A People's History of the United States* (New York: HarperCollins, 2003 [1980]), pp. 407–42.
51. *Merlin* II-3 editorial article, p. 224.
52. Ibid., p. 224.
53. This quotation is taken from *Merlin* II-4, 1953, p. 229; this same issue published Neruda and advertised editions by Alexandre Kojève and Robert Creeley.
54. *Merlin* III-1, 1954, p. 117.
55. Trocchi, *The Sigma Portfolio*, Paper 4, p. 3.
56. Ibid., p. 3.
57. Ibid., p. 4.
58. Ibid., p. 4.
59. Ibid., p. 5.
60. Trocchi, *The Sigma Portfolio*, Paper 5, 5; see David Cooper's *The Grammar of Living* (London: Allen Lane, 1974) and *Psychiatry and Anti-Psychiatry* (London: Tavistock, 1967) for a more fully Marxist and determinedly anti-psychiatric account of the psychosocial than can be found in Laing.
61. Trocchi, *The Sigma Portfolio*, Paper 5, p. 5.
62. Guy Debord, trans. John Shepley, 'One More Try if You Want to be Situationists (The SI *in* and *against* Decomposition)', originally in *Potlatch* 29 (French version), n.p., repr. McDonough, ed., *Guy Debord and the Situationist International* (Boston: MIT Press, 2004 [1957]), pp. 51–9.
63. Trocchi, *The Sigma Portfolio*, Paper 5, p. 6.
64. Ibid., p. 6.
65. Ibid., p. 6.
66. Trocchi, *The Sigma Portfolio*, Paper 6, p. 1.
67. Ibid., pp. 1, 2.
68. Ibid., p. 1; see various experiments in Bruce Andrews and Charles Bernstein, eds., *The L=A=N=G=U=A=G=E Book* (Carbondale, IL: Southern Illinois University Press, 1983).
69. Trocchi, *The Sigma Portfolio*, Paper 6, p. 3.
70. Ibid., p. 6.
71. Trocchi, *The Sigma Portfolio*, Paper 7, n.p.
72. Ibid., n.p.
73. Trocchi, *The Sigma Portfolio*, Paper 18, p. 2.
74. Ibid., p. 2.
75. Ibid., p. 2.
76. Ibid., p. 2.
77. Ibid., p. 4.
78. Trocchi, *The Sigma Portfolio*, Paper 21, pp. 1–2.
79. Ibid, pp. 2, 4, 3.

80. Ibid., pp. 7, 6.
81. Trocchi, *The Sigma Portfolio*, Paper 22, pp. 1–2.
82. Trocchi, *The Sigma Portfolio*, Paper 23, p. 1.
83. Ibid., p. 1.
84. Ibid., p. 3.
85. Ibid., p. 3.
86. As in Sigma Paper 37: 'Pool Cosmosnaut'.
87. 'Invisible Insurrection of a Million Minds', p. 192.
88. Cf. Paul Virilio and Sylvère Lotringer, trans. Mike Taormina, *Crepuscular Dawn* (Boston: Semiotext(e), 2002), pp. 21–45.
89. 'Invisible Insurrection of a Million Minds', p. 193; one of the most justly celebrated novels of the Gorbals Clearances is Jeff Torrington, *Swing Hammer Swing* (London: Secker and Warburg, 1992).
90. Trocchi, 'Invisible Insurrection of a Million Minds', p. 198.
91. Ibid., p. 199.
92. Ibid., p. 200.
93. Ibid., p. 197.
94. Ibid., p. 194; see 'By his friends and Admirers', *In Defence of Literature, for John Calder* (Oakville: Mosaic Press, n.d.).
95. Trocchi, 'Invisible Insurrection of a Million Minds', p. 194; see also Tom McGrath, *The Riverside Interviews*, with Gavin Selerie (London: Binnacle Press, 1983).
96. Trocchi, 'Invisible Insurrection of a Million Minds', p. 198.
97. Ibid., p. 186.
98. Ibid., p. 186.
99. Virilio, *Crepuscular Dawn*, pp. 21–45.
100. *McGrath: The Riverside Interviews*, p. 89.
101. Trocchi, 'Invisible Insurrection of a Million Minds', p. 188.
102. Ibid., p. 188.
103. Ibid., p. 190.
104. Ibid., p. 196
105. Ibid., p. 198.
106. G. E. Davie, *The Democratic Intellect: Scotland and her Universities in the Nineteenth Century* (Edinburgh: Edinburgh University Press, 1961).
107. Trocchi, 'Invisible Insurrection of a Million Minds', p. 199.
108. Davie, *The Democratic Intellect*, pp. xv, 4, 65–8.
109. Deleuze and Guattari, *Anti-Oedipus*, p. 166; nevertheless, elsewhere they describe the movement of heroin in the body-without-organs as a cancerous one, p. 285.
110. William S. Burroughs, *The Naked Lunch* (Paris: Olympia, 1959).
111. Bowd, 'The Outsiders', p. 39.
112. Danny Boyle, dir., *Trainspotting*, Miramax, 1996.
113. David Mackenzie, dir., *Young Adam* (Sigma, 2004).
114. Edward Dorn, 'Notes More or Less Relevant to Burroughs and Trocchi', *Kulchur* 7, 1962, pp. 3–22: 3.
115. Ibid., p. 3.
116. Ibid., p. 9.
117. Ibid., p. 5; cf. p. 10.
118. Ibid., p. 6.

119. Ibid., pp. 8–9, 18, 21, 15, 16.
120. Ibid., p. 9; we could compare this 'responsibility' with Peter McDougall, dir., *Shoot For The Sun*, BBC, 1986; cf. Duncan Petrie, *Contemporary Scottish Fictions: Film, Television, and the Novel* (Edinburgh: Edinburgh University Press, 2004), p. 90.
121. Dorn, 'Notes More or Less Relevant to Burroughs and Trocchi', p. 16.
122. Ibid., p. 10.
123. Ibid., p. 11.
124. Ibid., p. 18.
125. Ibid., p. 18.
126. Alexander Trocchi, *Helen and Desire* (Edinburgh: Rebel Inc., 1997 [1954]).
127. McGrath, *The Riverside Interviews*, p. 92.
128. Jacques Derrida, trans. Michael Israel, 'The Rhetoric of Drugs', in Elisabeth Weber, ed., *Points . . . Interviews* (Stanford, CA: Standford University Press, 1995), pp. 228–54.
129. Alexander Trocchi, 'The Junkie: Menace or Scapegoat', in Scott, ed., *Invisible Insurrection of a Million Minds*, pp. 210–15: 210.
130. Ibid., p. 211; Thomas De Quincey, ed. Barry Milligan, *Confessions of an English Opium Eater and Other Writings* (London: Penguin, 2003 [1822]).
131. Trocchi, 'The Junkie', p. 212.
132. Ibid., p. 213.
133. Ibid., p. 214.
134. Beverley R. Placzek, ed., *Record of a Friendship: The Correspondence of Wilhelm Reich and A. S. Neill, 1936–1957* (London: Gollancz, 1981).
135. Trocchi, 'The Junkie', p. 215.
136. See Jeanne Paslé-Green and Jim Haynes, eds., *Hello, I Love You!: Voices from within the Sexual Revolution* (New York: Times Change Press, 1977).
137. White, *On Scottish Ground*, p. 64.
138. Ibid., p. 61.
139. McGrath, *The Riverside Interviews*, p. 85.
140. Ibid., p. 84.
141. Ibid., p. 97.
142. Ibid., p. 23.
143. Ibid., p. 95.
144. Trocchi, 'Invisible Insurrection of a Million Minds', p. 203.
145. See Alec Finlay, ed., *Justified Sinners: Scottish Counter-Culture, 1960–2000* (Edinburgh: Pocketbooks, n.d.); Owen Dudley Edwards, ed., *A Claim of Right for Scotland* (Edinburgh: Polygon, 1989).
146. Bowd, 'The Outsiders', p. 30.
147. Letter from Edwin Morgan to Alec Finlay, January 2002, repr. in Fnlay, ed., *Justified Sinners*, n.p.
148. '[Laing's "sigma"] project was launched by Alexander Trocchi's brochure, "The Invisible Insurrection of a Million Minds", to which Laing contributed an enthusiastic note of sponsorship' – Peter Sedgwick, *Psycho Politics* (London: Harper and Row, 1982), p. 264; Edwin Morgan has stressed that 'they collaborated on various antiuniversity and similar projects': private correspondence, August 1999.

149. Described by Andrew Murray Scott, 'Mr. MacDairmid and Mr. Trocchi: Where Extremists Meet', in *Chapman* 83, 1996, pp. 36–9, and by Edwin Morgan, 'The Fold-in Conference', in *Gambit*, Autumn 1962, repr. in *Edinburgh Review* 97, Spring 1997, pp. 94–102.
150. Alexander Trocchi, 'Letters to Hugh MacDiarmid', in Andrew M. Scott, ed., *Invisible Insurrection of a Million Minds* (Edinburgh: Polygon, 1991), pp. 204–6: 204.
151. Ibid, p. 204.
152. Ibid., p. 205.
153. Ibid., p. 205.
154. Morgan, 'The Fold-in Conference', p. 97.
155. Edwin Morgan, 'Newspoems', from ed. Duncan Glen, *Graphic Lines* 1, repr. in Morgan, ed. Hamish Whyte, *Nothing Not Giving Messages: Reflections on His Life and Work* (Edinburgh: Polygon, 1990), pp. 261–3.
156. Edwin Morgan, 'The Poet's Voice and Craft', in Morgan, ed. Whyte, *Nothing Not Giving Messages*, pp. 213–26: 222.
157. Morgan, 'The Poet's Voice and Craft', p. 226; for more on how a poem may exist independently of its language, see 'The Translation of Poetry', in Morgan, ed. Whyte, *Nothing Not Giving Messages*, pp. 232–5: 233, 1976.
158. In Finlay, *Justified Sinners*, n.p.
159. Ibid., n.p.
160. Hamish Henderson, *Alias MacAlias* (Edinburgh: Polygon, 1992), pp. 2, 1.
161. Ibid, p. 53.
162. Ibid., p. 35.
163. Bowd, 'The Outsiders', pp. 6–7.
164. Ibid., pp. 7–8.
165. Ibid., pp. 9–10.
166. Ibid., pp. 21–2.
167. Ibid., pp. 7, 10, 17–19.
168. Ibid., pp. 37, 31.
169. Ibid., p. 120.
170. Ibid., pp. 125–6.
171. Cited in Duclos, 'Kenneth White et la France', p. 120.
172. Ibid., p. 144.
173. Ibid., p. 93.
174. Kenneth White, *Une Stratégie paradoxale* (Bordeaux: Presses Universitaires de Bordeaux, 1998), p. 28.
175. Ibid., p. 26.
176. Ibid., p. 83.
177. Ibid., p. 26.
178. Ibid., p. 27.
179. On a contrary war waged against the earth, see Paul Virilio, trans. Patrick Camiller, *Polar Inertia* (London: Sage, 1999 [1990]).
180. Cf. Deleuze and Guattari, *Anti-Oedipus*, p. 5.
181. Duclos, 'Kenneth White et la France', pp. 135, 125.
182. Ibid., p. 136.
183. White, *Une Stratégie paradoxale*, p. 28.
184. Ibid., pp. 41, 87–100.
185. Ibid., pp. 79–85.

186. Ibid., p. 79.
187. Ibid., p. 80.
188. Quoted in Stuart Kelly, 'Canons to the Left of Him, Canons to the Right of Him: Kenneth White and the Constructions of Scottish Literary History', in Gavin Bowd, Charles Forsdick and Norman Bissell, eds., *Grounding a World: Essays on the Work of Kenneth White* (Glasgow: Alba, 2005), pp. 186–96: 186.
189. Ibid., p. 191.

Chapter 5

The Author as DJ

States of emergency

At the time of writing, there has not yet emerged any Scottish state. Elsewhere I have contended that the current unpredictable process of devolution has little in common with the pattern towards Home Rule in the early 1910s sense, but rather forms part of a longer tendency towards democratisation (a 'future politics') within which context constitutional change in the UK had become unavoidable.[1] Since 'culture' was the only politically interventionist sphere left to the stateless nation (recognised since Trocchi and the all-or-nothing politics of Situationism), after the second world war any Scottish literary thought which has not been nationally navel-gazing has been angled towards the rights and individual powers usually associated with statehood – immigration, nuclear non-proliferation, civil rights, and so on. These concerns have replaced the pre-modernist (and even First Renaissance) 'Unionist Nationalist' condition of maintaining an eye-level Scottishness as nation within a greater empire, and even the British executive's 1997 dishonest presentation of devolution as Scotland's 'becoming a nation again'.[2] Here I again suggest, with reference to the poet-critic Edwin Morgan, that the movement towards these rights of citizenship, predicated on some contingent statehood but by no means simply state-happy,[3] is aesthetically linked to the concrete, the tactile and the ironic.

Again, there is a postcolonial context: a critically reworked concrete and *poésie trouvée* movement, pioneered in Scotland by Edwin Morgan and Ian Hamilton Finlay, can be dated from 1963, immediately after immigration laws made it more difficult to emigrate to the UK from the Caribbean in 1962, and after the last half-decade or so had seen strong immigrant movements, and a concomitant swelling of the loony right.[4] And although most of the immigrants initially settled in London, not only was much Scottish literary thought already 'doing postcolonialism' in its allegiances, it was in any case diasporic in relation to London, long-term base of the Sigma Papers and home to a base of writers which remains strong to this day. In the mid-1960s, there was also a sensitisation towards the ethics of diaspora via journals such as *Scottish International*. Morgan's work shows how, while the immediate impetus for concrete poetry came from the more politically fraught Latin American (as opposed to Beat American) quarters of Brazil, a 'de-authorising' thinking was ripe to be taken up in stateless Scotland. Here I split my thoughts on his work into three, corresponding to three of Morgan's works: two of the period of the *évènements* in the mid-1960s, during which I regard Scottish theory as performing a parallel role to French theory (*Newspoems* [1965–71] and *Emergent Poems* [1967]); and one from the mid-1980s (*From the Video Box* [1986], while touching on *Sonnets from Scotland* [1984]).

The idea behind *Newspoems* is by no means headline news; the method of cut-up from random sources was a staple of early modernism. But *Newspoems* also represents an important critical *re*-reading of the cut-up in a Scottish context, in its representation of 'dialect words' and contemporary concerns, as well as in its aesthetic politics. The technique can be traced back through an early modernist French tradition of picking poetry out of unexpected contexts – *poésie trouvée* – as well as of a formalist collage technique going back to nascent Soviet times. Though the origins of modernist visual collage are often placed much later, in 'Into the Constellation' Morgan points to Revolutionary Russia and 'Kamensky's "ferroconcrete" poems (the name curiously prophetic of the concrete poetry of recent years)'.[5] MacDiarmid's extensive references to modernist Russian literature, and more particularly his interest in Mayakovsky, also echo in Morgan's early 'clean-edged' collage form of concrete. The 1938 Glasgow exhibition, which impressed a formative Morgan, showed a strong architectural constructivist influence, especially in Tait's Tower.[6] Although a cursory look might suggest that the formalist-modernist influence was simply absent until about 1962, Morgan is himself reflective about having grown up aesthetically in a time when constructivism was around and being put to use.

In Central Europe, in the early 1940s, a tradition of 'concrete art' grew up around Max Bill, who would later directly influence Morgan, with Eugen Gomringer as his secretary. In 1947 Gomringer declared an interest in textual concrete art, followed six years later by his first book of 'Constellations', a term taken from the work of Hans Årp.[7] In 1954 Gomringer produced the first of his own manifestos, 'From Line to Constellation', regarded by many poets in the 1960s as the beginning of concrete poetry, and bearing more than a passing titular resemblance to Morgan's 'Into the Constellation'. Developments in 1950s Brazil grew from a surrealist-modernist bedrock and against the backdrop of a push for national definition. The name 'Noigandres', taken by the collaborative group of Haroldo de Campos, Augusto de Campos, and Decio Pignitari, comes from Pound's *Canto XX*, and it was from this group that Morgan would take his own initial ideas of concrete poetry. The Noigandres group's concerns encompassed, somewhat preceding the Situationists who pointed towards 1968, the interaction of semiotic codes buried in the poetic canon with their effects in the social. This is seen, for example, in their production of 'poster poems' from 1956, again rendering urban space polemic. Decio Pignatari's famous 'beba coca cola', for instance, uses the linguistic possibilities of the advertising slogan 'Drink Coca-Cola' to make subversive shadow-messages appear within the overall iconic form,[8] a technique picked up in Morgan's *Newspoems* and *Emergent Poems*.

Morgan's personal induction to concrete poetry came when a letter from E. M. de Melo e Castro appeared in the *Times Literary Supplement* of 25 May 1962, introducing the Noigandres movement.[9] Morgan replied the same day,[10] and Castro in turn replied on 3 June enclosing a copy of the Brazilian anthology *Poesia Concreta*.[11] Later that year Morgan passed on the *TLS* letter to Ian Hamilton Finlay, at that time unaware of concrete poetry.[12] In March 1963, Morgan began to experiment with the form, and in the same month Finlay's seminal journal *Poor.Old.Tired. Horse* published, among others, Augusto de Campos and Pedro Xisto.[13] Concrete poetry by Scottish writers appeared in Finlay's single-sheet (and single-issue) publication *fishsheet* in June 1963.[14] As well as the Brazilian connection, Morgan retained the European influence of Gomringer and his 'constellation', the high-formalist interest in the spatial arrangement of text. Gomringer published Morgan's now well-known pamphlet *Starryveldt* in 1965.[15]

In these concrete poems, questioning, like Debord, Trocchi and Virilio, the extension of space, the poem's 'image' is not simply a primary part of the piece, but *more than* primary – ironising the place that the visual has in verse and making *space* continuously dominate the reader's mind during the reading process. Huge single newspaper words often constitute a whole poem, exploding both lineation *per se* and the MacDiarmid/Muir language debate by twisting found poems in the native dialect, even if the 'original' has come from another language. 'Scotland joins the Common Market' is, for example, cut from its original context (whatever that was) to read 'All Ons/All Oot'.[16] Most of *Newpoems* work along similar lines of insinuating the unexpected, the twistedly humorous and the subtle incursion of 'foreign' dialects, for example, that of Glasgow, into 'someone else's' writing.

Scotland Enters the Common Market

All
ons.
all
oot!

There are four points I want to make here, all of which are common to concrete poetry: firstly and most obviously, attempts at lineation, prosody or similar forms of generic validification of poetry *as* poetry which have traditionally allowed for entry into the Eng. Lit. canon, become irrelevant. The carefully measured feet of Shakespeare and Dryden take their place alongside something which seems like a pictorial joke. But concrete poetry is merely, of course, 'disguised as' a pictorial joke. Another way of looking at this lineation is to say that the silence at the end of each traditionally prosodic line which measures out and validates a poem in Eng. Lit. terms has always acted as both poetry's impossible and its enabling element, a silence which rhythmically justifies (in both meanings) the work; linebreak is the promise that each new line will be discrete and well turned, the interpellation into prosody of the promise of prosody to come. In this sense concrete poetry's spreading linebreak all over the poem is a generalisation of the promise, the acceptance that that promise is not one which must be returned in kind as the graphetic immortality of canonisation, but has to be seen as pure gift, pure intervention.[17] Concrete poems were also case-expensive to print through the usual channels, and so resisted being market-led: '[p]oets have been the slaves of publishers and printers for far too long. They are now beginning to assert themselves.'[18]

Secondly and relatedly, the image in concrete poetry is pointedly given far more importance than an image normally has in poetry as we know it, so that the reader is aware of the overall image *at all times*. There is no reading 'process' at all in terms of the temporal expansion of special understanding according to naturalised habits of narrative. The looming down of the image over any naturalised reading works to make the single visual image powerfully ironic, and so to nullify the projection of space central to any seeing-knowing process as in the philosophical tradition which stems from the Enlightenment. Tom McGrath, founder-editor of *International Times*, has questioned with Morgan the ethics of the contemporary tendency to read Charles Olson, largely descended from Pound – loudly pronounced by MacDiarmid as his man – as saying that linebreak can be rationalised to the human breath, since this means that the visual, a vital component, is ignored, and lineation reverts to the 'universal' measures: 'I never actually believed . . . in Olson's theory about breath. I talked this over with Edwin Morgan in Glasgow and we both felt the same way about it. I don't believe the line is related to the breath as closely as Olson thought it was.'[19]

Despite common rearguard attempts in the 1980s to distance Morgan from anything which could be related to a fancy foreign intellectual field, the man himself, an arch-linguist, shows the kind of care to separate speech and writing as occupying different ethical spheres which should remind us of Derridean thought, and he is highly aware of modes of communication as 'translation' between the two. He realises that concrete poetry demands that the textuality of writing remains constantly in view, and constantly material. If 'reading' is pared down to a single look, the poem will never settle within any naturalised semantic control: given that the iconic image is always leaning into the reader, this method can be read as a form of deprogramming of how we have learned to follow the poetic line. To regain control of speech, in this case frequently Scots speech, the visual aspect of the poem has to be to be emphasised at least as much as the aural, as Morgan hinted in his contribution to the catalogue for the 1965 ICA exhibition *Between Poetry and Painting*.[20] Moreover, I would equate the phrase 'committedly visual', used by Morgan in this document, as 'committedly postcolonial', since power over visual space is a basis of empire.[21] In concrete poetry the visual is always there and is always undercut; it always has a message at a tangent to its 'content', disturbing fact-based lineation.

If we grasp this undercutting of the primacy of the seeing-knowing imperial subject, we need not go to the lengths of the obvious reading of Morgan's 'The First Men on Mercury' as postcolonial analogy: any poem in which the visual is awarded *too much* importance relative to mainstream narrative poetry, and in which prosodic 'reading' and image-formation ironise one another, can be regarded as critically postcolonial. Intelligent concrete poetry creates a situation in which vision is loaded with both humour and anxiety – a disordering which echoes the 'exchange of looks' in colonies described in Lacanian terms by Frantz Fanon.[22] Morgan further links Scotland to the postcolonial by transporting the scene of the colonial exchange of looks in highly Fanonian terms to Glasgow, when he describes the look of his home city as charged almost like a nervous disorder: '[t]o look too long at anyone is dangerous (in Glasgow at any rate – I don't know about other places), and so the rapid flickering scan is characteristic of the urban poet'.[23] The urban poet *in Scotland*, we should add: we are not here in the realm of the *flâneur*, and from the mid-1950s to 1968 the urban poet in Paris would do more than just look: she would use the 'plagiarised' visual as a degree-zero of the *dérive*, and watch out where you've parked your Citroën. In the likes of Debord's 'The Naked City', cognitive mapping is exploded as *arondissements* of Paris become bite-sized chunks of map joined by arrows, the whole forming a thing to be spun around, in other words 'psychogeographical turntables [*plaques tournantes*]' linking segments, each with a different 'unity of atmosphere'.[24] To the *plaque tournante* we shall return.

It is significant, then, that concrete poetry bypassed England to arrive in Scotland – though there were many underground English versions in the 1970s – since in my terms it represents a critical modernism in which every sign ironically partakes of the 'metaphorical' image (connotation – images triggered 'vertically' to the word)[25] during the reading process, meaning that 'metaphor' is, *pace* Deleuze, meaningless as a literary trope at all.[26] On the contrary, 'the primary question is that of form itself'.[27] Concrete poetry is a serious unsettling of literature as we have been educated to understand it, yet Morgan was writing it during his tenure at Glasgow University, where Kenneth White was finding it difficult to square his Jargon Papers with his job. Since, via connotation of the image on the page, concrete's image is also an image of the society which creates it (the Georgian poets' orderliness on the page embodied gentlemanly order, the New Apocalypse's indentations embodied psychological ferment, and so on), the state-society of Eng. Lit. is perpetually *sous erasure* in concrete's negative prosody, helping to explain why 1960s/1970s English publishers, scarcely among the vanguard in separating state and nation, were content to settle for Philip Larkin. Moreover, as time went on, Morgan abandoned 1950s mid-European concrete's tendencies towards the 'ideally isomorphic' (where content 'equals' form), to lean on the importance of the image, as a look at any of his *Newspoems* confirms.

Thirdly, most concrete poetry typically involves some kind of tactile process in the making, as in cutting, glueing or ripping (and William Burroughs did not, despite American literary mythology which would have him as the granddaddy of postmodern theory, invent the 'cut-up'). This is certainly true of *Newspoems*: words have been spotted in various publications, cut out, using scissors – the action of the hand on plastic and metal – pasted and stuck onto paper, then patted down and photo-copied.[28] The tactile has been raised above the visual in creative proce-dure. The process of making the poem incurs the *resistance* upon which Macmurray and Virilio have insisted – a hand feeling a simultaneous counter-pressure. Throughout ex-colonies, from the percussion banned in British Trinidad (thus, the invention of the steel drum) to the graffiti of the descendants of slaves in Philadelphia, we find that the aesthetic procedure of the tactile has been central to political resistance.

Fourthly, and perhaps most importantly to the extension of my argu-ment hereafter, the poem is not and never has been the property of the 'poet'; the poet renounces all authority to this thing which was really never his/hers in the first place. The text has a life unto itself, is *iterable* (though perhaps not 'speakable'), and lives on without the authority of the conduit whose touch merely gave it form.[29] A DJ's aesthetic is like this, a transitory manipulation of cultural material to hand, in this case other people's records. Historically, the newer the record the better; the 1960s Jamaican scene was, for example, fiercely competitive in terms of a tune's novelty (especially during the 'rocksteady' phase, which cor-responds almost exactly to Morgan's and Finlay's early concrete exper-iments). This process of spontaneous newness is another version of the *dérive* (and indeed was recognised as such by Paul Morley, who made good on the Situationist slogan and built the Hacienda, in Manchester) – when a DJ plays a certain record, there is an upsurge of energy in the crowd which disturbs conditioned urban space. In late 1950s and early 1960s Jamaica, major exporter of the Sound System into the UK, these crowd upsurges were unique to place, fleeting, unpredictable – and postcolonial, since the quest for a present collective action works to overcome the division of the time of experience in the colonial time-lag.

At any given time, the playing of a record by a DJ belongs either to no one or to everyone, in a circular influence which takes in the musicians, the producers, the remixers, the DJ, the crowd, then moves back to the DJ. Every last and every next record haunts every present one, and a good DJ will either play up the break to stress it, or render it seamless in a subtler aesthetic.[30] The performance of playing and dancing to the record passes, but precisely in its passing creates a moment of unassimilable political energy – in the terms of Hakim Bey beloved of clubculture theo-rists, a 'temporary autonomous zone' – untouchable by dominant norms and always productive of its own situation, promising an unpredictable freedom.[31] This is not an exclusively 'pop culture' phenomenon: one trace-line of the use of the turntable *as a hands-on instrument* dates back to *Composition #1* (1939) by John Cage – a figure who has fascinated Morgan – in which the composer uses a variable-speed deck, of the kind which would later become indispensable in disco, when one beat had to be fitted to another, in response to the crowd.

The DJ then does not simply play records in a specific order, but repeatedly creates a new 'canon' – an action radical enough, and one to which Scottish Eng. Lit. has been particularly open – but also makes the dancers, no longer merely the audience but the participants, understand re-mappings of orders of influence in their bodies and minds. A specific effect in early New York disco is, we realise, audible in tendencies in late 1980s London house, and so on; this understanding may also exploit the area of crossover during which both records are being played at the same time. While laying hands on vinyl, the DJ is creating connections which she can never claim for herself; they are also always geared, in Bakhtinian terms, towards a listener who must be present, and via whose participation the chain of authority is completed – in moving back to the receptive DJ.

In Morgan's take on concrete poetry from the early to mid-1960s onwards, canonical Eng. Lit. is similarly disturbed by the declaration that the work is not that of an individual author, but has instead been pulled out of a circulation of text which is itself responsive to our readership, or which is trying to awaken our own authority as co-producers of a reading-image – in a poetry which is so easy to make that for years Morgan's concrete poetry has been taught and imitated in schools. The juvenile or mature poet/DJ collates ideas or images rather than authors them. There is, indeed, no author, where the word implies 'authority'. The poet renounces any claim to individual fame within the canon that was the ladder to fame via Eng. Lit. Instead, the cut-and-paste merchant takes the role of DJ, bringing disparate materials together unexpectedly in both clash and concord.

In the case of latter-day *poésie trouvée* the writer is always a critic, if we absolutely must stick to these terms (and the French never really have). She has never 'made' the work, merely amplified a circulating authority, rather than the Thomas Carlyle–Jean Brodie trickle-down theory of culture which sees fixed audiences benefit from a Great Author. The poet of *Newspoems* has merely altered some other source – often crossing languages, a political act itself in Scottish literature – and brought the altered source to our attention in a creative way. Eng. Lit.'s most prestigious genre as guaranteed by a specific prosody, itself guaranteed by a specific author, disappears (or, as Muir might have wished it, poetic sensibility is not dissociated in the need to create special, 'owned' languages). Since the

Say

o

Scottish author-as-DJ wants us to rethink the context in which art is understood or socialised, the 'original' is altered by placing it in a context contrasting with the History-of-Eng. Lit. one.

The DJ is involved in an intimately tactile process, feeling out tunes by percussion, handling each vinyl and moving to the next using analogue and hand-controlled speed adjustment and pitchshifting. Found poetry, concrete poetry and cut-ups are all similarly tactile, and their irregular appearance reflects this, as do the scratches and rubs found on vinyl (but digitised away by CD). In Morgan's *Newspoems*, the imperfections of the text – the tendency to use type not perfectly 'black' all the way over, but to have lighter patches – is similarly integral to the aesthetic. This is a visual 'crackle', a graininess which arises from the text's tactility.

In English poetry this wasn't the case: it wouldn't have mattered whether Philip Larkin's *Whitsun Weddings* had been written longhand, typed or dictated, it would all have ended up looking the same, since the language itself, as a material, had no grain. In Scottish concrete poetry, language became the 'form' itself. The concern for the materiality of language, best articulated as one of Riach's Seven Types of Ambiguity, and seen at its highest extreme in concrete poetry, is one example of why we can legitimately regard much post-1960s Scottish thought as theory, rather than imagining that theory came from somewhere else, to be something against which Scottish literature is to be weighed. The time to 'decide about' theory has passed; the theory has already been done.

If Morgan's *Newspoems* uses his digits before the term 'cut-and-paste' came to have a digital meaning, his *Emergent Poems* measure distances from the sides of the paper then slice into a famous quotation. After the remaining letters are seen dropping down the page, the quotation reappears as the 'original', in its 'own' language at the bottom, but only after having undergone what we realise is a series of re-readings and translations made by cutting spaces out of the repeated quotation. Morgan DJs the 'original' by breaking it down so that new words appear in an entirely different form, yet as interpretations of the theme – as if the 'original' words had always had those cognates waiting for them. (In one poem a Lallans-like, unsustainable combination of writing becomes contemporary Scots.)[32] In *Emergent Poems*, as in *Newspoems*, as cuttings into the original text arise, they are, as well as being translated, visually 'wrong': they don't form 'proper' sentences written without gaps, and they have no proper linear prosody (although they are often cunningly rhythmic). The iconic is again the ironic.

As well as leading with an aesthetic based on linguistic change, the themes of *Emergent Poems* are humanistic and left-leaning, suggesting that social 'emergence' will be incorporative and open to alterity, another direct challenge to canonical Eng. Lit., which shrank down the conditions for personal entrance. Again there is a serious disturbance of politely lineated poetry and the image in modernism, which, even in imagism, shows little interest in the politics of the poetic image as a syncretic whole.

The 'original' quotation itself is thus both unauthorised and ironic: it is always in view and is never the full story. The quotation is broken up and each line offers a new critical reading, simply by exposing something that was already there. Latent possibilities also obliterate any conscious/unconscious distinction (horizontal versus vertical association, in the structuralist terms of Barthes or Jakobson) tied to a conscious reading of left-to-right, line-by-line.[34] Morgan's reading pattern points up the supplementary attributes of the 'original'. So despite the endemic misuse of the term deconstruction in literary studies, Colin Nicholson is right when, in his essay in a Morgan-dedicated number of the journal *Cencrastus,* he describes Morgan in *Emergent Poems* as 'playfully deconstruct[ing]' the original.[35]

If there is a modernist impulse here, it is a thoroughly critical-modernist impulse, not a slightly-late-and-peching-to-keep-up early-modernist one, one well aware of the temporal distance from what it's reading. It aims, like later North American L=A=N=G=U=A=G=U=E poetry, to track technological changes in how we understand and process narrative – and here I am thinking, for example, of Bruce Andrews and Steve McCaffery (and in England, of Peter Middleton and John Wilkinson). As often in

```
plea
        a                              l        l
      rea          ch              t h
  d        e          a        c t             l        l
   en    a           at        h
  de                      a                        ll
 a                 r              i              e
      k            r           i              n
 all   a        r                        all
  n   e   a   r                   i
   re        a  c  h           i        al
     t   r                i            n
  den                     i          al
     a  l              on         l
            b            on      e
   e   a      t             en
   n     e   r   y       allen
      bra           i      n
   n           u       h         l
        l    a             v        e
              bra          v       e
              b        i  v       e
   a   l       a        v      o
    le           a        t    e
   all             t        i f  e
    l   ea             h      v   e
  de   a        t            h  o
    n          a      r   t      o
    n                              o
    n          t ur                n
    a     rea                  o
    n                  u  r       o
         b u t                o
   e    a        ch           e
        b          o
  d   e   a   r   t   o
   e   a         c   h  i          n
 a                 l    l
denn alle kreatur braucht hilf von allen
```

American postmodernism, *Emergent Poems*' statements are arranged flush with the axis of lineation (Susan Howe comes most readily to mind here), and lineation is lost to irony – where in *Newspoems* lineation had been eschewed altogether.

The state of the *Emergent Poems* might be seen in the sense of condition (as in, by Christ you were in some state last night), or even in the Raymond Williams sense of a rising ideology.[36] But in the 2000s it's also easy to imagine the *emergence of a state* via the overwhelmingly, ironically, 'vertical' connotation of the image. My position has been that the changes in institutional power in devolution have been less important than the idea that a body like a state can be useful in guaranteeing civil rights to those not seen as ethnically Scottish – those maps of Picts, Scots and Angles in books at your local library. Morgan leaves open the possibility of the overwhelming image as image of a new society, in sidestepping the 'three languages of Scotland' model of the Second Renaissance, and writing in 'other' languages while remaining committed to Scottish sovereignty – and since 16 February 2004, while being 'Poet for Scotland', effectively a Scottish version of Poet Laureate (except that in Scotland this is a real poet, rather than a court jester).

This is, needless to say, not to co-opt Morgan to any party-political Nationalist cause (as the SNP, mercifully, have recognised, choosing not to use Morgan on their commemorative materials, still preferring the feedback-like screech of MacDiarmid). Morgan has always refused to see his poetry's Scottishness as an end in itself, but at times (he writes in 1971) it is necessary to acknowledge a Scottish allegiance in the name of further representation.[37] His Scots is not Synthetic, but rather performative, as in *Emergent Poems*, where 'original' languages are erased as interpretive messages appear from the same sentence: the sequence is an exercise in 'translation' *in so far as* it is an exercise in interpretation – thus readerly participation is a form of the emergence of voice. (The coda to all of the above is that this section's title, for those who haven't noticed, is taken from Björk's song 'Jóga', the video for which shows her native Iceland still *emerging* volcanically from the sea. Iceland was, of course, the first European country to have a modern parliament.)[38]

My third example of breaking the naturalised form of authoritative Eng. Lit. poetic narrative flow is altogether more obvious, and comes from sections 4–6 of 'From the Video Box' (1986), mimicking the action of scratching in music and, in this case, video.[39] The idea, inspired by Gus McDonald's Channel 4 series *Right to Reply* – an ingeniously deconstructive explosion of the Standard English, Standard Audience education ideal of Lord Reith, used on the medium developed by John Logie Baird, and a programme hosted, as if we need to ask, by another Scot. This is also a perfect example of a Bahktinian literature, in which an addressee is vital – also reminding us how seldom literature, other than drama, is written in second person.

Scratching has, from the early 1970s days of electro-disco, been a key technique of DJs (particularly black DJs: and it still, despite *Smash Hits*-level assumptions that scratching is *passé*, forms the musical breaks around which a lot of hip-hop regenerates its themes). Scratching also, of course, makes impossible any purely front-to-back reading of a record or poem – and its 'forwardness' is always under the present-tense control of the DJ's hand, the body being the ultimate analogue instrument, unlike digital allowing for an infinite number of variations, and born of pure resistance. 'From the Video Box' enacts a performance which uses the back/forward switch in conjunction with lineation for its effects, as twenty-seven viewers come in to voice their concerns, or just to misbehave. Person number four is even 'here to make a scratch video'.[40] Repetitions of phrases again recall the moment when the turntable became a popular instrument, as opposed to a device for listening to records, and the most postcolonial of instruments, one which allowed mostly black young people to take back someone else's music – a reversal of the way in which the history of pop music has appropriated black music – and impose primary rhythm (tactile) over metropolitan pop's primary melody (aural).[41]

The language of 'From the Video Box' 4–6 wears the tactile on its linear sleeves; it uses lineation and rhythm in apparently conventional ways, but again falls under the analogue of the human hand for its aesthetic effects. In a challenge much more serious than it first seems (Morgan's most lasting legacy will perhaps be to have made the aesthetically forceful seem merely playful), Eng. Lit.'s system of metrics and prosody is thus seen to be cut through as linebreak shuffles across for the contingent rhythmic measure of the body:

> my friend and I watched that scratch that scratch video
> last night we watched that last night I was
> on the black chesterfield and Steve was on the
> black chair not that that will interest viewers
> interest viewers but I want to be authentic
> on the black the black chesterfield just as the sun
> went down reddish outside and I could switch
> from the set to the sky and back sky and back
> and back back there was a squeezed sunset
> on the set between gables and a helicopter cut
> through the reddish screen like a black tin-opener
> while suddenly a crow flew suddenly a crow
> a crow flew through the real red outside what we
> call the real red and tore it silently it silently
> a scratch in the air never to be solved scratch
> in air Steve said never solved as inside
> back went the helicopter to start again
> to start again I said those gables don't
> grow dark those gables don't grow dark
> that's what I want to say they don't grow
> dark those cables on the set[42]

Here it is not so much that grammar and punctuation have 'disappeared' than that they have become subsumed. The poem remains rhythmically impeccable, and even lyrical: 'the sun/went down reddish outside'; 'I could switch/from the set to the sky'; 'a squeezed sunset'. In fact, its theme of a perceptual, quasi-spiritual ether which can be ripped, and its determination to stretch prosody, are for me reminiscent of Gerard Manley Hopkins. Rather, Morgan has allowed the Eng. Lit. poet's palate to be flooded by effects which are only accountable to contingent touch, to resistance. As Macmurray might have put it, a DJ makes history by coming into contact with the physicality of the original recording and choosing one contingent movement from an infinite number – the hand, unlike the digital switch, understanding the infinity of in-betweens made possible by mutual touch.[43] Unlike digitised material which can be reversed by reversing the binary code, the tactile cannot be undone; the tactile is an historical connection between forces, a Glasgow kiss.

States of emergency: remix

It is by now verging on the banal to say that translation and the experience of 'other cultures' (whatever that means) are centrally important to Edwin Morgan's work. This conclusion doesn't take an Arthur Conan Doyle: Morgan's range of translations, even as gathered some time ago in Carcanet's *Collected Translations* (1996), are vast, ranging from St Columba to Gennady Aigi, from Claudian to Otto Orban.[44] It is impossible while going through this breadth of translation not to be sensitised to the relation of dialect to power, and to the translator's responsibility. Morgan, moreover, has his 'own' languages, poetic experiment and remix which never stay fixed; he takes a philosophical stance which strongly resists the idea that there is such a thing as an impossible sentence. This echoes Veronica Forrest-Thomson but, *contra* any lingering logical positivism in her *Poetic Artifice*, Morgan is prepared to socialise meaning much more readily, to put fewer formal barriers between the poem and social change in the world, formalist though his poetry itself may be.

Morgan has also kept faith with Noam Chomsky's ideas of a deep common linguistic structure, which suggests that his prolific translation is really the coming-into-view of the passage of language from one mode to another.[45] Morgan also insists, somewhat *contra* MacDiarmid's lukewarm attitude to language-learning and that of most English modernism, that translation *strengthens* a nation, rather than watering down its 'own' language, for there is no 'own' language there. National identity during periods of relative flux is bolstered by changes necessitated by poetic translation.[46] In Morgan, poetic voices can thus even be 'devolved' from received definitions of humanity altogether:

> the idea of bringing things together and of giving things a voice through what I write, even if they don't have an actual voice – giving animals or inanimate objects a voice – that attracts me a lot, and I suppose that is a kind of translation in a way. If I write a poem called 'The Apple's Song', the apple is being translated if you like into *human* language.[47]

This also helps to explain Morgan's interest in technology – partly an extension of MacDiarmid's overtures towards science, but also partly a contrary commitment to finding the limits of humanity as a dysfunctional universal, or what would later be called post-humanism – which we have seen in White as early as 1964, and which is not, as the anti-theory lynch mobs claimed, the opposite of humanism; it does not mean 'not liking people'. In 'Poetry and Translation', following a post-humanist thread, Morgan speculates provocatively that those aspects of translation thought of as the most 'mechanical' and those thought of as he most 'artistic', may not be so easily separated. An older humanist resistance to 'machine translation' would always want to put a defaulted form of human judgement at the centre of every activity.[48] But the ethical question to be asked by Scottish philosophy has remained, whose judgement? The term 'post-humanism' was not as scary as it seems, despite the fact that in the late 1980s and 1990s anti-theorists set out to weed out any term connected to their poets which began with 'post-' or ended with '-ism' as not sufficiently down to earth, like Paw Broon making pronouncements on the world from behind his *Sunday Post*.

On the image of Paw Broon, Morgan has carefully been both attentive to MacDiarmid's demand not to continually write in an 'Anglicised' Scots, and reinvigorated by the new mixture of American Beat, French radical thought, and 1960s counter-culture which seemed to bring irruptions of newness from within himself. To repeat the answer to the bogus question of Chapter 2, post-1968 was *his* second life – the phrase is taken from his 1968 collection, and his output from here on represents some of the most challenging scientific Scottish poetry of the twentieth century, made cosmic (as in cosmonaut, rather than the 'cosmos' of the early Trocchi and White) from the time of *From Glasgow to Saturn* (1973).

Nevertheless the 'beatnik' attack made, in part on Morgan, by MacDiarmid in 1962, whose scientific Marxism was now failing to reach escape velocity, had been taken at its word in Morgan's considered

'The Beatnik in the Kailyaird'. MacDiarmid's attack on 'visual poetry' would be intensified in *the ugly birds without wings*.[49] Mark Scroggins quotes MacDiarmid in the *Letters* (on Finlay's *Glasgow Beasts*) defending the Synthetic Scots experiment at all costs – and the now rather panicky turn of tying nation to (artificial) language: '[Finlay's *Glasgow Beasts* is] not the kind of Scots in which high poetry can be written, and what can be done to it . . . is qualitatively little, if at all, above Kailyard level.'[50] Of course, the Glaswegian cat already was out of the bag; it had been sprung along with Tom Leonard, Ian Hamilton Finlay, Alan Spence and later Liz Lochhead, James Kelman, and later again cemented in theory as dialectic by a newly revived Morgan. In the 1970s none of the early contemporary Glaswegian dialect writers let up, and by 1979 Morgan was talking of 'more recent exploratory work from Ian Hamilton Finlay or myself which must complicate the impression of what "Scottish poetry" is really like to the outside eye (or ear)'.[51]

Morgan's 'Sonnets from Scotland' (1984) form part of the cosmic progression which runs through *The Second Life* and *From Glasgow to Saturn*, from within a darker political milieu, moving from the tiny to the inter-planetary, from the geologically ancient to the contemporary. What interests me here is not only the highly formalistic set-up of the poems, which are of a semi-Shakespearian sonnet type (abba cddc rather than abba abba), one of the dozens of poetic forms which Morgan has mastered, nor even that they were perhaps the first non-Lallans poetic attempt to define this region from a mass of temporal and geographical angles, but that they were directly inspired by the loss of the 1979 devolution vote, which demanded a counter-acknowledgement that the entity of the nation does exist discretely.[52] At the time of the UK's entry into the Common Market in 1972, Morgan was already discerning a broad consensus towards national, though not necessarily nationalist, cultural agreement: '[t]here is not only a very widespread feeling that some sort of devolution is necessary, but there is also, now, the awareness that the constitutional changes which must take place in Ireland, and even in the United Kingdom itself as a result of entry into the Common Market, give the first opportunity for hundreds of years of rethinking the whole constitutional situation.'[53] Two years before 'Sonnets from Scotland', a 'de-mythologising' tradition (tartan as a nationalist icon was a 'creation' of a later era, and so on: standard right-wing Cambridge revisionist history stuff) was epitomised and cemented by some essays in the collection *Scotch Reels*, which, as most critics realised, was disingenuous in implying that there was no 'real' Scotland at all.[54] England, Britain, the empire – there were still no ethical reasons perceived to draw distinctions. *Sonnets From Scotland* can be read in part as a reaction to this demythologising tradition. And Morgan, like Trocchi, is mindful of moments like 1919: the Westminster state has rarely grasped the 'state' of the Scottish nation, and continues to fail to do so today. This has left the problem to artists, and this has been the case since the First Renaissance, but was never more so than the time around 1984, when Morgan contrasted state policy to Scotland's overwhelming opposition to its own status as a nuclear 'region'. As Duncan Petrie hints, the literary and cinematic tradition of Clydesideism was in the mid-1980s giving way to that of Holy Loch.[55] For Petrie, the likes of Alasdair Gray, James Kelman and John Byrne were having to find such a post-Clydeside tradition.[56] Morgan also finds a post-Clydeside tradition in *Sonnets From Scotland*, after having paid his dues to Clydesideism, and, again like Trocchi, refuses the absolutism of West/East posed by New Criticism. (Despite being one of the mild-mannered characters on the Scottish poetry scene, Morgan can scarcely hide his disdain for the T. S. Eliot of the 'strategic bombing of Russia'.)

Sonnets From Scotland builds on an earlier and equally timely theme in Morgan's *Sovpoems* in pointing out that the Cold War nuclear buildup is against popular national consent, this time pushed by a Thatcher–Reagan alliance which ignored Mikhail Gorbachev's pleas to stop an arms race his people couldn't afford. Thus the B-side of the *oeuvre* of the national makar has a more jagged, acidic tone, coming from within the nuclear sights of the Soviet nation whose aesthetic he has supported:

> . . . Each machine,
> each building, tank, car, college, crane, stood sheer
> and clean but that a shred of skin, a hand,
> a blackened child driven like tumbleweed
> would give the lack of ruins leave to feed
> on horrors we were slow to understand
> but did.[57]

In similar vein, Colin Nicholson's recent study of Morgan for me fulfils two important functions: firstly, it provides an overall survey of the vastness of Morgan's work (adding to Crawford and Whyte's *About Edwin Morgan*);[58] secondly, it links Morgan's Soviet translations and influences to labour disputes in Scotland, drawing him further left than have previous critics. This is not to describe either Nicholson or Morgan as a Marxist (Morgan would certainly deny the term, as any other political stricture), but the historical parallels are telling.

For Nicholson, Morgan anticipates Kristeva in deviating from grammatical rules to get back to the phonic, which she regards as a primary function of poetry, and whose appearance she describes as irruption – showing similarities to the Russian formalism Morgan had already discovered:

> Twenty years before Kristeva published *La Révolution du langage poétique* (and thirty before its English appearance) Morgan was using Russian intertext to explore what Kristeva would call 'the sociality in which the (speaking, historical) subject is embedded'.[59]

That is, for Nicholson, Morgan's poetics occupy a space between the signifying code and the fragmented body as had modernism, but are free to refer, intertextually and proactively, to an outside world. (Derrida believed, therefore, that Russian formalism formulated literariness as such.)[60] Carefully avoiding the banal but common argument that Scots is simply more expressive than English, Nicholson notes that the choice of Scots for Morgan's translations of Mayakovsky shows the urgency of making literature available to the people as part of revolutionary work, just as Mayakovsky produced agitprop throughout the 1920s at the risk of accusations of squandering his talent.[61] (According to Morgan, the Mayakovsky of *Wi thi Haill Voice* wanted to stretch his lungs after being accused of incomprehensibility during that frantic period.)[62] Morgan's quasi-bolshevik sense of the connection between dignified labour and adventure never left him; it may even, he suggests, offer a way to track back to recover the Romanticism lost by the dissociation of sensibility: in *Star Gate* (1979), Morgan indicates that the edge of space was for late twentieth-century artists what the edge of terror, or the concept of the sublime, was for the English Romantics.[63]

Nicholson also reads as Kristevan the argument that Morgan's rendition of Mayakovsky is non-Saussurean in its 'dislocation' of signified and signifier (though, as poststructuralists will argue, they can never finally be connected anyway), and moreover that under circumstances of underrepresentation the disruption of official language is both inevitable and revolutionary. Nicholson thus presents a Morgan who has taken up Trocchi's absolutist worries by bearing the burden of Soviet (though not Stalinist) and East European modernist influence over their Anglo-American equivalents like Eliot and Pound, to whom MacDiarmid aligned himself (to Tom McGrath's disdain, as we have seen).

Perhaps nowhere is the choice of Eastern European over Anglo-modernism so clear as in Morgan's *Sovpoems*, composed in 1959–61, at a time of alarming transatlantic nuclear buildup, opposed by most Scottish people.[64] The sequence has an imperial analogue in the US/UK stockpiling of nuclear arms as in May 1968's analogue in disputes arising from the Algerian War of Independence. This all takes place beyond the ken of the Second Renaissance, which, MacDiarmid's *Hymns to Lenin* notwithstanding, had itself become exclusionist. Synthetic Scots is dead: long live Scots. Or, in Nicholson's words:

> In a textual movement eligising the death of an original speaker [MacDiarmid], a form of Scots that will always be a minority usage comes to speak the early twentieth century's golden-mouthed bid for social transformation.[65]

Here, Nicholson is using the term 'minority' in its numerical sense, but it could even more profitably be read in the Deleuzian sense of 'minor', as a language group within a language group, an idea I will develop in Chapter 7. Paradoxically, the Mayakovsky translations revive Scots at a time when the rift with MacDiarmid – who, as everyone knows, was a lifelong Communist (apart from the other times, like when he was SNP or Fascist) – was widening; the translations are not in Synthetic Scots, nor are they realist, but they do attempt to reproduce the kind of polemical Glaswegian Mayakovsky would probably have used over either SE or Synthetic Scots had his revolution been in George Square, as it almost was in 1919. And Nicholson is right to remind us that during the period in which Mayakovsky was writing, John Maclean, appointed by Lenin the first Soviet consul for Scotland, had the agenda of putting Glasgow on the front line of revolution. Morgan's celebrated translations of Mayakovsky's *Wi the Haill Voice* can also be seen in this constructivist-formalist-socialist light, and their composition and publication are both significantly timed: their composition coincided with a 1919-like gathering of shipbuilders' concerns, their publication the context of Clydeside action:

> In June 1971, a year before *Wi the Haill Voice* was published, the public space of Glasgow Green, venue for many of the meetings that helped give form and definition to a 'Red Clyde', earlier in the century, saw tens of thousands gathered in protest at the closure of Upper Clyde Shipbuilders. In August 1971, when an estimated quarter of all Scottish workers downed tools in solidarity, the George Square over which the red flag fluttered, and into which a panicked government in 1919 had sent troops and tanks to quash a feared Bolshevik insurrection, was crowded with 80,000 people demonstrating their support for what was left of the Clyde shipyards' work force. That work force intensified its opposition to redundancy by organizing a 'work-in' that became one of the most remarkable events in late twentieth-century industrial history. With high levels of local support the work-in was sustained for several months until, early in 1972, financial backing was secured for the shipyard's continued survival.[66]

It is in this sense, a sense more immediate than most realise, that translations of Mayakovsky into Scots represent a direct intervention – cultural, linguistic, political – on Morgan's part. This also links the years after 1919 (when MacDiarmid started publishing in Scots) to 1972 in a Scottish Marxist literary theory which sees material processes as connected – in an Althusserian rather than a Lucáksian sense – to aesthetic ones. Moreover in *Glasgow Sonnets* (1973) Morgan expressed his solidarity with this same workforce after their manipulation by Whitehall:

> 'There'll be no bevvying', said Reid
> at the work-in. But all the dignity you muster
> can only give you back a mouth to feed
> and rent to pay if what you lose in bluster
> is no more than win patience with 'I need'
> while distant blackboards use you as their duster.[67]

Some of the twelve 'Glasgow Sonnets', and in a less obvious way some of the 1984 'Sonnets From Scotland', and indeed the very context of the latter, represent a polemical broadside from a poet otherwise noted for his gentility. Scarcely ever noted at all for his gentility, James Kelman would develop another strain of Marxist polemic central to Scottish literary thought; we will come to him after pausing to reflect on World War III.

Notes

1. Michael Gardiner, *The Cultural Roots of British Devolution* (Edinburgh: Edinburgh University Press, 2004).
2. The phrase is taken from the second verse of the *de facto* national anthem, and was often used by 'revellers' at the time, with encouragement from the New Labour government, despite the fact that the national status of Scotland didn't change.
3. Cf. Gilles Deleuze and Felix Guattari, trans. Robert Hurley, Mark Seem and Helen R. Lane, *Anti-Oedipus: Capitalism and Schizophrenia* (Minneapolis: University of Minnesota Press, 1983 [1972]), pp. 217–62.
4. See Zig Layton-Henry, *The Politics of Immigration: Immigration, 'Race', and 'Race' Relations in Post-War Britain* (Oxford: Blackwell, 1992), pp. 71–7.
5. Edwin Morgan, 'Into the Constellation: Some Thoughts on the Origin and Nature of Concrete Poetry', *Akros* VI-18, March 1972, repr. Morgan, *Essays* (Manchester: Carcanet, 1974), pp. 20–34: 29.
6. On Tait's Tower, see Charles McKean, *The Scottish Thirties: an Architectural Introduction* (Edinburgh: Scottish Academic Press, 1987), pp. 185–8; unpublished conversation with Edwin Morgan, 3 October 1998.
7. Eugen Gomringer, *Constellations*, trans. as *The book of Hours, and Constellations*, by Jerome Rotherberg (New York: Something Else Press, 1968).

8. Decio Pignatari, 'bebe coca cola', in Mary Ellen Solt, *Concrete Poetry, A World-View* (Bloomington: Indiana University Press, 1968), fig. 15.

9. E. M. de Melo e Castro, letter to *Times Educational Supplement*, 25 May 1962.

10. Unpublished correspondence with Edwin Morgan, 31 July 1999.

11. E. M. de Melo e Castro, unpublished correspondence with Edwin Morgan, n.d.

12. Unpublished conversation with Edwin Morgan, 8 May 1998.

13. Ian Hamilton Finlay, ed., *Poor. Old. Tired. Horse* (1962–7), p. 6.

14. Ian Hamilton Finlay, ed., *Fishsheet* 1 (Edinburgh), 1962; I am indebted to Edwin Morgan for a copy of this.

15. Edwin Morgan, *Starryveldt* (Frauenfeld, Switzerland: Eugen Gomringer Press, 1965).

16. Edwin Morgan, 'Scotland Joins the Common Market', in Morgan, *Themes on a Variation*, (Manchester: Carcanet, 1998), p. 100.

17. Cf. Jacques Derrida, trans. Samuel Weber and Jeffrey Mehlman, 'Signature Event Context', in Derrida, *Limited Inc.* (Evanston, IL: Northwestern University Press, 1988), pp. 1–23.

18. Morgan, 'Into the Constellation', p. 32.

19. Tom McGrath and Gavin Selerie, *The Riverside Interviews* (London: Binnacle, 1984), p. 99.

20. Repr. as 'Concrete Poetry', in Edwin Morgan, ed. Hamish Whyte, *Nothing Not Giving Messages* (Edinburgh: Polygon, 1990), pp. 256–7.

21. Ibid., p. 257.

22. Cf. Frantz Fanon, trans. Charles Lam Markmann, *Black Skin, White Masks* (London: Pluto, 1986 [1952]), pp. 216–27.

23. Edwin Morgan, ' "For bonfires ii" and "Glasgow Sonnet i" ', *Words* 3, pp. 93–8, repr. in ed. Whyte, *Nothing Not Giving Messages*, pp. 252–3; 253.

24. See Guy Debord, 'The Naked City', repr. in Tom McDonough, 'Situationist Space', ed. McDonough, *Guy Debord and the Situationist International: Texts and Documents*, pp. 241–65: illustration 243, discussion 244.

25. Cf. Roman Jakobson, 'The Metaphoric and Metonymic Poles', repr. in David Lodge, *Modern Criticism and Theory: A Reader* (London; Longman, 1988 [1956]).

26. Cf. Claire Colebrook, *Deleuze* (London: Routledge, 2002), pp. 17–18.

27. Gilles Deleuze and Felix Guattari, trans. Brian Massumi, *A Thousand Plateaus: Capitalism and Schizophrenia* (Minneapolis: University of Minnesota Press, 1987 [1980]), p. 374.

28. For an account, see Duncan Glen, ed., *Graphic Lines* 1, repr. in Morgan, ed., Whyte, *Nothing Not Giving Messages*, pp. 261–3: 261.

29. Cf. Jacques Derrida, trans. Peggy Kamuf, ed. Christie V. McDonald, *The Ear of the Other* (New York: Schocken, 1985), p. 121; the classic account of iterability is Derrida, 'Signature Event Context'.

30. On a possible link between DJing and this 'haunting' as supplementarity, see Jacques Derrida, trans. Gayatri Chakravorty Spivak, *Of Grammatology* (Baltimore, MD: Johns Hopkins University Press, 1976), p. 158.

31. Hakim Bey, *T.A.Z.: The Temporary Autonomous Zone, Ontological Anarchy, Poetic Terrorism* (New York: Autonomedia, 2003 [1991]).

32. Edwin Morgan, 'Dialeck Piece', in *emergent poems* (edition hansjorg mayer, 1967), n.p.

33. Morgan, 'plea', in *emergent poems*, n.p.

34. The best history of connotation in the history of lineated Eng. Lit. poetry is still probably Anthony Easthope, *Poetry as Discourse* (London: Methuen, 1983).

35. Colin Nicholson, 'Living in the Utterance: In Conversation With Edwin Morgan', *Cencrastus* 38, Winter 1990–91, pp. 3–11: 4.

36. Cf. Raymond Williams, *Marxism and Literature* (Oxford: Oxford University Press, 1977).

37. Edwin Morgan, contribution to *Aquarius* 11, repr. 'What if [*sic*] feels like to be a Scottish poet', in Morgan, *Nothing Not Giving Messages*, pp. 201–2: 202.

38. Björk, 'Jóga', from *Homogenic* (One Little Indian, 1997).

39. Morgan, *From the Video Box*; see also Robert Crawford, ' "to change/the unchangeable": The Whole Morgan', in Crawford and Whyte, eds., *About Edwin Morgan*, pp. 10–24: 15.

40. Morgan, *Collected Poems*, p. 483.

41. See also my notes on Paul McGuigan, dir., *The Acid House* (1998), in *The Cultural Roots of British Devolution*, p. 123.

42. Piece #6 from *From the Video Box*, repr. in *Collected Poems* (Manchester: Carcanet, 1990), pp. 479–500: 484.

43. See my notes on The Aphex Twin, *The Cultural Roots of British Devolution*, p. 115; Deleuze and Guattari, *A Thousand Plateaus*, on the relation of the synthesiser to continuous change and the analogue, p. 343.

44. Edwin Morgan, *Collected Translations* (Manchester: Carcanet, 1996).

45. On translation as a *condition of* the 'original' text, see Jacques Derrida, trans. Joseph F. Graham, 'Des Tours de Babel', in Graham, ed., *Difference in Translation* (Ithaca, NY: Cornell University Press, 1985), pp. 165–205.

46. Edwin Morgan, 'The Translation of Poetry' (1976), reproduced in Morgan, ed. Whyte, *Nothing Not Giving Messages*, pp. 232–5: 234.

47. Edwin Morgan, 'Nothing is not Giving Messages', interview with Robert Crawford, *Verse* 5–1, pp. 27–42, repr. in Morgan, *Nothing Not Giving Messages*, pp. 118–43: 130–1; on the analogy between entering literacy and entering 'humanity', see Henry Louis Gates Jr, *Figures in Black: Words, Signs, and the Racial* Self (Oxford: Oxford University Press, 1987), pp. 17–18; Tom Leonard's position comes very close to Gates's persuasive account of 'literacy' as a means of entering 'the humanities'; Robert Young, *Colonial Desire: Hybridity in Theory, Culture, and Race* (London: Routledge, 1995), pp. 34, 66.

48. Morgan, 'Poetry and Translation', in *Nothing Not Giving Messages*, pp. 227–31: 227–8.

49. Hugh MacDiarmid, *the ugly birds without wings* (Edinburgh: Allen Donaldson, 1962).

50. Hugh MacDiarmid, *Letters*, ed. Alan Bold (London: Hamish Hamilton, 1984), p. 687; letter is from 1970, and quoted in Mark Scroggins, 'The Piety of Terror: Ian Hamilton Finlay, the Modernist Fragment, and the Neo-classical Sublime', flashpoint Web Issue 1, 1997: http://webdelsol.com/FLASHPOINT/ihfinlay.htm.

51. Morgan, 'What if [*sic*] feels like to be a Scottish poet', p. 202.
52. Cf. Colin Nicholson, *Edwin Morgan: Inventions of Modernity* (Manchester: Manchester University Press, 2002), pp. 137–42.
53. Edwin Morgan, 'The Resources of Scotland', in *Essays* (Manchester: Carcanet, 1974 [1972]), p. 159; see also p. 160 on consensus, p. 162 on the race to remake the national language; p. 163 on London publishers' flattening out Scots speech – except in Alan Spence.
54. Colin McArthur, ed., *Scotch Reels: Scotland in Cinema and Television* (London: BFI, 1982); cf. David McCrone, Angela Morris and Richard Kiely, eds., *Scotland the Brand* (Edinburgh: Edinburgh University Press, 1985).
55. Duncan Petrie, *Contemporary Scottish Fictions: Film, Television, and the Novel* (Edinburgh: Edinburgh University Press, 2004), p. 31; cf. James Kelman, 'My Eldest', in *The Good Times* (London: Vintage, 1999 [1998]), pp. 47–50.
56. Petrie, *Contemporary Scottish Fictions*, p. 39.
57. Edwin Morgan, *Collected Poems* (Manchester: Carcanet, 1990), p. 453.
58. Robert Crawford and Hamish Whyte, eds., *About Edwin Morgan* (Edinburgh: Edinburgh University Press, 1990).
59. Nicholson, *Edwin Morgan*, 59; cf. Julia Kristeva, 'Revolution in Poetic Language', in Toril Moi, ed., *The Kristeva Reader* (Oxford: Blackwell, 1988 [1974]), pp. 89–136.
60. Jacques Derrida, trans. Alan Bass, *Positions* (Chicago: Chicago University Press, 1981), p. 70.
61. Nicholson, *Edwin Morgan*, 61–3; Edwin Morgan, 'Introduction to "Wi thi Haill Voice": 25 Poems by Vladimir Mayakovsky Translated into Scots', in *Essays* (1972), pp. 58–66, on his choice of Scots – 'There is in Scottish poetry (e.g. in Dunbar, Burns and MacDiarmid) a vein of fantastic satire that seems to accommodate Mayakovsky more readily than anything in English verse', see p. 66.
62. 'Introduction to "Wi thi Haill Voice"', pp. 58–9.
63. Edwin Morgan, *Star Gate: Science Fiction Poems* (Glasgow: Third Eye Centre, 1979); Nicholson, *Edwin Morgan*, p. 127.
64. Nicholson, *Edwin Morgan*, p. 83.
65. Ibid., p. 69.
66. Ibid., p. 75.
67. Morgan, *Collected Poems*, p. 290.

Chapter 6

Life During Wartime

The long revolution

It is telling that Edwin Morgan's book *Crossing the Border* (1990), which ranges across the history of Scottish literature, ends with three essays on the themes of Ian Hamilton Finlay, Alexander Trocchi and the question of voice.[1] If Morgan has been seen as relatively diplomatic about the clash between MacDiarmid and the vermin – praising MacDiarmid's interdisciplinarity in another essay in the same book,[2] and mindful of the paralysing silence which preceded the 1920s and the 1960s – in equivalent special numbers of the journals *Chapman* and *Cencrastus* Ian Hamilton Finlay is equally expected to be argumentative, and thus also, the logic goes, a more overt purveyor of theory (theorists being lippy bastards). *And* he's a visual artist. Finlay certainly felt that Synthetic Scots was unable to adapt to an aesthetics we would now describe as either late-modern or postmodern, saying, for example, in 1964, '[w]e have a whole school of poets here who write in Scots, but they use only old-fashioned forms, and their language too is from earlier centuries, and not the Scots that is still spoken'.[3]

In his passage through concrete poetry to plastic art in the 1970s, Finlay threw open the question of the materiality of text in ways that are more provocative than any cosy critical truisms about a continuum between text and image. In 'Into the Constellation' Morgan had already taken concrete back to constructivism, describing text/image combinations as an aesthetics of formal organisation which survived in the Soviet Union, in film, sculpture and art deco, at least until the mid-1930s. Constructivism became one early modernist giant along with surrealism – leading to two separate 'formalist' and 'organic' tendencies, and Scots tended to pick up on the former, suggesting a concern with the material. Similarly later, a wish to dissociate with the more organic 'patterning' tendencies of the late 1960s was one factor which led to Finlay's virtual abandonment of concrete poetry in journal/book form around 1968, and a reworking of the poetic 'ideogram' as a post-Enlightenment critique throughout the 1970s and 1980s.

By the turn of the 1960s, Finlay had been submitting to journals poems from what would become the now well-known *The Dancers Inherit the Party*. There is a close relation between Finlay and the Olsonian-Creeleyan circles in which Trocchi collaborators moved; there was also an American postmodernist interest in Finlay which long preceded Anglo-British appreciation. Still, a little-discussed aspect of letters from Lorine Niedecker to the early Finlay is the tendency at the time among even radical American poets to see his dialects as quaint and earthy, and comparable to Burns's 'delightful' language, spookily portending a 'Finlay Cult'.[4] After this, whether the early Finlay's dreadful translations into 'Scots' which Niedecker describes in 'A Posse of Two' are sincere or parodic, is unclear. In a letter to Louis Zukofsky, Niedecker says:

> Ian's *Glasgow Beasts* (funny he didn't write beas*ties* – Burns would have??) came, a tiny book – O *wee*, is of course what I should say. Charming, charming illustrations (papercuts) and Ian's *wee* verses – I hope they don't alienate him forever from his Highlanders!![5]

The possibilities of post-MacDiarmid anti-epic which Finlay discerned in concrete certainly ran the risk of celebrating quaintness – the 'reductive' diagnosis diagnosed by Marjorie Perloff, and a misreading of the Poundian ideogram.[6] Morgan's 'second life' impetus was however shared by Finlay, who was more proactive in terms of self-publishing. Four of his poems appeared in Michael Shayer's Olsonesque *Migrant* 7 and 8, and of these 'Orkney Interior' would later be one of the most striking entries in the collection of wacky avantgardes which made up Michael Horovitz's infamous and wonderful *Children of Albion*.[7] The tonal control of poems like 'Orkney Interior' was not simply abandoned in concrete, but provides a clue as to how native images could be brought to bear on classical contexts.

Finlay's journal *Poor.Old.Tired.Horse* ran from 1962 to 1967, and provided a Scottish outlet for American late modernists like Lorine Niedecker, Robert Creeley, Lawrence Ferlinghetti and Larry Eigner, as well as such respectable domestic Lallansographers as Robert Garioch and Helen Cruickshank. *POTH* 6 followed Morgan's lead back to Brazilian concrete, and *POTH* 8 to Russian constructivism. The journal retained a concrete tendency until 1967, numbers 10, 12, 14, and 24 were more or less explicitly concrete-anthologising. In 1965's 'Between Painting and Poetry' exhibition, whether or not most of the viewers noticed it, he helped show how far Scottish literary thought had shifted from and within Eng. Lit. origins.

Finlay is also the only Scottish poet discussed in what is probably the classic explication of American late-modern/early postmodern poetics, Perloff's *Radical Artifice*. This postmodernism, which, as in Morgan, reasserts form *sui generis* far more than did the final Olsonian phase of modernism, leans on native contexts: Perloff and other American critics have been insightful in arguments asserting the 'provinciality' of modernism (as in William Carlos Williams), which are probably most familiar to Scots through Robert Crawford.[8] In 1968, Mary Ellen Solt described Finlay in a weighty worldwide anthology as 'the concrete poet who has been most imaginative [in the world] in his use of materials'.[9] Solt also partially anticipates Perloff's argument in *Radical Artifice* about how the mass media have affected poetry by reproducing the site of enunciation:

> The realisation that the usages of language in poetry of the traditional type are not keeping pace with live processes of language and rapid method of communication at work in our contemporary world.[10]

Perloff's *Radical Artifice* emerged from the University of Chicago three years before Homi Bhabha's *The Location of Culture*, and also, perhaps not coincidentally, contains a chapter entitled 'Signs Are Taken for Wonders'. Perloff's argument is that, during the course of modernism, mass media reproduction has shifted the scene of writing, multiplying and standardising the Poundian image – 'that which presents an intellectual and emotional complex in an instant of time'.[11] Typographic art and found poetry in advertising become the poet's source material, and attention has shifted to the formal circulation of images. The ideogram is thus deliberately commodified in American L=A=N=G=U=A=G=E poetry, and becomes part of the production of an image-heavy poetry ironising the naturalisation of space in literary art, as we have seen to some extent in the last chapter. Perloff dates the denaturalisation of space in poetry to the time of George Oppen's *The Materials* (1962),[12] once common thinking in L=A=N=G=U=A=G=E circles, but it could also be dated to the time of Finlay's passage into and out of concrete.[13] By around 1967 Finlay was exploring the materiality of the neoclassical concrete image, as in his 'wave-rock' poem-sculpture from around that time, as discussed by Perloff.[14] 'Wave-rock' is text sandblasted onto glass, recalling Pignatari's 'beba coca cola'; the two words clash to produce the beachy word 'wrack' (sea meets land) straddled across wave and rock.

In Scotland, the path of Finlay's acceptance in anthologies has been chequered. Major recognition came via Yves Abrioux's collection *Ian*

Hamilton Finlay: A Visual Primer, and the critical collection *Wood Notes Wild*, edited by Alec Finlay, both 1985.[15] The radical American connection was maintained in *POTH* as it had been by Trocchi, as described by Mark Scroggins in 'The Piety of Terror', which logs some of the most graphic accounts of the MacDiarmid–Finlay skirmishes as found in Finlay's correspondence with Lorine Niedecker.[16] In *Cencrastus* 22 (1986) Kenneth White makes a move, now understandable via geopoetics, towards describing Finlay in terms of the claiming of space and 'grounding'.[17] This poetics, traceable for White through Melville, Whitman and Pound, and fertile ground for many early 1970s Scottish writers, stresses the person–environment relationship, as Finlay set his sights on the canonical place of the English literary garden, central to Eng. Lit.

The gardening Finlay can be seen as ending pro-Union images which contrasted the wild and dark Scottish garden to the ornate and cultured English one. In his Little Sparta project (1970s, 1980s), the neoclassical is deliberately forced up against the surrounding countryside, forcing a reconsideration of both Scotland's necessity to Eng. Lit. and the contingent nature of 'universal' civility. The pastoral terror of the neoclassical within the Scottish countryside can also be likened to Morgan's identification of science fiction as a neo-Romantic step into the wild unknown, in its imagining a nationalist Romanticism. Finlay makes the contrast more overt and more critical: in his installations, and in Little Sparta, classical images are deliberately bound up with natural ones; Roman and Nazi imagery with lakes and grasses, weaponry with idyll, and images of culture with images of nature. The weapon, as Virilio said, invents speed, rather than vice versa, in an era of mass media and remote weapons which are forever approaching the instantaneous.[18] Terror is not, as in the liberal mind, as easily separated from justice – thus our unwillingness to look at what Hume left out of humanity – the non-white, the female and the unpropertied. The consequences of this are depicted in *SF* – a booklet with George L. Thomson based on *Osso*, in which the archaic form of the letter 's' is made to morph into an SS slash (1978).[19] Finlay's 1983 Battle of Little Sparta, in which he fought, with 'weaponry', a Strathclyde Regional Council who defined Little Spartan temples as secular and therefore unworthy of funding, were simultaneous with Edwin Morgan's *Sonnets From Scotland*, which were in turn coincident with nuclear buildup in Scotland. When violence is airbrushed out of the picture of civility, we are left only with a supplementary horror-in-peace housing a 'deterred people'. Finlay remained undeterred.

From the mid-1960s, Finlay had been refusing mainstream publishing's production of the book form – an influence on many subsequent

Scottish small presses and experiments – as in his collaboration with Audrey Walker in 1966, 'Autumn Poem',[20] the screenprint 'Acrobats' (1966, Tarasque Press), the 'floating poem' 'frogbit' (1968)[21] and in the many home-made formats used by *Poor.Old.Tired.Horse*. In the 1960s words were ever gaining materiality in his sculptures and inscriptions. Perhaps better known are the lettered slabs which lie in the front garden at Stonypath (cast concrete with Michael Harvey, 1974).[22] 'The Present Order' is a similar piece taken as the cover of Cairns Craig's 1996 literary-state-of-the-nation book *Out of History* (stone with Nicholas Sloan, 1983).[23] 'Tristram's Sail' (slate and stone with Michael Harvey, 1971)[24] continues to interrogate the separation of 'absolute' justice and barbarism, in its 'Elegaic Inscription' 'Bring back the birch' (1971, stone with Michael Harvey).[25] Around the early 1970s, and throughout his Little Sparta project, Finlay moves to roman script, forming a tense relationship between the classical and the violence it leaves behind. (This is given extra pique by the fact that the area around Little Sparta was as far north as the Roman empire got.)

Here, weaponry is concealed in the Enlightenment pastoral ideal of the garden – *Aircraft carrier bird-table* (1972),[26] *Aircraft carrier fountain* (1972) and *Lyre* – a depiction of a gun (metal and inscribed slate, with John Andrew, 1977).[27] The chilling *Nuclear Sail* (1974), a rounded monolith in slate, plays out his earlier 'sailboat' imagery in a Cold War tension we have come to associate with literary protest.[28] Finlay's increasing interest in the Terror following the liberal and universalist French revolution invites parallels between a Scottish theory which sees a similar self-destruction of Humean 'sympathy' – and this is almost simultaneous to Derrida's reading of the contract-driven Rousseau. These 'models of order' both require *and* repress the excess of the universal, a process concretised in the state effort of warfare, as critically framed by Finlay.[29]

In his essay 'Adorno's Hut: Ian Hamilton Finlay's Rearmament Programme', Drew Milne describes Finlay's neoclassical poetics as finally undoing the organic images which lingered in Anglo-modernist-New Critical tendencies:

> Finlay's work represents the unnatural history of aesthetic domination through a transhistorical classicism, a mode of Eurocentric internationalism whose faith in aesthetic clarity is satirical, objective, and anti-romantic in tendency . . .
> a concrete poetry which is critical of modernist aesthetics.[30]

What Finlay is demonstrating, in Derridean mode, is that every revolution, every political event, is merely a promise of a perfect democracy which will never arrive, and which must be imagined anew, albeit through a *via nega-tiva*, by artists.[31] Finlay is thus vigilant(e) to the ambivalence of 'politics'; but if Morgan's Mayakovsky was building ships for the Soviet future, Finlay sets out only in little carved boats, onto a future made of what Morgan called the 'languageless sea'.[32]

The Terror

In 1985, the French Minister for Culture commissioned Finlay to create a bicentennial monument (usefully supporting the old truism that the 1960s to 1980s Scottish avantgarde artist was more recognised outside of her own country). Finlay, however, had in mind a work that would tease apart ideas of universal justice and equality – extended to the Scottish context, 'sympathy' – which formed the basis of the Enlighten-ment and then revolution (which, as any Burns or 1790s/1800s scholar will attest, had great effect in Scotland).[33] Gavin Bowd takes up the story of the ensuing bicentennial débâcle by first drawing on strong evidence for Scottish support for the French revolutionaries in the early 1790s, including Robert Burns's activities in Dumfries.[34] Finlay had already ironically invoked the name of St Just to repel Strathclyde magistrates who tried to seize works from Little Sparta on 4 February 1983 – medals were struck for service in the Battle of Little Sparta in 1984.[35] Finlay's argument is, like his comrades on the other side of the Channel – that with the liberalisation of the revolution, as with the liberalisation of Strathclyde, a tendency to revert to militaristic bureaucratic struc-tures remains built in (and here he is, of course, dealing with a region whose state government had saddled it with very real nuclear weapons in any case). As Deleuze and Guarrati argued, the war-machine is not entirely down to the state, but war has 'fallen under' the state.[36] Finlay's 'nomadic' war-machine is, moreover, *de facto* antithetic to the state as a stable fortress.[37] Capitalism demands, from its inception, total war; Finlay merely points this process up.[38] Meanwhile, perfectly exemplifying the violence of liberalism, the 1980s saw France nuclear testing in its ex-colonies in the South Pacific.

Finlay's medallions for Spartan veterans followed the pointed 'double-sidedness' of liberation and war in the medallion series *Heroic Emblems* in 1977.[39] *Heroic Emblems* is classically postmodern; the typesets are Roman (not, this time, neoclassical), and the text/image combinations match heroic scenes with pastoral ones. Inscriptions are in Latin – 'Et in Arcadia Ego', 'Hinc Clarior' – or martial English – 'Thunderbolt Steers All', 'Out of the Strong Came Forth Sweetness'.[40] Second World War

motifs are mixed with the arcadian, or as Finlay says, countering Plato, the 'neopreSocratic'.

The imposed form of the found object has a relation to the social of a kind of symbolic map, as in the allegorical mapping out of battleships as beehives on a lawn.[41] But these replete and rational forms are never allowed to stand alone; each has its own metatext underneath, a commentary, an unnecessary supplementary explanation, by Stephen Bann. There can be no simple reference to the artwork as self-contained object, to image as free of textual distortion, or vice versa. Terror and justice are not so easily separated. The medallion form also makes the image an ironic metaphor, or an unstable metaphor, so that bees can look like helicopters and battleships mingle with trees, with no clear indication of which of the two is the more fundamental.[42] But these medallions are also subject to a slippage of terms: bees can be summoned by the linguistic sliding, as in the name of a battleship, 'Hornet' (a scratching on the syntagmatic axis, in structuralist parlance).[43]

The overall iconic image thus often comically fails to tame the slippage and cultural undecidability of the piece. The insight of Finlay's post-modern aesthetics is to turn attention to the formalising process which manipulates language and image into such an unstable partnership. Cleo McNelly Kearns, in the only essay-length discussion of *Heroic Emblems* in popular circulation, notes their strong Foucauldian/Derridean spin, but asserts the work itself as separate from the status of 'a commonplace of postmodern literary theory, truths often complacently rehearsed by the *literati*' (meaning the twentieth-century American *literati*, not the eighteenth-century Scottish one).[44]

For their bicentennial celebrations the French republic, of course, got more deconstruction than they'd bargained for. In 1987 Paris City Art Museum exhibited Finlay's *Osso*,[45] and was simplistically denounced by *Art Press* and *Galeries Magazine* the next year as anti-Semitic; Catherine Millet followed the banal argument further to cite the presence of 'weapons' at Little Sparta as proof of neo-fascism.[46] But terror, the kind of terror that follows when the logistics of Enlightenment are in place, is, as Finlay recognised, a form of post-fascism, a total war – or a total deterrence – both are equally terrifying.[47] What the French state reaction seems to show is a strain of hyper-sensitivity indicating that the dismantling of the Enlightenment in French theory and in 1968, though hugely influential for literary-political thought around Europe, was diluted by post-1968 crises in the French left (PCF). The burden of demonstrating terror-in-universalism from the early 1970s through the dark Thatcher years had fallen back on the other Enlightenment giant, Scotland. Correspondingly, Finlay was forced to retire from the bicentennial sculpture because of the controversy, while in France the PCF lurched towards Stalinism in an uncanny echo of post-revolutionary Terror, going a long way towards vindicating Finlay's reading:

> En effet, les années soixante-dix quatre-vingts ont donné lieu à une relecture de l'histoire de la revolution française qui c'est faite au détriment de la Terreur jacobine. Cette tendence à coincidé avec le recul du marxisme chez les intellectuals français.[48]

This is further contextualised by the fact that in France the Russian revolution is customarily and strongly distinguished from that of 1789 – encouraging knee-jerk splinters between Trotskyite and Stalinist factions in the PCF.[49] For the republican public, the French revolution, rather than being a total social overhaul based on class consciousness, was deemed acceptable because it represented a reorganisation of the state along contractual lines (thus, Derrida's interrogation of Rousseau within the context of the hamstrung PCF). In Finlay's case, the PCF had been pressurised into a pro-1789 stance by the early 1980s – also exactly when the controversy was being stirred up around Little Sparta – thus the lack of intelligent readings from a French left.[50]

Finlay's aesthetic for the bicentennial celebrations was a continuation of the one he had worked out through the 1970s (and indeed goes back to Scotto-French Situationism; 'Dans la Révolution, la Politique devient la Nature';[51] that is, nature and power are mutually implicated in both Rousseau and Hume, however persuasively they separate them: '[s]on *œuvre* s'interroge sur les liens entre culture, nature et pouvoir: la Culture s'apprivoise-t-elle la Nature, ou garde-t-elle en elle un fond de barbarie? La Culture existe-t-elle indépendamment du pouvoir?'[52] Thus, Bowd argues, Finlay is to an extent in line with Kenneth White's statement about the need to leave the highway of history, since that history itself, as typically understood, has a form of cruelty buried within it, more or less visible according to the times (a line via which we can also trace through Derrida back to Nietzsche). Or, more accurately, Terror is a result of accepting history-as-given:

> On peut dire que Finlay pratique lui aussi une certaine forme de géopoétique, dans son jardin de Little Sparta, ses diverses réalisations, ses livres. . . . Quant à Finlay, dans une sculpture comme 'Osso', il montre la nature à l'œuvre de la cruauté de l'histoire.[53]

The post-Enlightenment critique of violence within culture (in the Humean sense of the term) was reflected not only in a battle but in a whole war with governmental authorities: The Fulcrum Dispute, the Little Spartan War, The Follies and the War of the Letter. All of these were staged by Finlay and sympathisers as full war and recorded much in the way of Situationism, and yet were fought 'on Scottish soil' (or at least the authorities thought it was Scottish soil). Finlay 'takes up arms' against the council – a funny point, except that British foreign policy was planting Weapons of non-humorous Mass Destruction in Strathclyde as the battles went on.

The Finlay of perpetual discursive violence and will-to-power reads like a guide to French theory, despite, and in tandem with, his disfavour with the bicentennialists. Violence, like power in Nietzsche, Foucault and Derrida, is not an option, not an object of volition, in the civic – it is always and has always been present, and has allowed the citizen's sense of belonging to 'evolve'. In imaging the social – city-state, republic, nation – like Derrida's Nietzsche, Finlay avowedly goes back to the rhetorical mythscape of the pre-Socratic, following its phases through what Bann calls the 'Western aesthetic codex'.[54] His medallions, *Heroic* and *Little Spartan*, are threatening not because they are a remembrance of live bullets fired, but because they threaten to show the disruption of the relationship between Enlightenment and the 'perpetual peace' (the phrase is Kant's) it promised.

Warfare/Welfare: Janice Galloway, Cairns Craig and the Home Front

Edward Said's reading of Jane Austen's *Mansfield Park*, a novel standing right at the edge of the British empire, remains one of the most influential pieces of literary thought of the past few decades, and one which demonstrates how the home, surrounded by the garden, must itself ultimately be surrounded by empire, which is what grounds the heroine[55] via an integrated cultural centring dependent on suitably remote colonial outsides, 'assuming . . . the importance of an empire to the situation at home'. But Fanny Price's socio-geographical journey to the Bertrams' well-appointed house can also be read as the creation of a specifically *English* national home, as indeed does Said, without saying so. Finlay provides a clue as to what happens to this home if we reflect that British imperialism, with Eng. Lit. as its cultural backbone, is in large part not English at all. Since the British Union which led to the early nineteenth-century colonial rivalries described by Said was largely led by aspiring Scots during and after the Enlightenment, it is not coincidental that so much Scottish culture of the period leading up to devolution, as in Finlay's wild gardens, seems to be casting around for a way in which to enunciate (Riach's *voice*) or position (Riach's *place*) a national home, since this represents something like the reversal of the 'Britishing' process Said describes. Janice Galloway's 1989 *The Trick is to Keep Breathing* – a story describing a young schoolteacher losing her mind and her *sense of place* – takes problems in this imperial British development of home to a new level, and moreover acts as a corrective to Said's influential model.[56] Her first novel is as unhomely as are the wild bushes of Finlay.

Galloway's novel is representative of a wider writerly search for a register of representation, the object of MacDiarmid's and Muir's 1930s fears, exactly bisecting the period between the failed and successful devolution referendums (1979–97). This period, as we have seen, also brings a concern with the process of writing itself, when the unwritten British constitution, squarely behind the tradition and precedent constituting imperial power, was being questioned. Galloway's novel appeared a year after the Owen Edwards edited version of *A Claim of Right for Scotland* (1988), a multi-authored attempt to write the democratic rules for at least one part of Britain, breaking down the imperial equation of politics and tradition.[57] From this volume, Cairns Craig continued to series-edit the 'Determinations' series of interdisciplinary critical works which set out to thoroughly rework Scottish Studies in the early 1990s. Craig's *The Modern Scottish Novel* (1999) valuably connects rhetorical and philosophical strategy in key novels throughout the century, and contextualises the work of Galloway. However, I suggest that Craig's account in general might have taken a more postcolonial turn, particularly concerning the land, violence, and homeliness.

Firstly, the modern Scottish narrative strategy Craig discerns (from *A Scots Quair* [1932–34]), one 'which displaces the third person, omniscient – and anglocentric' author in favour of a narration organised through the voices and the gossip of the folk themselves', certainly usefully points towards a later collapsing of first and third person which would challenge the fixation of narrative voice relative to Standard English, in James Kelman and then in Janice Galloway.[58] Yet it also sets up a dichotomy in which identification with otherness can seem a matter of mere volition. Gibbons's Chris Guthrie, educated in Standard English but locating herself at home in Aberdeenshire, makes a 'choice [which] allows her a perspective upon the community that can chart its failings without transferring to an entirely different cultural environment all her potentiality for growth and development'.[59] This perspectival commuting back and forth between the inside and outside of home implies that the self can completely assume one or other position at any time. Yet, as Craig recognises, the syntax of Kelman and Galloway is more ambivalent, more concerned with recovering action in all its untidiness, than with occupying any one perspective – even in a shaky third person – from which to 'know'. Kelman and Galloway, rather, confuse the *time of experience* of Standard English, a strategy so traumatic to Eng. Lit. that it demands an alternative orthography – no purloined apostrophe to finish words '–in'.

Nor does the ideally proactive movement between the positive and negative poles of the self square with Craig's otherwise highly convincing use of Macmurray.[60] In Macmurray the negative, fearful aspect of the self – the subject – is *incapable* of action or recognition, and is withdrawn from the world entirely.[61] In Macmurray, moreover, it is possible to discern a sub-British *agent* struggling within a standardised British *subject*: for Macmurray, in pragmatic societies the relationship of persons becomes impersonal rather than personal, subjective as opposed to active, and characterised by fear – an emotion Craig rightly identifies as a characteristic of many protagonists of modern Scottish fiction.[62] But in Macmurray, when the fearful self becomes subject, it becomes incapable of choice altogether; indeed the personal split between subject and agent can only ever be identified *analytically*, and so can't happen at the same time as the agent's action. Craig's model thus risks too easily making pure agency an object of choice, implying objective knowledge of an inactive seeing-knowing subject, a history with no cruelty (though *A Scots Quair* is full of heartbreaking cruelty). Despite his impeccably post-Enlightenment ethics, here Craig risks repeating an impulse behind the eighteenth-century *literati's* dividing of types of knowledge – which also divided the place of home.

The second point of postcolonial contact here with Craig's protagonists relates to his very extended discussion of Alisdair MacIntyre, which convincingly provides a Scottish theoretical framework with which to render opaque viewpoints which seem ethically transparent.[63] Here Craig approaches Said in quoting MacIntyre's own analysis of Austen:

> The novel, as MacIntyre's analysis of Jane Austen ([in *After Virtue*] 239–243) enforces, has been one of the major modes through which modern societies have shaped the argument about the 'goods' of their tradition and therefore about the very nature of the tradition of which they are a part.[64]

This jars with Said's account of Jane Austen's fixing of home, in which the 'national' goods become paradoxically English as they become British-colonial. This misfit is striking given Craig's concern with the interaction between the Scottish narration of 'home' and the British standards which displaced it – 'Scots is not at home in the novel; English is not at home in Scotland'.[65] Said's Mansfield Park is located in a form of home culturally and economically located within concentric fields of significance reliant on the colonial world of the Americas; yet the mutual influence between Scotland and the colonial Americas was even stronger than that between England and the Americas, and Scotland's economic links with America were largely behind Scotland's agreement to British Union. The republican US, of course, maintained a hypnotic attraction for Hume and Smith, who were British with grudging enthusiasm.

Enlightenment and early nineteenth-century Scots' investments, concentrated in the Americas, provided the economic comfort which enabled the conditions of Enlightenment – as did the investments of Austen's Thomas Bertram. Scottish involvement required a 'global' cultural adjustment which took the form of a Unionist Enlightenment, placing aspirations *outside* of the homeland. This may have heralded a homing process in a sense, but it was also a de-homing one: the same year as *Mansfield Park* (1814) saw the publication of Walter Scott's *Waverley*, the first of a series of novels portraying the final knockings of the dissociation of speech and spirit we have seen diagnosed by Edwin Muir – a context extensively discussed by Craig in his 1996 *Out of History*.[66]

At the same time as Austen was silently adducing 'home' to an ill-defined England, Scott was showing a very different home at work within Eng. Lit. Scott's home was of necessity displaced as part of a wider pragmatic displacement. The Waverley series, indeed, can be seen then as a distorted mirror to the centring of the home Said sees in Austen's 1810s England: in Scott we see a centring in empire which is never really centred. Despite the efforts of the Edinburgh *literati*, home has ceased to be *at home*, as it is projected outwards in the process of British imperialism. The dangerously replete Britishness of Britain – indeed the tendency to grasp at Britishness where the English were barely interested in Britishness at all until the mid-Victorian era – is what is missed by Said, who in *Culture and Imperialism* frequently describes the importance of colonial culture to the 'English' state. What is at stake in Said's collapse of British state and English nation is the adaptation of nations, especially Scotland, to the state, which was squarely behind the civilising imperative of imperialism's grand narrative; rethinking home is one of the major ways in which Scotland is participating in postcolonialism.

Said, perhaps *the* key figure of Postcolonial Criticism as we know it, is nevertheless a cautionary read: he sees Enlightenment, incredibly, moving around continental Europe and becoming 'accepted in . . . subsequently, England'.[67] He rightly describes the rationality of Carlyle's racism, but then fails to tie this to the arch-rationalism which Carlyle's newly stateless nation had needed to become globally central. Carlyle's *The Nigger Question* (1849) is only one example of a neo-Enlightenment equation of progress with cultural whitening.[68] Conversely, in the Scotland in which, *pace* Finlay, no one is really at home under Enlightenment conditions, a 1980s wave of *unheimlich* culture, exemplified by Galloway's Joy's inability to feel at home in her own home, must trigger a rethinking of the Enlightenment context's being coupled with a discussion of Scotland's complex position as imperialist.

The Trick is to Keep Breathing cleverly locates the subject-self in the shell of the Welfare State's final attempt to create a consensually British civil society. (In terms of its take on the Welfare State, this novel could profitably be compared with the early Muriel Spark.) Joy has to deal with a health visitor and a housing officer, and being a teacher, experiences all three of the main bases of welfare. She struggles to fend off the intrusions of family friends and colleagues, which never connect her to her *self*. Over-drinking and under-eating, she is eventually hospitalised, only to return to her *home* to find that it seems to have been occupied by someone else.

If Said's description of *Mansfield Park* shows a heroine being dragged towards the centre of concentric cultural and economic worlds whose geographies are defined by colonial concerns, Galloway's Joy shows what is left when imperial geographies are *not* concentric. Her struggle to get herself to the centre of her community, her work, her body and her mind, takes place in a loveless housing estate just far away enough from the metropolis to be inconvenient without being picturesque. Said's home, unlike Finlay's and Galloway's, misses the unhomeliness of this post-Enlightenment British abode. Fanny's Mansfield Park, buried in a verdant and rich English heartland, really is a *park*, though not a public one; Joy's Bourtreehill, conversely, is a public housing estate, but with no real *trees* or *hills*. In Galloway as in Finlay, nature always bears the burden of culture, and vice versa.

In looking at what has become unhomely for Joy in the Anglo-Britain where Fanny Price felt perfectly at home, it may be instructive to rethink Linda Colley's influential description of an empire-building Britain via the earlier critique of Tom Nairn: for most Scottish critics, Colley overstates the importance of Romantic nationalism in drawing Britons together as an organic whole during the Austen period of consolidation.[69] Nairn's *The Break-Up of Britain* (1977) had already characterised the period as one of a resignation to participation in a wider empire, ceding Romantic nationalism (an account for which Nairn was nevertheless unloved by some Scottish nationalists, who saw his reading as 'pessimistic', since it seemed to them to portray later nationalism as an atavistic and unmodern process).[70] English Romanticism, charged with creating the backbone of the 'British nation', generally didn't see the Scottish landscape or the Scottish vernacular as part of the national identity at all: although Edinburgh was 'Athenian' – a reputation enhanced by the mixture of classical and contemporary English examples in Adam Smith's *Lectures on Rhetoric* – the main attraction of the rest of the country was, and largely remains, its picturesque bleakness, made possible by the Highland Clearances.[71]

Joy's Bourtreehill is a hangover of the Austen era, when, via a popular and disastrous reading of Smith's 'free trade', the Highland Clearances emptied hundreds of thousands abroad or into a Glasgow so swollen by colonial trade that it later further spilled out into 'New Towns', faint echoes of nature, system-built and punctuated by unconvincing shrubs. Joy's story thus represents the last stand of the British organic metaphor, and is wide open to parody – of which her version is wry and painful. And although theory was trying to do away with the term 'organic' in the 1980s, the organic metaphor was still hanging on in the speeches of Margaret Thatcher and John Major, whose representations of British home were based on Georgian, Anglocentric 'villagey' images which had in fact originally arisen to counter nineteenth-century urbanisation and cultural mixture – a fear of ethnic dilution, much as we are seeing today.[72]

The senility of the British home of the Thatcher–Major era is seen in the kind of homes people lived in; the era began with 1981's candidly neo-racial legal redefinition of what kind of person could call Britain their home,[73] and proceeded via a division between responsible house-holders and deserving poor, encouraged by council house sales. Their infrastructure crumbling, those areas which remained public became increasingly uninhabitable, whether in the way described by Galloway in her impossible and loaded discussions with the authorities, or as in *Trainspotting*'s West Granton, where an HIV-positive Tommy is not expected to survive a winter.[74] Joy's house has already lost its marks of belonging before she enters it, since the number plates have been taken from the door by the previous occupant, leaving only a pair of colons – ' : : ' – a double narrative stop with no ongoing clause.[75] With a fragile stoicism, she concedes that her house doesn't deserve a place in society, and describes the number plates as 'a signal I could do without'.[76] Joy's relationship with nature is therefore pointedly not the organic ideal of Austen's Anglo-Britain: the greenery around the flats merely *connotes* countryside, and the food which is nearest to her is also the furthest from any knowable process of cultivation. Cultivation, with its over-tures of 'culture', may take place in her name, but, unlike those belong-ing to an Anglo-British tradition of planters and civilisers, her nature is drawn through the culture of the estate.[77] (A decade later George Monbiot would powerfully critique the New Labour government's support of supermarket chains' *laissez-faire* destruction of environ-ment and community, exemplifying the same chain – Tesco – as does Galloway's story.)[78] Joy's lack of control over her diet is central to her inability to feel at home: everywhere her attempts to centre herself in her own body (to *keep breathing*) are fraught with anxiety. Nothing in her world that makes sense to her is within reach. The earth itself is deterritorialised.[79]

Like Kelman's narrators, Joy thus slips between first, second and third person, and registers amazement at her 'own duplicity'.[80] She loses the sense of her own progress through any kind of narrative – seen in her misunderstanding of times and misreading of clocks. She is almost relieved when completely fixed into a circuit of objectification on being hospitalised – like Macmurray, Laing and other imperially off-centre writers, Galloway uses the clinical relationship to exemplify the imper-sonal. Being on the wrong side of the clinic invites a *reductio ad absurdam*, since the field of the visual is at last completely lost:[81] 'I don't know what I'm doing any more. I look myself in the eye and see nothing I recognise.'[82]

But appropriately, it is in her own home that Joy has most trouble telling the time or locating herself relative to any familiar narrative. She frequently falls asleep and wakes up in confusion, losing grasp of time and space, in sharp distinction to the extensive space-time of Enlightenment. When she returns to her house after the doctors let her go, it is with the sense of being a stranger, of realising the duplicity of the key to her home, which has somehow locked her out when it should keep her safely inside: '[s]omeone else had my keys. The place I lived in wasn't my home any more'.[83] Appropriately, Joy turns to writing as an interface between self and environment. She leaves notes to herself around the house, trying to give her life some unifying narrative:

> I'm leaning back on the worktop with the cup between my hands when a note twitches on the lino.
> PHONE DR. STEAD
> Could be an old one: it's hard to tell. I check the clock and worry in case it's stopped. Sometimes I have to haul it off the wall and listen for the tick to be absolutely sure.[84]

Unlike Fanny Price, Joy still struggles to use writing to fix herself in a time and environment – a critical point which makes the novel an ideal snapshot of late 1980s Scottish writing. The reader painfully watches the context of her original notes to herself disappear, while Joy takes faltering and often impetuous steps towards recognition. When hospitalised, Joy has become resigned to the loss of her letters, yet retains the habit of writing: 'I get over-excited and forget things. I keep the notepad with me just in case.'[85] This 'in case' ironically lacks any other contingent action, since both she and the reader by now know that her unhomeliness is also a cultural forgetting for which conventional narrative has long provided no solution. In the clinic, Joy is treated by relieving her of the necessity of trying to locate herself; she is not even allowed to wander into the corridor:

> You can't wait about in here like that.
>   At first I can't work out who's speaking. Then he comes closer: a white face and a white coat.
>   Are you listening? You can't wait here.
>   I say What? in a little girl voice, hoping for the best.
>   You heard me. You know you can't wait here like that. Come on now. Go and get your dressing gown.[86]

The staff want Joy to *wait* somewhere else, for they don't expect her to be engaged in any action other than waiting. Waiting – pointedly failing to grasp the present – is both a source of existential pain and a habit for those accustomed to a loss of participation in history. It is also a theme absolutely central to the writing of James Kelman, which charts the attempts of characters to move away from hanging about and towards history and action. Kelman's characters often also recognise the need to get over the spatial separation of individuals, in acts as simple as handshakes, but feel so accustomed to auto-placement that they can't risk the action of contact, 'no in the off-chance'.[87] Kelman's 'off-chance' is like Galloway's 'just in case', attributing a lack of agency to luck, while showing the reader the materiality of the inaction which inheres in what we call luck. Both Kelman's and Galloway's characters edge towards action over luck, the 'just in case', trying to find a sense of home, in super-markets, betting shops, and the degree zero for community, the *public house*.

Galloway's is a rhetorical strategy indebted to Kelman's, with very similar prose – short sentences with truncated or unexpected contexts, slides between first and third person, rapid movements from narrative to general statements, stoic signatures denoting despair and commitment. In her better moments, we can see that Joy, like a Kelman punter with a rush of blood to the head, has taken action (she is agent); in less good ones she describes her activity as a mere 'accident' (she is subject) – the kind of analytic distinction Cairns Craig describes in Kelman.[88] The struggle is to keep the meeting of persons at a dialogic level: as Said shows in the emotional growth of Fanny Price, in an imperial context having a home also depends on positioning oneself rather than being positioned, on acting rather than being acted on. This involves more than volition, and is the result of a complex set of political causes.

We might add finally that, although Said approvingly quotes Wole Soyinka's 1976 call to get beyond a dualistic siege mentality in decolonising literature,[89] he also takes Ireland as an example precisely because it is *not* in-between but oppositional – he describes it as a hundred per cent colony, despite centuries of Anglo-Irish settlers – whereas that most foundationally British-imperial territory of Scotland is more problematic, neither friend nor foe, neither specifically colonial nor specifically colonised, but merely displaced, becoming swept along by the British export of the familiar. If Said's Irish Dedalus cannot say 'home', then Said cannot say that Scottish speakers cannot say 'home'. This tongue-tiedness accompanying culture which is 'western' – and this is a crucial term: if 'westernisation' means individually adapting to civic standards which outweigh and seem to precede any given local experience, the 'western' is largely made in Edinburgh – would develop after Enlightenment in Scotland into a pathology, the silent shout of the subaltern who knows that her speech will often by silenced not only by her enforced Britishness, but also by the knowledge that she herself partakes of a cultural history complicit with the centre-margin topology of home.

Notes

1. Edwin Morgan, *Crossing the Border: Essays in Scottish Literature* (Manchester: Carcanet, 1990), pp. 292–329.
2. Edwin Morgan, 'MacDiarmid's Later Poetry', in Morgan, *Crossing the Border*, pp. 188–204; 'MacDiarmid at Seventy-Five', in Morgan, *Crossing the Border*, pp. 205–12.
3. Ian Hamilton Finlay, 'Letter to Ernst Jandl', in Alec Finlay, ed., *Justified Sinners: Scottish Counter-Culture* (Edinburgh: Pocketbooks, 2000), n.p.
4. See Jenny Penberthy, 'A Posse of Two: Lorine Niedecker and Ian Hamilton Finlay', *Chapman* 78–9, November 1994, pp. 18–20.
5. Ibid., p. 20.
6. See Marjorie Perloff, *Radical Artifice: Writing Poetry in the Age of Media* (Chicago and London: University of Chicago Press, 1991).
7. 'The Dancers Inherit the Party' and 'Orkney Interior', Michael Horovitz, ed., *Children of Albion: Poetry of the Underground in Britain* (Harmondsworth: Penguin, 1969), pp. 70–1.
8. Robert Crawford, *Devolving English Literature* (Edinburgh: Edinburgh University Press, 2000 [1992]).
9. Mary Ellen Solt, *Concrete Poetry, A World-View* (Bloomington: Indiana University Press, 1968), p. 44.
10. Ibid., p. 10.
11. Perloff, *Radical Artifice*, p. 94.
12. George Oppen, *The Materials* (San Francisco: New Directions, 1962).
13. For a detailed historical account of the progression of objectivism/projectivism from a L=A=N=G=U=A=G=E viewpoint, see Ron Silliman, *The New Sentence* (New York: Roof, 1987).
14. Perloff, *Radical Artifice*, pp. 114–16.
15. Yves Abrioux, ed., *Ian Hamilton Finlay: A Visual Primer* (Edinburgh: Reaktion, 1985).
16. See Mark Scroggins, 'The Piety of Terror', *flashpoint* web issue 1, 1997: http://webdelsol.com/FLASHPOINT/ihfinlay.htm.
17. Kenneth White, 'Poetics of the Open Universe', *Cencrastus* 22, Winter 1986, pp. 17–19.
18. Cf. Gilles Deleuze and Felix Guattari, trans. Brian Massumi, *A Thousand Plateaus: Capitalism and Schizophrenia* (Minneapolis: University of Minnesota Press, 1987 [1980]), 395; here they are discussing Virilio.
19. Ibid., p. 231.
20. Abrioux, *Ian Hamilton Finlay*, p. 228.
21. Ibid., p. 11.
22. Ibid., p. 51.
23. Ibid., p. 46.
24. Ibid., p. 49.

25. Ibid., p. 42.

26. Ibid., pp. 74–5.

27. Ibid., p. 187.

28. Ibid., p. 179.

29. The phrase comes from Stephen Scobie, 'Models of Order', in ed. Alec Finlay, *Wood Notes Wild: Essays on the Poetry And Art of Ian Hamilton Finlay*, (Edinburgh: Polygon, 1995) pp. 177–205: 188–9.

30. Drew Milne, 'Adorno's Hut: Ian Hamilton Finlay's Neoclassical Rearmament Programme', *Scottish Literary Journal* 23–2, November 1996, pp. 69–71.

31. On the perfect and unrealisable democracy, see the discussion of the *arrivant* in Jacques Derrida, trans. Peggy Kamuf, 'Passages – from Traumatism to Promise', in Derrida, ed. Elisabeth Weber, *Points . . . Interviews* (Stanford, CA: Stanford University Press, 1995), pp. 372–95.

32. Ian Hamilton Finlay, *Evening will come they will sew the blue sail*, ed. and designed Graeme Murray (Edinburgh: Graeme Murray, 1991).

33. Gavin Bowd, 'Ian Hamilton Finlay et la revolution française', in David Kinloch and Richard Price, eds., *La Nouvelle Alliance: Influences francophones sur la littérature écossaise moderne* (Grenoble: Ellug, 2000), pp. 91–114: 97.

34. Ibid., pp. 91–2.

35. Ibid., p. 84.

36. Deleuze and Guattari, *A Thousand Plateaus*, p. 354.

37. Ibid., p. 420.

38. Cf. Gilles Deleuze and Felix Guattari, trans. Robert Hurley, Mark Seem and Helen R. Lane, *Anti-Oedipus: Capitalism and Schizophrenia* (Minneapolis: University of Minnesota Press, 1983 [1972]), p. 421.

39. Ian Hamilton Finlay with Ron Costley, introduction and commentary by Stephen Bann, *Heroic Emblems* (Vermont: Z Press, 1977).

40. Ibid., pp. 7, 19, 1, 37.

41. Ibid., p. 48.

42. Ibid., pp. 45, 15.

43. Ibid., p. 45.

44. Cleo McNelly Kearns, '*Armis et Letteris*: Ian Hamilton Finlay's Heroic Emblems', in *Wood Notes Wild*, pp. 82–9: 87.

45. Abrioux, *Ian Hamilton Finlay*, p. 283.

46. Bowd, 'Ian Hamilton Finlay et la revolution française', pp. 97–9, 101.

47. Cf. Deleuze and Guattari, *Anti-Oedipus*, p. 421.

48. Bowd, 'Ian Hamilton Finlay et la revolution française', p. 103.

49. Ibid., p. 104.

50. Ibid., p. 106.

51. Cited in ibid., p. 111.

52. Ibid., p. 107.

53. Ibid., p. 112.

54. Ibid., p. 31.

55. Edward Said, 'Jane Austen and Empire', in *Culture and Imperialism* (New York: Vintage, 1994), pp. 80–97, p. 89, his italics.

56. Janice Galloway, *The Trick is to Keep Breathing* (London: Vintage, 1999 [1989]).

57. Owen Dudley Edwards, ed., *A Claim of Right for Scotland* (Edinburgh:

Polygon, 1989 [1988]); cf. Michael Gardiner, *The Cultural Roots of British Devolution* (Edinburgh: Edinburgh University Press, 2004), pp. 131–55.

58. Craig, *The Modern Scottish Novel*, p. 65.
59. Ibid., p. 66.
60. Ibid., pp. 89–91; cf. Cairns Craig, 'Beyond Reason – Hume, Seth, Macmurray and Scotland's Postmodernity', in Eleanor Bell and Gavin Miller, eds., *Scotland in Theory* (Amsterdam: Rodopi, 2004), pp. 249–80.
61. John Macmurray, *The Form of the Personal I: The Self as Agent* (London: Faber and Faber, 1969), p. 91.
62. John Macmurray, *The Form of the Personal II: Persons in Relation* (London: Faber and Faber, 1969), p. 138.
63. See Alisdair MacIntyre, *After Virtue: A Study in Moral Theory* (London: Duckworth, 1985), pp. 239–43.
64. Craig, *The Modern Scottish Novel*, p. 23.
65. Ibid., p. 78.
66. Cairns Craig, *Out of History: Narrative Paradigms in Scottish and British Culture* (Edinburgh: Polygon, 1996); an account uncannily similar to Scott's from more recent times, of Scottish 'nationalist' pride behind British imperialism, is to be found in Michael Fry, *The Scottish Empire* (Edinburgh: Birlinn, 2001).
67. Edward Said, 'Connecting Empire to Secular Interpretation', in *Culture and Imperialism*, pp. 43–61: 44.
68. Thomas Carlyle, *Occasional Discourse on the Nigger Question* (London: T. Bosworth, 1853 [1849]); Henry Louis Gates Jr, *Figures in Black: Words, Signs, and the 'Racial' Self* (New York and Oxford: Oxford University Press, 1989), pp. 17–19; Robert Young, *Colonial Desire: Hybridity in Theory, Culture, and Race* (London: Routledge, 1995), pp. 34, 66.
69. Linda Colley, *Britons: Forging the Nation 1707–1837* (New Haven, CT: Yale University Press, 1992).
70. Tom Nairn, *The Break-up of Britain: Crisis and Neo-Nationalism* (London: NLB, 1977); cf. Ronald Beveridge and Craig Turnbull, *The Eclipse of Scottish Culture: Inferiorism and the Intellectuals* (Edinburgh: Polygon, 1989).
71. Adam Smith, *Lectures on Rhetoric and Belles Lettres*, ed. John M. Lothian (Carbondale and Edwardsville, IL: University of Southern Illinois Press, 1971 [1776]).
72. Raphael Samuel, *Theatres of Memory* (London: Verso, 1994); Patrick Wright, *On Living in an Old Country: The National Past in Contemporary Britain* (London: Verso, 1985); Alun Hawkins, 'Rurality and English Identity', in David Morley and Kevin Robins, eds., *British Cultural Studies* (Oxford: Oxford University Press, 2001), pp. 145–56; Jeremy Paxman, *The English: A Portrait of a People* (London: Penguin, 1999), Chapter 8. See also Rider Haggard, *A Farmer's Year* (London: Longman Green, 1899); Arthur Quiller-Couch, *The Oxford Book of English Verse* (Oxford: Oxford University Press, 1900); Alex Potts, 'Constable Country between the Wars', in Raphael Samuel, ed., *Patriotism: The Making and Unmaking of British National Identity Vol. 3: National Fictions* (London: Routledge, 1989), pp. 160–86; Stanley Baldwin's 1924 'corncrake' speech – see Peter J. Taylor, 'Which Britain? Which England? Which North?', in Morely and Robins,

British Cultural Studies, pp. 127–44: 136; J. B. Priestly's *English Journey* (Harmondsworth: Penguin (1977 [1934]); on New Criticism, which returns to organic metaphors, see Ken Worpole, 'Village School or Blackboard Jungle', in Samuel, *Patriotism*, pp. 125–40; Francis Mulhern, *The Moment of Scrutiny* (London: NLB, 1979).

73. Cf. Zig Layton-Henry, *The Politics of Immigration: Immigration, 'Race', and 'Race' Relations in Post-War Britain* (Oxford: Blackwell, 1992); Ian Baucom, *Out of Place: Englishness, Empire, and the Locations of Identity* (Princeton, NJ: Princeton University Press, 1999).
74. Irvine Welsh, *Trainspotting* (London: Secker and Warburg, 1994 [1993]), pp. 314–17.
75. Galloway, *The Trick is to Keep Breathing*, p. 14.
76. Ibid., p. 14.
77. On the links between culture, cultivation, and colony, see Young, *Colonial Desire*, pp. 30–6.
78. George Monbiot, *Captive State* (London: Pan, 2001), pp. 162–207.
79. Cf. Deleuze and Guattari, *Anti-Oedipus*, p. 309.
80. Galloway, *The Trick is to Keep Breathing*, p. 83.
81. Cf. Frantz Fanon, *Black Skin, White Masks*, trans. Charles Lam Markmann (London: Pluto, 1986), pp. 194–9.
82. Galloway, *The Trick is to Keep Breathing*, p. 156.
83. Ibid., pp. 144–5; on the key as both opening and locking, see Jacques Derrida, trans. James Hulbert, 'Living On', in Harold Bloom et al., *Deconstruction and Criticism* (New York: Seabury, 1979), pp. 75–176.
84. Galloway, *The Trick is to Keep Breathing*, p. 11.
85. Ibid., p. 119.
86. Ibid., p. 137.
87. James Kelman, 'It happened to Me Once', in *The Good Times* (New York: Anchor, 1999), pp. 51–5: 55.
88. Galloway, *The Trick is to Keep Breathing*, p. 19.
89. Said, 'Yeats and Decolonization', p. 229; Wole Soyinka, *Myth, Literature and the African World* (Cambridge: Cambridge University Press, 1976).

Chapter 7

Kelman's Interventions

So far I have proposed that, in a reversal of Edwin Muir's 'twentieth-century condition' of Scottish muteness, after the failed 1979 referendum, and during the years when the nation was least represented by the state, Scottish writers most exerted the need to distinguish themselves. We have seen that Edwin Morgan's sequence *Sonnets From Scotland* (1984) arose in part as a result of anger at the (partly gerrymandered) negative 1979 result. A decade after this, *The Claim of Right for Scotland*, produced by a cross-party body ranging across an impressively wide range of consultants, demanded constitutional change and representation.[1] Around this time, the Scottish urban dialect novel as we now know it became popularly established (Cairns Craig cites Kelman's *The Busconductor Hines* [1984], as a primary influence), and Polygon's influential *Determinations* series (sharing its name with a 1934 collection of essays edited by F. R. Leavis, presumably accidentally), of which an edited version of *A Claim* was one, made the 1990s the most confident decade since the First Renaissance, despite Scotland's remaining economically and politically disadvantaged compared to the rest of the UK, echoing the local depression of the 1920s. If a single discrete example of Scottish cultural theory of the time were to be given, the *Determinations* series would be it: here the invisible absorption into Anglo-British polity, which had kicked in after 1979 as it had after the 1740s, is critiqued from interdisciplinary viewpoints setting sail from education, philosophy and cultural economics. In particular the series can be seen within a Davie-esque tradition of historicising education, of rendering general critical thought viable again.[2]

1987 also saw the publication of Cairns Craig's *History of Scottish Literature*, the most comprehensive and ambitious of its kind, and a mammoth task in its context (though similar productions have seemed less formidable since the late 1990s).[3] The late 1980s and 1990s were a time when a specifically Scottish form was sought – after the phase of merely accumulating grievances, a 'consciousness-raising' phase Gavin Wallace and other critics attribute to the 1970s.[4] As Alan Riach summarises this stateless state of affairs:

> the scene changed most in the 1980s and 1990s with such seminal work as Roderick Watson's *The Literature of Scotland* in 1984, the four-volume *History of Scottish Literature* (1986–1987) edited by Cairns Craig, Duncan Macmillan's *Scottish Art 1460–1990*, John Purser's *Scottish Music* (1992), Marshall Walker's *Scottish Literature Since 1707* (1996), *A History of Scottish Women's Writing* edited by Douglas Gifford and Dorothy McMillan (1997), Cairns Craig's *The Modern Scottish Novel* (1999), Duncan Petrie's *Screening Scotland* (2000), and the 2002 publication of the 1269-page *Scottish Literature in English and Scots* edited by Douglas Gifford, Sarah Dunnigan and Alan MacGillivray.[5]

For Christopher Harvie, the 1980s packed as much cultural punch not only as the First Renaissance of the 1920s but also as the Enlightenment.[6] Much of the impetus behind the movement to establish a separate Scottish culture was anger at the apathy and chicanery behind 1979. But this continued with the unpopular and thoroughly, etc. (this point need not be Laboured) Conservative administrations which ruled for the next eighteen years. Mid-referendums, when a depressed and often furious Glasgow was named European City of Culture in 1990, and large sums of money were to be passed into the hands of the city's rulers, James Kelman, already claimed as the country's highest-profile dialect novelist, wasn't backward in coming forward with his own interpretation of the situation.

Culture in the 'City of Culture'

The fact that Kelman published his critique of the Year of Culture in an important yet relatively unknown volume with AK Press, a smallish anarchist publisher, shows a will to stick with imprints he considers to have high integrity (eight years after he won the James Tait Black Memorial Prize and two before winning the Booker).[7] Kelman is speaking from a Marxist position, but one which recognises (as did anyone living near Glasgow) that local government for much of the twentieth century had been run by a minor mafia aware of the impossibility of any party other than Labour being elected, and free to play fast and loose with socialism. Stressing that an artist is still a worker (as in Morgan's Mayakovsky's 1920s assumption of the position of writer of art-agitprop), and the economic loss to the public forced to shoulder the costs of local government schemes, Kelman demonstrates the local government's underwriting (in older Marxist terms, its forming its 'base' of) arts partnerships which were not in themselves subject to any democratic process.[8] For Kelman, the local council's abuse came to light with European City of Culture status, when 'mixed-economy', non-public arts initiatives were encouraged. It is no coincidence that the Year of Culture almost perfectly bisects the long years of Conservative rule; a corporate culture seems to have seeped down from state to city level as if by historical necessity (three years before *Trainspotting*, which either 'mirrors' or 'critiques' Scottish life under Thatcher, depending on who you read). After 1979, corporations and culture funding seemed to share objectives. As Noam Chomsky has often observed, if you look for direct censorship, you're barking up the wrong cultural tree: a government doesn't have to 'censor' news, since both government and corporation point in the same direction: maximising share prices, confidence, audience viewing figures.

Kelman's critical response represents a *je t'accuse* of local government's appeal to sponsorship to the detriment of art as most art practitioners in the city understood it. With European funds at stake, art's value became determined not by its creative value, but 'by its potential "sale" value to the private sector'.[9] And work value was 'privatised': the 'workshop' system, for example, gave playwrights the right to pay less than Union fees, a blow to integrity defined by Kelman again as an 'external value', which functions like censorship as a disincentive to artists to produce their own work.[10] This represents an intensification of Trocchi's earlier worries in *Merlin* almost four decades before, as writers become increasingly market-led.[11] Literature became increasingly corporate and paradoxically removed from the social – in a sense an unspoken tenet of the British administration, bought into by city government.

Kelman's anger also attaches to the way that to both state and local government the appreciation of art by Glasgow's largely working-class population seemed unfeasible to funders, in a circular logic which worked to bar artistic production by city natives. The 'City of Culture' thus incorporated a remarkably low proportion of the city's residents.[12] This left the nominally left-leaning local council with a paradoxically elitist vision of working-class art – which what we might compare to aspects of the logic of Synthetic Scots. More concretely, as Kelman points out, the City of Culture funding, £50 million, coincided with state-level cuts in the arts, which meant that the redistribution of funds was actually *upwards*:

> Major cuts have already taken place in these areas precisely concerned with art and culture. The public funding of libraries, art galleries, and museums; swimming baths, public parks and public halls; are all being cut drastically . . .[13]

As is now well known, Thatcherite policing methods perfected during the miners' strike were brought to bear on anti-Poll Tax demonstrations happening at precisely the same time in the same city. Kelman's writing was nevertheless charged with 'bringing the city into disrepute' for questioning a situation in public in which spending cuts meant that the overall situation of cultural producers was made more difficult.[14] Even journalists who were otherwise expected to be colloquially leftish laid into Kelman for detracting from a scrap of fame for Glasgow, as in the columnist for the populist tabloid, the *Daily Record*, Ruth Wishart.[15]

As Kelman is aware, Wishart's hushing up of the bare economics of the Year of Culture broadly repeats the Enlightenment situation in which the 'Merchant City' traders made their fortunes by sending slaves to maddening deaths. The irony of the Year of Culture, when Scottish culture itself was undergoing a vital period of renewal against the state, was that state government had drawn local government into a funding situation in which governmental management, efficiency at all costs, had increasingly taken the place of politics itself, demanding the silencing of counter-voices:

> Taking its lead from the Tory national [*sic*] government, local officials of Labour-controlled District Councils up and down the country are suppressing and censoring voices of dissent, content to do so publicly when forced into it. When that fails they try to punish those who dare speak out.[16]

In one edition of the comedy series *Rab C. Nesbitt* from 1990, two hard-man wide-boy councillors are required to entertain delegates from the previous City of Culture, Paris – which by comparison took its socialism seriously (a sad reflection on the Trocchi years). A Parisian delegate being shown round a hospital decorated in Mackintosh style where the machines aren't plugged in is shocked to see that Rab's son, described by the councillors as 'scum', has lost a finger, to general disinterest. As a microsurgeon, the outgoing Parisian is able to sew the boy's finger back on. The context is humorous, but the point serious: a socialism which has rotted to the core, which neglects welfare in the name of fame and forgets where its financial wellbeing came from, and moreover that many of its own population still live in poverty, is not fit to speak for 'the people', whether about art installations or microsurgery.[17] In both cases, the victims are blamed for being victims; they get in the way of the distribution of arts funding.[18] For Kelman, it is not art and business which should be in partnership, but art and subversion. In this sense, he is indeed writing in the tradition of Trocchi and John Calder, and of the Morgan who translated Russian revolutionaries during other times of key change for Scotland. He is recalling the conditions behind the labour movement which embraced art *both* as spiritual nourishment and as agit-prop, and establishing himself as a major Marxist cultural commentator of the period.

In the next essay in the same collection, 'Some Recent Attacks on the Rights of the People', Kelman continues by documenting the removal of a Citizens' Rights Office in a Labour-controlled council, pointing out that since only this office had been fit to deal with specific race issues, the idea that Citizens' Rights problems can all be undertaken by a managerial-style 'One-Stop Centre' indicates that the organs of local government are them-selves racist.[19] We should note moreover that, since this already comes at time when the 'Scottish' in the title of this book urgently needs to drop its *Brigadoon* overtones for a democratic, bordered mandate, citizenship advice for incomers is a matter of urgency in the nation/state division. For the council, it was imperative to avoid awkward questions over this closure (exactly the questions Kelman brings up).[20] The point which strains nation against state for Kelman here is the complicity of the par-liamentary Labour Party, which falls into line with Westminster policy.[21] Under such circumstances, members of the top managerial classes can lack basic skills while administering help ('race' being the example at hand) and those bringing council problems to light are labelled dangerous radicals.[22] Rights are redefined as privileges, and, in a passage reminiscent of Louis Althusser's description of Ideological state Apparatus, Kelman lists the agencies via which state rights are being privatised:

> [o]vertly this happens by means of the political and legal systems; by the forces of law and order, the police and the penal system, the military; by state immi-gration controls, the DSS, the education system and so on. These institutions and structures are designed to control the vast majority of people who con-stitute society, the public.[23]

Thus the 'public' is gradually pared down to individual wants, making public culture impossible (elsewhere I have noted how, bizarrely, after 1994 a 'gathering' of two persons could in the UK legally constitute a dangerous crowd).[24] Even in Glasgow, in a dramatic echo of the events of 1919, every public gathering was seen as a potential threat. The classic example of the closing down of culture comes during the Year of Culture, when Pat Lally, the 'socialist' Council Leader, plotted to sell off a third of Glasgow Green, the traditional gathering place and relaxing ground for the public:

> The authorities prefer a situation where the only meeting place is the pub. By the time you've talked your way through the problem you're too drunk to do anything about it . . . In 1990, at the height of their attack on culture, Pat Lally

and the Glasgow 'socialists' tried to sell off one third of Glasgow Green to private developers, the very land where people have gathered for generations, as of right, to air and address their political grievances. That's the sinister side of it, if we need reminding, the Green is not only a prime site for the cash profit brigade it is also dangerously, it represents a political threat to local security.[25]

In his 1990 installation 'Proof', the Scottish artist Douglas Gordon creates a monument to this spiv-like attempt to privatise the public of Glasgow Green, echoing Kelman's identification of the Green as a site of grass-roots culture on grass.[26] Glasgow Green has typically been conceived as *the* public space of Scotland's largest city; what is extraordinary is that the attempt to sell off a third of it has not registered more strongly in cultural history.

Chomsky and common sense

In 1990, and largely through the intervention of Kelman, Noam Chomsky (invited to give a Gifford Lecture in Edinburgh) spoke on 'Self-Determination' at the Pearce Institute in Glasgow, and was briefly active in that most cultural of cities during that most cultural of years.[27] Kelman would later persuasively link Chomsky to the late-Enlightenment Scottish philosopher Thomas Reid, whose ideas (we now realise) twist the Humean scepticism which would later form the backbone of Anglo-British logical positivism. In 'A Reading from the Work of Noam Chomsky' Kelman describes how Reid's critique of Enlightenment implied not only an inter-disciplinarity *per se*, but also an interdisciplinary education (in media as well as universities), one within the reach of anyone:

> No matter the subject under scrutiny, certain factors remain the same, we apply our reasoning devices and these devices are inter-disciplinary. We apply them in physics, in astronomy, in domestic economy, in horse-race betting, in joinery, in the creation of art . . .
> If we are restricted to one subject only then our ability to reason may stagnate . . .[28]

Like G. E. Davie, Kelman here reworks the ethical implications of high generic borders in education:

> What seems clear is that restricting yourself to one particular method will just make life more difficult . . .
> If the educational system is to thrust groups of people into separate compartments then none will be equipped to take the wide view necessary.

No longer does it become possible for the poet to discuss methodology with sculptors and electricians.[29]

Chomsky is similarly interdisciplinary and thus anti-behaviouristic.[30] He would also, therefore, similarly be a target for efficiency-raising agencies in broadening the terms of any given debate – as in the attempt to increase the number of media outlets available (and Chomsky has also written for AK Press, and indeed been foreworded by Kelman).[31] Kelman's Chomsky also breaks with the art-as-mirror-of-ideology form of vulgar Marxism in seeing new forms of enunciation (as in the dialect novel) as the creation of new linguistic, and therefore new social, forms. Common Sense, in a Reidian and then in Chomskian sense, leads, for Kelman, through a viable Scottish Romanticism – which in Tom Nairn's reading had gone underground at best and at worst disappeared into a sub-British seam of anti-empiricism – reflected in the aesthetic formalism which we have seen is a standard in late twentieth-century Scottish literature. The role of Scottish universities from the Reidian eighteenth century was thus to reconcile economic and moral expansion to the needs of given communities, whereas Oxbridge typically created hierarchies of communities, a role aided by its proximity to London.[32]

Like Macmurray, Kelman correspondingly reverses the Anglo-British positivist precedence of concepts over experience; the assumption of objects 'out there' viewed by a prior subject-self is dehumanising, and, at its worst, as in Trocchi's warnings in *Merlin*, can lead to absolutism and thus to totalitarianism, and to torture, silencing, fascism.[33] Judgement, in the Macmurray–Chomsky–Kelman line, should be seen to come *before* knowledge; there is no pure knowledge, no knowledge uninformed by prior social conditions. The concepts-first method can now be seen as the last stand of Britishness, coincident with logical positivism (and, we might say, with the idea that a specialism was more useful than general criticism in empire). Concepts-first thinking is exclusivist, since 'only those who specialise in discussing topics will be admitted', and, when its exclusiveness is filtered through a linguistic lens, 'splitting hairs' in the quest for correctness is a form of violence – as is reflected in the trajectory of the idea of democracy through liberalism and utilitarianism to the present:

> [according to the definitions of Lord Justice McGonigal, i]nhuman treatment is . . . treatment causing *severe* suffering. Torture is an *aggravated* form of inhuman treatment and *degrading* conduct is conduct which *grossly* humiliates.
>
> At which point experts who specialize in encountering concepts can instigate a further debate on the meaning of grossness or severity, or the meaning of the concept 'aggravation'.[34]

Where the Anglo-British reading of Hume delights in his 'hair-splitting' scepticism, empiricism and factuality (as in logical positivism), this stress is less certain in the Hume 'who spoke of those parts of our knowledge that are derived "from the original hand of nature" and that are "a species of instinct" '.[35] Moreover, via Hamilton, then Maxwell, then Ferrier, Reid's interest in 'the relation of sight and touch' also represents a direct intervention into the seeing-knowing subject upon which positivism typically rests.[36] The aesthetic of touch and resistance (physical and political: in Macmurray, as we have seen, the two are closely related) also troubles the producer/consumer division by creating a shared present with shared experience. A form of Reid's aesthetic can be, as below, linked to Kafka, but Kelman also attributes the same existential method to Tom Leonard, generally accepted as one of the first writers to use narrative Scots in an entirely serious way, *resisting* Standard English.[37]

Franz Kafka's narration

In his unusually long critical essay 'A Look at Franz Kakfa's Three Novels' (2003), Kelman considers Kafka's entire novelistic *oeuvre* and outlines a narrative stance similar to that which has formed the ethical basis of his own narration – a form of free indirect discourse, or a strategic switching between first and third persons.[38] Kelman's voice is in part a transmission of the possibilities for the poetic reconfiguring of the relation of speech and writing as in Edwin Morgan, Ian Hamilton Finlay and later, Tom Leonard; via Kelman, as Cairns Craig has noted, 'voice' then opens up paths for Janice Galloway, Alan Warner and Irvine Welsh.[39] (And Welsh's voice is no more than Kelman's a 'realist' one.)

Kafka's *Amerika*, for Kelman, moves towards a third-person narration without accruing any noticeable authority to the third person, leaving the narrator full of uncertainty: '[t]he narrative is hardly a recognisable third-party voice at all, unless it is presenting Karl Rossman's interior perception of how things are'.[40] But *Amerika* is merely a rehearsal: *The Trial* is an allegory in which God's workings, the magic behind the omniscient third person, is made incomprehensible yet definitely material. As this kind of critique suggests, Kafka is both bound to the social and straining at the existential, in which the self is the ultimate arbiter of experience. 'Within the existential tradition the distinguishing feature, typically, is the use of the first-party narrative',[41] but in this case the God-voice is represented by the move to third person – and Kelman will pick up on Kafka's ability to shift between these two, positing an authority which is always material but always beyond comprehension, the secularised 'God' of authority. So *Amerika* seems, at first glance, to buy into the naturalistic third person, but it's clear from Kelman's tone where Kafka is going:

> The conventional perception of third-party narrative derives from a naturalistic view of the world and sees it as objective and unbiased. If somebody is giving us an opinion from within the narrative we are informed that this is what we are getting, an opinion; and by definitions opinions are subjective. The traditional third-party narrative, as a general rule, takes the form of an 'unbiased', 'objective' voice that reports, depicts or describes reality in a way that allows the term 'God-voice' to appear valid.

The final 'appear' is key here: Kelman's fiction uses rapid shifts between the first and the third person to disturb the sense of the God-like presence that the third-person narrator has had in the Eng. Lit. novel. In Scots, this switching has never been fully achieved, even in the classics. Hogg's Scots, for example, could only be taken seriously as adding local colour in dialogue:

> [t]he novel [Hogg's *Confessions of a Justified Sinner*] is written in standard literary form and the Edinburgh *literati* use precisely that linguistic expression when involved in dialogue. But when Hogg gives himself a couple of lines in reply to them he speaks in the supposedly culturally inferior dialect of a couthy Scotch shepherd.[42]

In other words, despite Reid, during Nairn's failed-Romantic phase, the national voice disingenuously renounced claims to native third-person narration, meaning that authority was always something 'out there' (and 'correct'). Kelman thus begins by eschewing the need for a narrative as we have come to understand it at all, a move which could be seen as Deleuzian in its unwillingness to acknowledge some originary lack driving the story by seeking a conclusion.[43] This certainly provides one source of comparison between Kelman and the determinedly inconclusive Beckett who was championed by Trocchi. Kelman's process is highly formalist and mindful of the materiality of enunciation: one of the main emphases that comes through in his reading of *Amerika* is the amount of time spent by the anti-hero Karl in studying English[44] – reminiscent of the implication that Kelman wasn't using proper English from those Booker Prize judges who failed to see how the movement between first and third person works in conjunction with a humorous, rhythmic and controlled movement between Broad Scots and Standard English.

In *The Trial*, various cultural and political authorities are interdependent, and their conglomeration forms a single authority which is nominally material yet just beyond human understanding. This fearful authority corresponds to the prior position of the universal subject – the factual before the personal – at which existentialism had started to chip away, and which was certainly in Kafka's sights. The workplace, the family and the police are all concretised in the objectivity of the out-there of 'the law', as the law itself becomes the external sum of a life. This is most famously demonstrated in the story 'Before the Law', explicated by Jacques Derrida, in which a single man waits a lifetime for entry to the omniscient law, only to find out that he has always already been singled out for denial.[45] Kelman, as he acknowledges in this essay, has taken on a narration which, after the idiom of Kafka, struggles to demonstrate the perplexing materiality of the third-person God-position, as in the law, by sliding between first and third person narration.

In Cairns Craig's influential 1994 essay on Kelman, 'Resisting Arrest', Kelman's form of free indirect speech represents a recognition of, and an attempt to overcome, a society atomised into abstract powers. On Kelman's *A Disaffection* (1989) Craig says:

> The third-person narrative voice that relates facts in the world – 'he swal-lowed . . . Pat glanced . . . They both looked' – merges into the reflective third-person voice that interprets characters' states of mind – 'He was quite sad' – which then fuses with the characters' own thoughts and the language in which they speak to themselves – 'he couldn't give him anything. He didn't deserve to be given anything. So how come he should be given it?' – which in turn becomes true interior monologue – 'so fuck off'. Kelman's particular use of free indirect discourse not only allows modulation between different per-spectives (third-person narrator, first-person thought) but also allows modu-lation across different linguistic registers. In particular, what is characteristic of Kelman's voice itself can take on the characteristics of a speaking voice. By this method, Kelman has found his own very specific means of overcoming the distinction between English (as the medium of narration) and Scots (as the medium of dialogue) which has proved a constant dilemma to Scottish writers. The liberation of the narrative voice from the constraints of written English is an act of linguistic solidarity, since it thrusts that narrative into the sane world which its characters inhabit.
>
> The interweaving of spoken and written forms of speech is made more emphatic by Kelman's refusal to use inverted commas as speech markers. The text is designed visually to resist that moment of arrest in represented speech of a character, and what this does is to create a linguistic equality between speech and narration which allows the narrator to adopt the speech idioms of his characters or the characters to think or speak in 'standard English' with no sense of disruption. The text, therefore, constructs a linguistic unity which resists the fragmentation and isolation that the novels chart as the experience of their characters.[46]

The function of Kelman's fiction, as Craig sees it, is to give us a kick up the Ares, the Are-ness, the complacency of *being* in Standard English while speaking and probably thinking in Scots.[47] While Eleanor Bell (2004) and others have persuasively argued that Craig attempts to 'explain' form and style with recourse to socioeconomic conditions – thus flying close to vulgar Marxism (and we can get a hint of this with the 'therefore . . . experience' in the quotation above)[48] – in Gavin Wallace's 1993 account Craig's Kelman is spearheading the search for what a Scottish form might become, a search which dominated the 1990s.[49]

Kelman's reading of *The Trial* is particularly important, not least because it recalls Macmurray in implying that if there is in a novel no recognition of others, in the full philosophical sense, then there is no moral life to be described therein.[50] In *The Trial* the law, the material-but-abstract, is in practice greater than society itself, so that social life is founded on a deception, which the novelist must implicitly de-narrate. Josef K is, as in 'Before the Law', bound to his quest of returning to a zero point, which he knows to be overdetermined by surveillance and compliant subjects. Every site in the novel becomes one of judicial activity.[51] Mere doubt makes Josef K guilty of a crime which is unspecified, a state of mind which can be read as (Humean) scepticism taken to the furthest degree, to paranoia. In paranoia the reader is placed, disconcertingly, in an omniscient third-person position, sharing Josef K's doubts, but all too aware of his predicament: 'Kafka has placed the reader in a position that a supreme being would occupy if in existence. It is only through being on the outside that the reader has the power to recognise the truth about Josef K's society'.[52] This authority, although third-person, really has no 'outside'; everyone acts within it while simply becoming used to it, as one would get used to, to use the older Marxist terminology, ideology: '[h]e was not having lies told about him: he was living a lie'.[53] The law is never under the control of any one person, nor does it embody any person. Persons are merely the law's functionaries:

> Everything about this mysterious Law suggests that it is under the control of human reason. Yet it is a peculiar form of reason. It seems to be attempting to translate something that must remain outside human understanding into a form which human beings can understand.[54]

This Law must appear to be 'just', where 'justice' is drained of political meaning and can only mean 'efficient' – recalling the thrust of British governments from 1979 to the present day away from politics and towards management. Josef also realises though that he can have no belief outside the Law. And yet, in the terrifying shadows, he feels something of the human well up inside him, or as Kelman powerfully puts it: 'logic is doubtless unshakeable, but it cannot withstand a man who wants to go on living'.[55]

In *The Castle* the third-person narrative even more effectively approaches pure description while hinting at a denial of authority which comes with being on the 'historical highway' over which the use of a material force, History in the use of the law, has come to have power: '[i]f within the third-party narrative there had been a pause for a report of past actions it would have become, in effect, the *perception* of a narrator, a "third-party voice" '.[56] So situational judgements run alongside Josef's ignorance and take the place of omniscient narration: '[w]ithin *The Castle* almost all judgements are contingent and the mood is essential. Since the narrative keeps pace with K., his lack of certainty must be embedded in it . . .'[57] This perpetual contingency acts like a time-lag which ensures that official information is always one step ahead, and that personal experience never becomes personally historical. The ultimate authority is for most beyond and beneath the omniscience of the third person, as judgement arrives via a non-existent supremacy; within the story, only the Land Surveyor has grasped that authority cannot remain abstract, but must be made up of specific voices – thus the key to his bureaucratic success.[58] The Land Surveyor though, the apparent actor, also – in Deleuzian terms – bears no metaphor; he is not fully human, since he simply is what he does.[59] For in Kelman's Kafka, humanity, historicised and socialised, is greater than logic, and resists any form of writing which would describe experience in terms of mere jurisprudence.

For Kelman in Kafka's deliberate pseudo-third-person narration, ultimately a *readerly* judgement is demanded: '[t]he reader who seeks any cause for unrest among the villagers has to judge for him- or herself'.[60] Following this is a description (again, readable via postcolonialism) of the gap between villagers and castle residents; yet Josef is both a refugee without status and a representative of the Law.[61] Like inactive Scottish Britons, he is stuck: received respectability would lead to loss of integrity, and disobedience of the rules to pointless punishment. The reader is thus left in a position from which 'sympathy' for a character – the third-person novelistic standard – rather than seeing that character's socialisation – is impossible: '[t]he reader who has rationalised those "cases" and started considering how the characters might have avoided their present condition, has fallen into the trap'.[62] Characters don't have the free will to manipulate their positions, and even if they did, they wouldn't recognise it as free will. In other words, the absurd logic of the castle requires acceptance of a supreme authority beyond any person, leading Josef to conclude that everyone is subject to some other, inexplicable, power.[63] He is a materialist who nevertheless posits ultimate authority, for example the castle, as paradoxically transcendental. His materialism requires Kafka's language to be shorn of metaphor, that is of any value outside itself, as is Kelman's language, and as is a condition of literariness in Deleuze.

Kelman/Deleuze

Although their significance was accelerated by questions of being and becoming which accompanied the cultural push for determination in the 1980s and 1990s, many of the ideas behind Kelman's work correspond to a longer intellectual tradition based in Glasgow. As we have seen, Scottish culture was also highly politicised in the mid- to late 1960s and concerned with Sartrean and post-Sartrean existentialism and with anti-psychiatry, as in R. D. Laing. Many of Laing's concerns pre-date those of Deleuze, and indeed are referred to by Deleuze, though this fact seems to have been little noted by Scottish intellectual historians.[64] By 1972, when the links between capitalism, subject-interpellation and paranoia were sketched in Deleuze and Guattari's *Anti-Oedipus*, Laing had been pushing similar connections for over a decade; just over a decade later again in Laing's Glasgow, Kelman's *The Busconductor Hines* (1984) signalled a new direction in narration in its shifting – in Deleuzian terms, a schizoid shifting – between first and third persons, and idioms (in the Scottish case, English and Scots), as we have seen sketched out in Kelman's Kafka. This narratology of recovering action by unsettling voices was perfected by Kelman for a further decade, to *How Late It Was, How Late* (1994), the book for which he won the Booker Prize, and the one I am here describing as his most Deleuzian.

This novel describes, to the tune of almost 400 pages, a protagonist determined to 'batter on' in the face of imprisonment, breakup and inexplicable blindness. Its hero, Sammy Samuels, has typically been described as 'hardy' or 'stoic'; I think we can take this more seriously and describe how Sammy's walking round the streets blinded, ceaselessly present and ceaselessly in action, shows an unwillingness to accept *lack*. Deleuze and Guattari's argument in *Anti-Oedipus* is that lack is not, as Freud describes it, an originary state which creates desire, but a *blockage to* desire, produced by capitalism working through the law (of the father and of the state):

> To a certain degree, the traditional logic of desire is all wrong from the very outset: from the very first step that the Platonic logic of desire forces us to take, making us choose between *production* and *acquisition*. From the moment that we place desire on the side of acquisition, we make desire an idealistic (dialectical, nihilistic) conception, which causes us to look upon it as primarily a lack: a lack of an object, a lack of the real object.[65]

Thus,

> [i]t's a game but so it is man life, fucking life I'm talking about, that's all ye
> can do man start again, turn ower a new leaf, a fresh start, another yin, ye just
> plough on, ye plough on, ye just fucking plough on, that's what ye do, that
> was what Sammy did, what else was there I mean fuck all, know what I'm
> saying, that's what ye do, that was what Sammy did, what else was there
> I mean fuck all, know what I'm saying, fuck all.[66]

As in Kafka, the law enacts various types of violence, physical and epis-
temological, on Sammy, who remains unaware of any 'original' reason for
this, having blacked out and then co-operated with the police to the best
of his abilities. Nevertheless, he has built up a resistance to seeking any
transcendental metaphor to explain the law's behaviour:

> Ye cannay make contact with them; all you would have got was sarcasm and
> wee in-jokes . . . [a]nd it was always them, these bastards, always at their con-
> venience, every single last bit of time, it was always them that chose it; ye never
> had any fucking choices.[67]

Trying to get him to understand that there is something originally
wrong with him, the law tries to force upon Sammy a sense of lack.
Rather than simply acting by walking to his next point, he is required to
be on a quest for something missing, to be 'normally dysfunctional' in
the Oedipal sense of having experienced a deflection of his desire by law.
He is even pre-Oedipalised by a beating which has blinded him, like
Oedipus, at some 'traumatic' point before the start of the action. But
while the law sends him on a quest to search for something wrong with
himself, Sammy frustrates the law by registering the unknown origin of
his blindness without any great wish to return to a primal scene and
'solve' the problem:

> He studied roundabout, looking for chinks of light, to where the screw would
> be watching, the flash of the eye maybe; but nothing. He reached his hand
> ower the bunk and felt about the floor and found something, a shoe; he lifted
> it to in front of his face. He fucking smelled it man it was fucking ponging,
> but he couldnay see it; whose fucking shoes were they they werenay fucking
> his, that was a certainty. He was definitely blind but. Fucking weird. Wild. It
> didnay feel like a nightmare either, that's the funny thing. Even psychologi-
> cally. In fact it felt okay, an initial wee flurry of excitement but no what you
> would call panic-stations. Like it was just a new predicament. Christ it was
> even making him smile, shaking his head at the very idea, imagining himself
> telling people; making Helen laugh; she would be annoyed as fuck but she
> would still find it funny, eventually, once they had made it up, the stupit
> fucking row they had had, total misunderstanding man but it was fine now, it
> would be fine, once she saw him.

Now he was chuckling away to himself. How the hell was it happening to him! It's no as if he was earmarked for glory!
Even in practical terms, once the nonsense passed, he started thinking about it; this was a new stage in life, a development. A new epoch![68]

The law in response sets up endless series of questions designed to undermine Sammy's sense of fullness as a human; as he shuffles around blinded, like Beckett's Molloy, he is asked unanswerable questions about time he has forgotten, by those under the umbrella of the law: '[a] fag got put in his hand. The auld psychology. The one place they acted like people was when they were in their own wee office going about their own wee bits of business, wage-earners, time-servers, waiting for the fucking tea-break.'[69]
In the early stages of *Anti-Oedipus*, Deleuze and Guattari similarly describe the questioning of Molloy in Beckett, and the police's relentless demand that Molloy keep forcing himself to 'clarify' by saying and fixing names, even when the repetition of names undermines sense – producing a lack in the apparent move toward completeness.[70] The law's aim of course is not to get information anyway – it has all the information it needs, indeed is in control of the very conditions via which information is legitimised – but rather to place Sammy, to *subject* him. Sammy would be obeying the law, like Kafka's Josef K, by becoming an unfaithful recorder, in sticking to one voice or register as *the* story.[71] Instead, as Timothy Murphy points out of Deleuze and Guattari's Beckett's anti-heroes, and like Alan Warner's *The Man Who Walks*, in the one without lack proactively walks, *resisting* lack, striding uphill,[72] Sammy is disarmingly straight and unmetaphorical: no metaphor, no lack.[73] *Anti-Oedipus*, and more so, *A Thousand Plateaus*, are known for breaking the law by breaking down generic categories; here the 'literary' is concerned with effects stripped of metaphor, of the need to automatically naturalise. All narrative, all law, begins in fiction.[74] Thus it is for Sammy.
But *pace* Deleuze, and despite the claim Kelman makes at the outset of his paper on Kafka, the majority of 'critics' do not attempt to provide 'meanings' for literary texts, and most haven't done so since the 1960s.[75] The claim itself, though probably directed at academics Kelman feels are misrepresenting his stories, shows a disappointing bad faith in fencing off the literary (as 'novel', 'poem', and so on) – even in the middle of an essay he would himself plainly view as 'critical'. As Deleuze realised, the literary does not work in terms of an opposition of the creative and the critical: what makes a text literary is its effects rather than its typology, what it makes happen in the world rather than its signifying something absent. But it is precisely this proactiveness of the literary that prevents

any one writer from bracketing off her own work as literary – a problem remaining where Scotland is market-led into creating artificial 'schools', with 'writing' and 'criticism' still strongly separated. Indeed, this closing down of the literary possibilities of all writing – rather than only those texts which have passed through a publishing filter for generic approval – is in Deleuzian terms itself classically bourgeois.

Sammy, far from classically bourgeois, rather than accepting his 'lack' and seeking a Freudian cure, takes each of the innumerable problems the law hands him as another starting-point for an endless *becoming*. He is not in search of any final signified – or, to put it into a Scottish context, of the dream of a 'correct English' which haunted Scots from Adam Smith's *Lectures on Rhetoric* through James Beattie and Thomas Carlyle and Lord Reith's BBC to the anti-theory squads of the 1980s. (Nor, indeed, is he interested in Synthetic Scots or 'correct Scots', whose moment(s) have certainly passed.) Where lack would interpellate him, it doesn't strike him to think of himself as being *in debt*. He is indebted to no one, the bold Sammy, the bold yin, and, struggling to take steps in the present, refusing to swallow the idea that a solution to an interpellated lack would allow him one day to get back to square one, wherever that was.[76]

Sammy's having to pay for his black-out with his sight is also a terrible Humean playing out of the two Renaissances' sponsorship of drunkenness and the wearisome nationalist sponsorship of 'Scotch whisky' – most obviously in the MacDiarmid of 'A Drunk Man Looks at the Thistle' and 'A Glass of Pure Water', but also in the research of David Daiches and others into 'our' national drink – a critical tendency which we can see at its peak pre-1979. The contradiction is that alcohol is a corporeal form of debt *par excellence*, not merely in the Kelman-anecdotal sense of owing folk rounds and navigating one's way round Glasgow by pubs (like Beckett's any-space-whatever, pub-Sammy's space is not only physical but also fucking mental),[77] but also in that alcohol acts with a depressant effect, a relief at the time but always to be paid for with interest later. Societies that rely heavily on alcohol as an everyday drug are also likely to be those that rely heavily on debt (note, for example, the United Kingdom's disposition towards credit cards and heavy mortgaging). The reliance on alcohol disappears, most obviously, in Irvine Welsh, Alan Warner and other writers falling under the tired phrase 'chemical generation' (partly behind Christie March's flawed argument that these writers have somehow overtaken Kelman),[78] and in other rave-influenced aesthetics, in which there is a sense of looking back over the ecstasy revolution. Writers in particular influenced by the aesthetics of ecstasy tend to be much more interested in the tactile than the what-are-you-looking-at culture of vision. And the cultural 'value' of alcohol flags throughout

Kelman's *oeuvre* as a whole, whose talk of pubs and carry-outs is as first glance crass, but on closer inspection increasingly subtle and sometimes despairingly proactive, especially in his later work.

In Sammy's proactively schizo narrative, again in the Deleuzian terms used of Kafka, first-person often takes the habit of third-person talk.[79] Kelman writes in Deleuzian free indirect style, which 'uses the third person to describe single characters from the point of view of a received and anonymous language'.[80] Via this narrative technique, whose sophistication is missed by critics who see his 'demotic' prose as a simple 'downward identification',[81] Kelman takes advantage of a habit of third-person address in Scottish English speech ('up he gets'; 'he's off and running'; 'the bold Sammy') to enact a prose not fixed to the first person, but always *becoming* a nominal third person who never reaches omniscience. Cairns Craig's convincing and detailed account of how Kelman 'translates' between persons and dialects can be read in this sense: Sammy is 'resisting arrest' by resisting placement in any one normative neurosis, by being, as it were, a walking schizophrenic – the character with whom Deleuze and Kelman start their 1972 study.[82] Like Kafka, Kelman takes on and temporarily occupies 'other' registers, rendering them strange and discordant, always 'translated'.[83] And as in Wilhelm Reich, an identification with the individual leader, father of the familial/state law – or in Deleuze, with the abstract 'man' as such – and the need to get back to a perfect form or an abstract law, is rejected in the endlessly contingent schizo stroll.[84] Sammy votes with his feet.

Where lack fixes the person to a life of working for some final purpose, of earning her way back to normality (in Freud, the 'normally neurotic'), for Sammy, as for Deleuze's schizoid, the only thing that doesn't change is that things are always changing. He continues to batter on without any nostalgic or clinical wish for things to be as they once were, or as the law in its many forms may want him to believe they once were. Nor even does he view his blindness as a lack, rather seeing it as part of a continuous process of transition. For Sammy there is no question of a hidden referent. His speech doesn't relate to something which is missing, in an effort to recover it; rather, he is constantly becoming through his speech, that is, he is aware (as Kelman writes it out, in Scottish existentialist terms) that his language is more about effect than reference. He is more interested in what his communications cause to occur than in whether they place him satisfactorily within any given social narrative. Nor is his track of time any too reliable: he often, as in both *Anti-Oedipus* and *A Thousand Plateaus*, imports memory into the present in an irreducible doubleness.[85] His aims change throughout according to what is happening to him, and he doesn't hold one single ideal of returning to any teleology promising to take him back to some originary position.[86] His experience is a constant process of repetition with difference, a distancing himself from what he once was and what he is supposed to be, in order to become something slightly different and thus to acknowledge the personal nature of his participation in history. Even his name, Sammy Samuels, enacts this difference-within-repetition and stands as a kind of affront to the kinds of names respectable people should have.

Moreover, in *How Late*, impressions are registered on a *recording surface*. Blinded, Sammy has to feel the grain of his environment; he is reliant on the pure contingency of present contact, of being *in touch*. Like Josef K, Sammy is out of touch with a material yet unknowable law, being perpetually pushed from one inadequate explanation to the next.[87] His given role is forever to try to recover a stable place before the law; yet his struggle as a participant in history is to create difference from this given position.[88] His personal future as underwritten by the law of lack is always *avenir*, to come, always postponed and requiring a wait which is really an action, during which he goes on *becoming* a new man.[89] And since he is blind, the world is inscribed, historically, on his body. He records like a record[90] – unlike, for example, a CD. (As Uwe Zagratzki argues, the black American blues voice, familiar from scratchy old vinyls, can be heard throughout *How Late*.)[91] Both *Anti-Oedipus* and *How Late* have a record-like spiral structure:[92] where *Anti-Oedipus* introduces concepts briefly and then returns to them periodically in modified forms, *How Late* allows personal concerns to arise, be forgotten and reappear as if for the first time after some event has moved Sammy into another situation.[93] This is another post-Humean process which removes Sammy from the state-happy police/*polis*: as Paul Patton and John Protevi put it, 'reading strategies and interest in institutional powers have an affinity'.[94]

In this sense Kelman and Deleuze are modernist in the manner of Gertrude Stein; leitmotifs appear throughout their texts without any overall structuring principle to them, making them, in a sense 'difficult'.[95] But this does not imply an Adorno-esque division of high and low culture.[96] Nor, however, does it mean that Kelman is playing class-hero by identifying with the 'bottom'. Such perspectival, hands-off topographies are done away with if one takes seriously Deleuze's ideas on *becoming* rather than identifying a place of being.

And, as in Deleuze and Guattari's definition of Kafka, Kelman fits the bill as a *minor* writer. His is a literature of affect and becoming, rather than a majoritarian one of representing something assumed to be already there. In the Deleuzian sense Scotland as a whole is a minor nation, having no state citizenship and always having to 'become' out of, or to create a repetition with difference from, essentialist images, since there is nothing else of substance. In Deleuze's *Essays Critical and Clinical*, literature is no less than the creation of a people.[97]

Here, of course, 'minor' does not imply unimportant, or somehow small,[98] though Kelman's work is also 'minor' in the less Deleuzian sense of a refusal to court marketability. Rather, Deleuze and Guattari define the minor this way:

> A minor literature doesn't come from a minor language; it is rather that which a minority constructs within a major language. But the first characteristic of minor literature in any case is that in it language is affected with a high coefficient of deterritorialisation . . . The impossibility of not writing because national consciousness, uncertain or oppressed, necessarily exists by means of literature . . . The second characteristic of minor literatures is that everything in them is political . . . The third characteristic of a minor literature is that in it everything takes on a collective value.[99]

In *A Thousand Plateaus*, 'major' and 'minor' are even separated out as two treatments of the same language, or further as two functions of language as such, where the two terms are in relation.[100] And the powerful minor writer can '[u]se the minor language to *send the major language racing*' (an apt term given the frequency of betting-shop chancers in Kelman's early stories).[101] Kelman is thus at a proactive tangent to 'English Literature', where this phrase means not 'literature from England' or 'literature in English', but a literary discourse of moving towards a central authority relying on a nebulously globalised 'English' and traditionally working via characters looking towards a major socio-historical centre.[102] English Literature has in the main been marked by this activity of pointing towards a pre-existent subject – for example, Georgianism, a reaction to urbanisation and multiculturalism, was, it is strange to reflect, contemporary with Kafka, and Claire Colebook rightly exemplifies Rupert Brooke's 'The Soldier' as major literature – language pointing back to a self-pre-existing the language used, further stabilised by an unplayful obedience to the metre most connoting correct English Language as it has been fixed in tradition.[103] A more extreme example of this would be the poetry of the even more Georgian Enoch Powell (first-class headcase and Tory powerbroker behind the coming to power of Thatcher), metrically perfect in a Latinate way (and late-imperial prescriptive grammars typically assumed Latin constructions as being somehow more authoritative than English ones),[104] pathologically averse to switching a metrical foot, and standing for an idea of England so 'prior' that its Thatcherite echoes in effect split a British Union which looked almost nothing like England at the time Kelman came to prominence.[105] Britishness in the 1980s and 1990s pressed ahead with increasing puzzlement in its role of building on a prior subject, and preventing the becoming of Britain's 'minor' nations – including England itself.

How Late is not the only Kelman story to have a highly Kafkaesque turn; another example is his brilliant short story 'The Block', which again shows marked similarities to the interpellated guilt or lack of *The Trial*, and sees a milkman witness a man fall from the sky, to find that this act of witnessing puts him in some vague way in trouble with the police.[106] A further irony is the fact that in Glasgow pronunciation 'block' can be very close to 'bloke' – did he see *a man* or a thing? Is he really somehow involved? A further irony comes in the shape of the Deleuze/Guattari notion of the block in *A Thousand Plateaus*, in which 'every becoming is a block of coexistence',[107] and a block is formed by two asymmetrical movements.[108] Kafka's concern with the guilt of witnessing the grey area between human and inhuman, the omniscient and experiential, is a recurrent theme in Scotland at about this time. Irvine Welsh's story 'The Granton Star Transfer' (1994), for example, candidly pinches the idea of Kafka's 'The Metamorphosis' by turning the speaker into a bluebottle.[109]

So, sensitised to the problems of representation in the largest city of a nation with no state, one in which learning a foreign dialect/language was a requisite of passing into a realm of 'global' success,[110] Kafka, like those immediately before him, was deeply concerned with the relationship between representation and effect, and this returns in 1970s–1990s Scottish Literature. In Edwin Morgan's celebrated 'The First Men on Mercury', travelling earthlings with broadly well-intentioned imperialist designs, far from having their desired affect, are gradually corrupted by incomprehensible sound in a face-off with native Mercurians, whose phonetic nonsense appears more and more meaningful until the groups exchange places,[111] while they even seem to have a phonetic affiliation with Glasgow speech.[112] The 1960s Glasgow movement of concrete poetry/sound poetry for which representation was central has no real equivalent in English Literature, at least until the 1970s, and even then in a depoliticised form.[113] This Scottish movement of concrete poetry is also exactly coincident with Laing's refusal to accept the placement of the solid subject, again predicated on lack, in capitalist societies, a thinking that would feed into *Anti-Oedipus*. Laing's unjustly ignored 1967 prose-poem 'The Bird of Paradise' can be seen as having a Morgan-like concern with the sliding affective image.[114] One of Laing's most significant early (co-written) works was a guide to the thought of Jean-Paul Sartre.[115] Kelman, as I have suggested, belongs to the same tradition, read via a Sartrean and post-Sartrean existentialism signalled by a close relationship with French literature and domesticated by as likely figures as Alex Trocchi and unlikely figures like Muriel Spark. Deleuze and Guattari, along with other architects of 1968, are part of this post-Sartrean existential tradition, their main beef with Laing being that he sees the policiticisation of psychiatry as an event rather than a process.[116] In any case, the next time you hear someone moaning about not being able to find a 'story' in Kafka's novels, I suggest this is because they're *all* process, all becoming. It is about philosophical brass tacks, but it is also playing around.

Notes

1. Owen Dudley Edwards, ed., *A Claim of Right for Scotland* (Edinburgh: Polygon, 1989).
2. See, for example, Andrew Lockhart Walker, *The Revival of the Democratic Intellect: Scotland's University Traditions and the Crisis in Modern Thought* (Edinburgh: Polygon, 1994); Craig Beveridge and Ronald Turnbull, *The Eclipse of Scottish Culture: Inferiorism and the Intellectuals* (Edinburgh: Polygon, 1989).
3. Cairns Craig, ed., *The History of Scottish Literature*, 4 Vols. (Aberdeen: Aberdeen University Press, 1987).
4. Gavin Wallace, 'Voices in Empty Houses: The Novel of Damaged Identity', in Wallace and Randall stevenson, eds, *The Scottish Novel since the seventies: New Visions, Old Dreams* (Edinburgh: Edinburgh University Press, 1994 [1993]), pp. 217–23.
5. Alan Riach, *Representing Scotland: The masks of the Modern Nation* (Basingstoke: Palgrave, 2005).
6. Christopher Harvie, *Scotland and Nationalism* (London: Routledge, 2004 [1977]), p. 200; for Douglas Gifford, twentieth-century Scottish literature has come in 'waves'; cited in Duncan Petrie, *Contemporary Scottish Fictions: Film, Television, and the Novel* (Edinburgh: Edinburgh University Press, 2004), p. 10.
7. James Kelman, 'Art and Subsidy, and the Continuing Politics of Culture City', in *Some Recent Attacks: Essays Cultural And Political* (Stirling: AK Press, 1992), pp. 27–36.
8. Ibid., p. 27.
9. Ibid., p. 28.
10. Ibid., p. 29.
11. Ibid., p. 30.
12. Ibid., p. 30.
13. Ibid., 32.
14. Ibid., 32.
15. Ibid., 33.
16. Ibid., 34; cf. Anthony Barnett, *This Time; Our Constitutional Revolution* (London: Vintage, 1997), pp. 43–6.
17. Colin Gilbert, *Rab C. Nesbitt*, series one, episode six (1990), BBC TV.
18. Kelman, 'Art and Subsidy', p. 35.

19. James Kelman, 'Some Recent Attacks on the Rights of the People', in *Some Recent Attacks*, pp. 37–45: 37.
20. Ibid., p. 38.
21. Ibid., p. 39.
22. Ibid., pp. 40–1.
23. Ibid., p. 43.
24. Cf. Michael Gardiner, *The Cultural Roots of British Devolution* (Edinburgh: Edinburgh University Press, 2004), pp. 117–19.
25. Kelman, 'Some Recent Attacks on the Rights of the People', p. 44.
26. Douglas Gordon, 'Proof', in *Kidnapping* (Eindhoven: Stedelijk Van Abbesmuseum, 1998), p. 11.
27. http://www.scran.ac.uk/database/record.php?usi=000-000-136-825-C&PHPSESS; cf. the account in the *Times Literary Supplement*, 26 January 1990; cf. Alan Taylor, 'Noam Chomsky: Still Furious at 76', *Sunday Herald*, 20 March 2005.
28. James Kelman, 'A Reading from the Work of Noam Chomsky and the Scottish Tradition in the Philosophy of Common Sense', in *And the Judges Said* (London: Vintage, 2003), 140–86: p. 141.
29. Ibid., pp. 147, 161.
30. Ibid., p. 151.
31. Ibid., pp. 152–3; Noam Chomsky, *Terrorizing the Neighborhood: Amercian Foreign Policy in the post-Cold War Era* (Stirling: AK Press, 1991).
32. Ibid., pp. 113–14.
33. Ibid., pp. 174, 166, 169.
34. Ibid., 169.
35. Ibid., 179.
36. Ferrier quoted in ibid., p. 183.
37. Ibid., p. 181.
38. James Kelman, 'A Look at Franz Kafka's Three Novels', in *And the Judges Said*, pp. 264–334.
39. See the stress on Kelman's *The Busconductor Hines* (London: Orion, 1992 [1984]) in Cairns Craig, *The Modern Scottish Novel* (Edinburgh: Edinburgh University Press, 1999), pp. 99–103.
40. Kelman, 'A Look at Kafka's Three Novels', p. 288.
41. Ibid., p. 267.
42. Ibid., pp. 269–70.
43. Ibid., p. 272; cf. Jacques Derrida, trans. Peggy Kamuf, 'Dialanguages', in *Points . . . Interviews* (Stanford, CA: Stanford University Press, 1995), pp. 132–55.
44. Kelman, 'A Look at Kafka's Three Novels', p. 283.
45. Franz Kafka, 'Before the Law', in ed. Nahum L. Glatzer, trans. Willa and Edwin Muir, *The Complete Short Stories* (London: Vintage, 1999 [1933]), pp. 3–4; Jacques Derrida, 'Before the Law', trans. Avital Ronell and Christine Roulston, in Derek Attridge, ed., *Acts of Literature* (London: Routledge, 1992), pp. 181–220.
46. Cairns Craig, 'Resisting Arrest: James Kelman', in Gavin Wallace and Randall Stevenson, eds., *The Scottish Novel Since the Seventies* (Edinburgh: Edinburgh University Press, 1994), pp. 99–114: 103; for a refined version of

this, see Cairns Craig, *The Modern Scottish Novel* (Edinburgh: Edinburgh University Press, 1999), pp. 99–106.

47. Craig, 'Resisting Arrest', p. 112.
48. Cf. Eleanor Bell, *Questioning Scotland: Literature, Nationalism, Postmodernism* (London: Palgrave, 2004), pp. 80–6.
49. Wallace, 'Voices in Empty Houses' p. 221.
50. Kelman, 'A Look at Kafka's Three Novels', p. 290.
51. Cf. Ronald Bogue, *Deleuze on Literature* (London: Routledge, 2003), pp. 98–9; see also state deterritorialisation in Deleuze and Guattari, *Anti-Oedipus*, pp. 234–5, and Deleuze's notion that judgement must start with false judgement, 'To Have Done With Judgement', in trans. Daniel W. Smith and Michael A. Greco, *Essays Critical and Clinical* (Minneapolis: University of Minnesota Press, 1997 [1993]), pp. 126–35.
52. Kelman, 'A Look at Kafka's Three Novels', p. 301.
53. Ibid., p. 204.
54. Ibid., p. 305.
55. Ibid., p. 308.
56. Ibid., p. 309.
57. Ibid., p. 310.
58. Ibid., p. 314.
59. Ibid., p. 316.
60. Ibid., p. 317.
61. Ibid., p. 319.
62. Ibid., p. 321.
63. Ibid., pp. 324, 329.
64. Cf. Craig Beveridge and Ronald Turnbull, 'Recent Scottish Thought', in Cairns Craig, ed., *The History of Scottish Literature*, Vol. 4, pp. 61–74; Gardiner, *The Cultural Roots of British Devolution*, pp. 90–6; Claire Colebrook, *Deleuze* (London: Routledge, 2002), p. 5; Gilles Deleuze and Felix Guattari, *Anti-Oedipus: Capitalism and Schizophrenia* (Minnesota: University of Minnesota Press, 1983 [1972]), pp. 84 *et passim*.
65. Deleuze and Guattari, *Anti-Oedipus*, pp. 25, 58–61, 306–7.
66. James Kelman, *How Late It Was, How Late* (Vintage 1998 [1994]), p. 37.
67. Ibid., pp. 19, 32.
68. Ibid., pp. 10–11.
69. Ibid., p. 15.
70. Deleuze and Guattari, *Anti-Oedipus*, pp. 12–14.
71. Franz Kafka, *The Trial*, trans. Edwin and Willa Muir, in *The Complete Novels* (London: Vintage, 1999 [1935]), pp. 11–128.
72. Timothy S. Murphy, 'Only Intensities Subsist: Samuel Beckett's *Nohow On*', in Ian Buchanan and John Marks, eds., *Deleuze and Literature* (Edinburgh: Edinburgh University Press, 2000), pp. 229–50: 231; Alan Warner, *The Man Who Walks* (London: Cape, 2002).
73. Cf. Deleuze and Guattari, *Anti-Oedipus*, pp. 38–41.
74. Cf. Jacques Derrida, trans. Avital Ronell and Christine Roulston, 'Before the Law', in Derek Attridge, eds., *Acts of Literature* (London: Routledge, 1992), pp. 181–220: 191–9.
75. Kelman, 'A Look at Kafka's Three Novels', p. 265.
76. Cf. Deleuze and Guattari, *Anti-Oedipus*, p. 247; the debtor must also be

kept alive to keep the debt alive – see Deleuze, 'To Have Done With Judgement'.

77. Cf. Deleuze, 'The Exhausted', in *Essays Critical and Clinical*, pp. 152–74.
78. Cristie L. March, *Rewriting Scotland: Welsh. McLean, Warner, Banks, Galloway, and Kennedy* (Manchester: Manchester University Press, 2002).
79. Cf. the plateau 'Memories of a Haecceity', in Gilles Deleuze and Félix Guattani, *A Thousand Plateaus: Capitalism and Schizophrenia*, trans. Brian Massumi (London: Athlone, 1987 [1980]), pp. 260–5.
80. Colebrook, *Deleuze*, p. 114; in Deleuze and Guattari, *A Thousand Plateaus*, 'the essential thing, precisely in free indirect discourse, is to be found neither in language A, nor language B, but "in language X, which is none other than language A in the actual process of becoming language B" ', p. 106.
81. On the dangers, perceived or real, of a counter-Thatcher proletarianisation of culture, see Petrie, *Contemporary Scottish Fictions*, p. 19.
82. Craig, *the Modern Scottish Novel*, 99–106; Cairns Craig, 'Resisting Arrest', pp. 99–114; Deleuze and Guattari, *Anti-Oedipus*, pp. 1–8.
83. Gilles Deleuze and Felix Guattari, *Kafka: Towards a Minor Literature*, trans. Dana Polan (Minneapolis: University of Minnesota Press (1986 [1975]), p. 19; cf. Deleuze and Guattari, the plateaus 'Memories of a Haecceity' and 'Memories of a Molecule' in *A Thousand Plateaus*, pp. 260–86; cf. Colebrook, *Deleuze*, pp. 126–9; Craig, *The Modern Scottish Novel*, pp. 99–106. Kelman makes this 'translation' absolutely explicit in *Translated Accounts* (London: Secker and Warburg, 2001); cf. Drew Milne, 'Broken English: James Kelman's *Translated Accounts*', *Edinburgh Review* 108, 2001, pp. 106–15.
84. Wilhelm Reich, *The Mass Psychology of Fascism*, trans. Vincent R. Carfagno (Harmondsworth: Penguin, 1975 [1933]).
85. Cf. Deleuze and Guattari, *A Thousand Plateaus*, pp. 291–8; Gilles Deleuze, *Cinema 1: The Movement-Image*, trans. Hugh Tomlinson and Barbara Habberjam (London: Athlone, 1986); cf. Colebrook, *Deleuze*, p. 33.
86. Cf. Gilles Deleuze, *Difference and Repetition*, trans. Paul Patton (London: Athlone University Press, 1994 [1968]), pp. 291–3.
87. Deleuze and Guattari, *A Thousand Plateaus*, p. 14.
88. Cf. Kafka, 'Before the Law'; Jacques Derrida, ed. Derek Attridge, *Acts of Literature* (London: Routledge, 1992), pp. 181–220.
89. Cf. Jacques Derrida, *Voyous: Deux Essais sur la raison* (Paris: Galilée, 2003).
90. Cf. Deleuze and Guattari, *Anti-Oedipus*, pp. 76–9.
91. Uwe Zagratzki, ' "Blues Fell This Morning": James Kelman's Scottish Literature and Afro-American Music', in *Scottish Literary Journal* 27–1, Spring 2000.
92. Cf. Deleuze on Beckett in 'The Greatest Irish Film (Beckett's "Film")', in Deleuze, *Essays Critical and Clinical*, pp. 23–6.
93. Cf. Michael Hardt, online guide to *Anti-Oedipus* taken from his own university guide: www.duke.edu/~hardt/Deleuze&Guattari.html.
94. Paul Patton and John Protevi, introduction to Patton and Protevi, eds., *Between Deleuze and Derrida* (London: Continuum, 2003), p. 3.
95. As in, for example, Gertrude Stein, *Three Lives: Stories of the Good Anna, Melanetha, and the Gentle Lena* (New York: Dover, 1994 [1909]).

96. Cf. Theodor Adorno, 'Perennial Fashion: Jazz', in Brian O' Connor, ed., *The Adorno Reader* (Oxford: Blackwell, 2000), pp. 267–79.
97. Deleuze, 'Literature and Life', in *Essays Critical and Clinical*, pp. 1–6: 4.
98. Cf. Deleuze and Guattari, *A Thousand Plateaus*, p. 291.
99. Deleuze and Guattari, *Kafka*, pp. 16–17.
100. Deleuze and Guattari, *A Thousand Plateaus*, pp. 103–5.
101. Ibid., p. 105.
102. Cf. Edward Said, 'Jane Austen and Imperialism', in Said, *Culture and Imperialism* (New York: Vintage, 1994), pp. 80–97; Said, 'The Cultural Integrity of Empire', in Said, *Culture and Imperialism*, pp. 97–110.
103. Colebrook, *Deleuze*, pp. 119–20.
104. Cf. Lynda Mugglestone, ' "Proper English" and the Politics of Standard Speech', in Kevin Robins and David Morley, eds., *British Cultural Studies* (Oxford: Oxford University Press, 2001), pp. 181–94.
105. Cf. Anthony Barnett, *This Time: Our Constitutional Revolution* (London: Vintage, 1997).
106. James Kelman, 'The Block', in Kelman, *Not Not While the Giro* (London: Minerva, 1989 [1983]), pp. 99–106.
107. Deleuze and Guattari, *A Thousand Plateaus*, p. 292.
108. Ibid., pp. 293–4; the section on blocks is pp. 291–309.
109. Irvine Welsh, 'The Granton Star Cause', in Welsh, *The Acid House* (London: Vintage, 1995 [1994]), pp. 120–36.
110. Cf. a number of essays in Robert Crawford, ed., *The Scottish Invention of English Literature* (Cambridge: Cambridge University Press, 1998).
111. Edwin Morgan, 'The First Men on Mercury', in Morgan, *Collected Poems* (Manchester: Carcanet, 1990), pp. 267–8.
112. W. N. Herbert, 'Morgan's Words', in Robert Crawford and Hamish Whyte, eds., *About Edwin Morgan* (Edinburgh: Edinburgh University Press, 1990), pp. 65–74.
113. Cf. Michael Gardiner, 'Towards a Post-British Theory of Modernism: Speech and Vision in Edwin Morgan', *Pretexts: Literary and Cultural Studies* 11.2, November 2002, pp. 133–46.
114. Deleuze, *Difference and Repetition*, 265–6; R. D. Laing, 'The Bird of Paradise', in Laing, *The Politics of Experience and the Bird of Paradise* (Penguin: Harmondsworth: 1967), pp. 171–90; Gardiner, *The Cultural Roots of British Devolution*, pp. 90–6.
115. R. D. Laing and David Cooper, *Reason and Violence: A Decade of Sartre's Philosophy* (London: Tavistock, 1964).
116. Deleuze and Guattari, *Anti-Oedipus*, p. 320.

Chapter 8

After Genre

After genres, plateaux?

One of the obvious difficulties in a post-theoretical age in writing about Scottish books not deemed 'creative' (or even simply 'writing') is being told that you're anachronistically 'doing theory' – often at the same time as the contradictory argument that there has never been any Scottish literary theory anyway. Theorists write prose, in Standard English but with 'jargon', while writers plumb the real human experience and write whatever they want (except, perhaps, theory). A transgression in this book will have occurred to those disciplinary fundamentalists who have made it to the last chapter: here, some smart arse has done this book on 'Critical Theory' containing a chapter on Muriel Spark, who is a *novelist*: check it on Google if you don't believe me. And so on. But, as the title of this section implies, my dream is of a Scottish literature which ignores genre as we understand it altogether. It is a literature that Scotland is well placed to create, and for help in fleshing this out, I press on with my post-Humean companion, Gilles Deleuze.

For Deleuze, calling Hume's bluff, literature is a set of 'good habits' of language use.[1] By this, though, Deleuze implies a heavily 'philosophical' language, which he sees, in a reversal of what we might expect, in certain forms of Anglo-American literature (though certainly not in what we know as Anglo-American philosophy). Ian Buchanan and John Marks see no generic boundary between the critical/philosophical and the literary in Deleuze at all.[2] As Deleuze himself stresses in *Essays Critical and Cultural*, it doesn't occur to him to separate out his favourite philosophers and artists: both are merely in the business of creating concepts. Nietzsche's thinkers are physicians, Kafka is a post-clinical observer of symptoms, and so it goes.[3] The question is one of orientation towards style, rather than of publishing categories. Or as Jean-Luc Nancy has put it, there is no conflict between poetry and philosophy, '[b]ut this is not because philosophy would like to think itself strictly scientific or logical: it is rather because it behaves, altogether naturally, as another poetry . . .'[4] For Derrida, more forthrightly, all good literature is always already critical.[5]

In Deleuze and Guattari's *Anti-Oedipus*, writing is an effect of the decoding and re-conjunction of social flows;[6] the creation of semantic 'debt' arises through a surplus value of code, as a condition of the coding itself, as we have seen, but is inconsequential in a healthy literature (it isn't used 'for metaphor', for example).[7] A healthy, non-generic production of concepts would inhere in the production and multiplicity of flows (or, as they say in *A Thousand Plateaus*, expression takes the form of an assemblage of semiotic systems).[8] But since one popular form of that semantic coding, money, is ultimately regulated by the state via its various apparatus (a truism as inflammatory for the Scottish 1980s as for Paris 1968), a condition of perpetual debt – and thus, of perpetually schizo behaviour – is supposedly natural to all citizens.[9]

For Gregg Lambert, Deleuze's treatment of schizophrenics is like his treatment of genre – thus the pairing of 'Critical and Clinical'.[10] As always, effects are primary over typology. Bruce Baugh argues that:

> [a] literary work *works* when the reader is able to make use of the work's effects in other areas of life: personally, socially, politically, depending on the reader's desires, needs and objectives. 'It is a question of seeing what use a text is in the extra-textual practice that prolongs the text' . . .[11]

There is in Deleuze, as in Derrida, no 'interpretation' of texts, merely hypothesis on what texts do, based on knowing a lot about the words of which these texts are made.

But why is this particularly pertinent to Scotland? Ronald Bogue picks up on the idea of the minor to suggest that a small nation digests its literature more thoroughly, and that in the small nation literature and politics are closer.[12] (Certainly throughout twentieth-century Europe, from Yeats to Havel, this was the case.) For Bogue, minoritarian status demonstrates that action *is* language:

> Linguists generally analyze language in terms of constants and invariants, whereas Deleuze and Guattari argue that the standard, fixed forms of language are secondary effects produced by regular patterns of action.[13]

Irish literature, in Kafka's reading of Beckett, has already been accounted for in its minority; it may be that minoritarian thinking on Scottish literature will be imported in the way that postcolonialism has trickled over.[14] In *Anti-Oedipus*, the repressed are, *pace* Beckett, disfigured – and who better to demonstrate the disfigurement enacted by the sciences of man than the myth-keeper for modernism who also represents the con-clusion of the Scottish encyclopaedic tradition, James Frazer, flagged up early in *Anti-Oedipus*?[15]

Similarly, Fanon's 'first stage' in his tripartite model in *The Wretched of the Earth* involves a collectivity of 'foreign' actors (and in Deleuze's terms, one can be a foreigner on one's 'own' soil), who 'vomit out' – let's think of that phrasing in terms of lines of flight – their first identification.[16] This vomiting is like stuttering, a becoming-minor which is of particular relevance to Broad Scots as it works within English. Between the minor-ity and the majority language arises a grey area where the author is tongue-tied, causing a kink in the major, a point where *language itself* stutters. To Beckett's version of this Deleuze devotes a chapter in *Essays Cultural and Clinical* ('He Stuttered'), but the model is also highly apt for the coming into being of a literature in Scots in the 1980s, as in the tiny markers of linguistic activity found in, for example, James Kelman – 'he sniffed', 'he chuckled'.[17] And within the 'dialect novel' as a whole, stut-ters abound in those speaking Scots natively but educated in Standard English. Another understandably underrated example is Irvine Welsh's *Trainspotting*, in which the carefully inserted dialect stutters add rhythm and humour and help make the novel what it is, before being airbrushed out of the film and in foreign translations.[18] Chapter 4 here has shown how Edwin Morgan's concrete is a visual 'stutter', an irruption of Scots into Eng. Lit. Where Deleuze is keen to show the decomposition of the self in Beckett's *Malone Dies*, a similar claim could be made for Morgan's de-authorising texts, in which the Eng. Lit. narrative relationship breaks down.[19] In *A Thousand Plateaus*, the movement of language in lines of flight creates assemblages, and the assemblages are procedurally formed into plateaus, knots of expressions in a semiotic system which have a high degree of de- and re-territotialisation – aiming at a flickering nullity of self – '[t]he point where it is no longer of importance whether anyone says'.[20]

As Paul Patton shows, both Deleuze and Derrida orient their ideas on literature – and their writing of literature – towards a future which is necessarily unknown. Deleuze and Guattari view philosophy/literature as the invention of concepts for a yet unknown people.[21] We don't have to look far for such an unknown people – for the idea that Scots have always been the same people is an ethnocentric nonsense used to sell shortbread. Becoming a people is an ongoing process directed at a demo-cratic ideal which will never, in the conventional sense, 'arrive'. But devo-lution and its surrounding cultural hype underscore and accelerate the process of becoming a people, and this people is literary (as seen in Edinburgh's status in 2005). The result of this process is in Deleuze's terms anarchically unknown, in Derrida's a future 'danger', and in Paul

Virilio's an 'accident'. Paul Patton stresses the difference, common to Deleuze, which Derrida maps out in '*Psyché: Inventions de l'autre*', between ordinary invention and pure invention, read as specific historical incarnations of democracy versus the truly unthinkable notion of a democracy to come. The first involves modifications or concretisations of extant materials and the second, to which devolution is closer than most people think, partakes of something entirely unknowable.[22] The current Scottish literary-political process has less to do with the bureaucratic separation of reserved and devolved matters in devolution than the undoing of the categories of thought through which the eighteenth-century *literati*, and the nineteenth-century champions of Great Author-style Eng. Lit., sought to classify things.

And yet, despite the increasing confidence in this literary-political process and the stress on Scotland's democratic-intellectual tradition, Scottish universities have remained more or less passive in the face of the Research Assessment Exercise (RAE). For the non-academic reader, how the RAE works is this: if you write in a generically specific tone within a recognised format, typically in an academic journal which will never go on sale in bookshops and will never be known to 99 per cent of the population, you get 'a point'. The university can then use these points in league tables and the individual can (and must) use them in her career. Perhaps not surprisingly, most universities claim the 'top' RAE grade of 5, and those which are even higher than top, 5*. Why not 6? Maybe everyone just loves a star. It's like in infant school: if you wrote exactly what made the teacher's life easier, a gold star was stuck in your jotter. And Scots, three decades after *The Democratic Intellect*, had to go along with all the nonsense of league tables, holding out their homework to Tony Blair.

Beam me up

According to David McCrone, whose *Understanding Scotland* was hammered by nationalists for what seems nevertheless like a fairly accurate sociological picture of the nation, the Scottish semi-state in the Union made a decision to 'travel light'.[23] Here I'd like to reverse this proposal to suggest that since 1707 pragmatic Scots have worked towards *light travel*: since the En-light-enment, many of the huge proportion of Scottish inventions have involved scientific observation, communications technology, the pursuit of speed unto its very C. What would have been left had the London-to-Scotland railway remained unbuilt and television unimagined – a colonial time-lag, which imperialist Scots wanted to avoid at all costs. Since the time of the joining of the empire state, Scots have struggled to be in central, seeing-knowing positions. Michel Foucault's account of Jeremy Bentham's panopticon (a starfish-shaped prison) as a tendency of total surveillance is well known.[24] Less remarked on is the fact that the panopticon was a direct model for William Stark's *Glasgow Asylum* (1804–20),[25] or that in 1824 *The Glasgow Mechanics' Magazine* was suggesting that the city undergo total surveillance, so that 'the necessity of sending out emissaries to reconnoitre the conduct of the lieges would be superseded, since everything would then take place, as it were, under the eye of the Police'.[26] Also forgotten has been the fact that, as recently as November 1992, the first town in Britain to have CCTV cameras installed in its streets was the working-class Glasgow satellite town of Airdrie.[27] In *Star Trek*, the character Scotty can easily be read taken as hangover of Clydesidism, of a James Watt engineering tradition that boldly went where brown people didn't want them, but do we also reflect that Scotty is the only crew member able to take the ship beyond warp speed – speed greater than light? This is the ultimate Scottish Enlightenment dream: to be in London at the same time as the Londoners. And we're pretty much there. C is the limit, and for Virilio, all happens at once, everywhere: for Scots, it seemed the only way out of the eighteenth-century condition.

This semi-conscious realisation is perhaps behind the numerous monographs which have attempted to rethink Scotland over the past few years: as in Virilio, no human, in so far as she wants to remain human, really wants to reach light-speed, to arrive without leaving, to be virtually spread out in a simultaneous time of experience – to have no narrative at all. Eleanor Bell notes the comment in Alasdair Gray's *Lanark* that '[m]etaphor is one of thought's most essential tools. It illuminates what would otherwise be totally obscure. But the illumination is sometimes so bright that it obscures instead of revealing'.[28]

The Poets' Pub is now closed

In his essay in an edited book on Kenneth White, Stuart Kelly speculates that Sandy Moffat was urged to paint the ubiquitously known *Poets' Pub* with the words, 'before it's too late'.[29] This absurd phrase (used by Kelly to arch effect) hides the fact that the work is, in its overtly figurative sense, one of pure conjecture, since when the painting was made in 1980, two of its figures had already died. Where was the pub anyway, and did the living ones sit nicely together? More to the point, why is Scottish literature here doing nothing more than trying to keep up with Eng. Lit.

by forming a central famous group – a canon – around which other more minor figures will be ranged – thus the slightly unhinged desperation of the phrase 'before it's too late'? As Kelly puts it: 'It is fundamentally a fiction, a response to some yearning for a "group" or "movement" that Scotland could hold up against Bloomsbury Square, the Cabaret Voltaire or the Algonquin Hotel.'[30] And yet, this act of canon-formation has been bought into by Scottish critics and academics who ought to know better: '[i]t is on the homepage of the Scottish Poetry Library's website [as well as the cover of about a thousand books on anything to do with Scotland] . . . [e]very anthology, twentieth century or otherwise, uses this grouping [of figures] as its spine.'[31]

So '*Poets' Pub*, fundamentally, is a desire for "a canon" that became its realisation'.[32] Who are these people? Everyone in the picture is male, and all had to be pally with Hugh MacDiarmid to some degree to get in.[33] Kelly convincingly suggests that another half-dozen or so names had their fivers cocked at the bar but have remained just out of frame; we could name White himself, Trocchi, Thomas Clark, Liz Lochhead, Iain Sinclair and Douglas Oliver, all of whom were alive in 1980, and Veronica Forrest-Thomson, who had passed away just before. What concerns me (and, I think, Kelly) more, however, is the way in which Scottish literature felt the need to expunge some of its most interesting poets in order to make way for an instantly recognisable group in a manner which took its cue from the Great Names model of Eng. Lit. 'The "Scottish School" of Twentieth Century Poets': the idea is a nonsense, yet this nonsense itself has to be remedied by Scots: the *literati* were largely behind the urgency of catching up to/creating the study of schools which eventually gave structure to the Bloomsbury Group, in their late eighteenth-century separation out of university disciplines, of which the nascent Eng. Lit./good English was one. (Ironically, the most convincing account of this process comes from Robert Crawford [1992], fingered by Kelly for over-canonical editing practices regarding White.)[34]

Canons have for the British empire been a doorkeeper to the law of social improvement; they have represented the conservation of the greatness of the perfected language as a model for social order. In empire they have acted with the violence, as Kelly's title wryly implies, of 'cannons'. Such was the backbone of Eng. Lit., its set of officially recognised examples of Great Work keeping up the spirits of jaded diplomats in Calcutta via Good English in their libraries peopled by Great Men, as they were described by the manically Anglophile Scot Thomas Carlyle. Cracking the code linking the Great Men, grasping the canon's core aesthetic – though there never really was one – became essential to greatness for the individual career in empire.

There is, however, no reason why these circumstances should even come up in a separate Scotland. Scotland has never had its own empire, and, *pace* Tom Nairn, its nationalist Romanticism slid under that of Anglo-British English Romanticism. And while Robert Crawford power-fully demonstrates that the codes of Eng. Lit. arose from an aspirational movement originating outside England – an influential critique and a blueprint for a Scottish re-reading of theory if ever there was one – he still uses the techniques of Eng. Lit. to do so: biographical explication, judge-ment by literary merit in terms of prior standards, personal connection.

In 'Poets' Pub', as in the idea of a sub-Eng. Lit. Scot. Lit. canon, a highly figurative realism creates a file of the new Greats. And after all, what could better connote the great spiritual vistas and unimagined potential of a national literary culture than a crowd of guys getting pished? What were they thinking, 'before it's too late', if not that Scot. Lit. is a cap-in-hand subset of Eng. Lit.? Iconic use for teaching in Schools? The produc-tion of collections and anthologies? Places on university curricula? None of these aims has finally worked: look, for example, at the critical inter-est now in, for example, Ian Hamilton Finlay as against Sydney Goodsir Smith. And a Scottish version is more noxious than would be an English one, since it clings to a sense of marginality while appropriating the means of the centre. Of the painting's six poets, only one writes in a language other than English, that area where, for the emotionally challenged, voice meets 'race' – Gaelic – and only one is a real linguist in a way which most European literatures take for granted – Edwin Morgan. (MacDiarmid, of course, subscribed to the Ezra Pound school of good-enough translation.) Morgan, moreover, has always stressed that the area between 'artist' and 'critic' cannot but overlap: even 'pure' critics like F. R. Leavis (do they come much purer?) can show a great *creative* flair.[35] None of the pub poets writes in any of Scotland's *other* languages (than the 'three'). All are white and male; one is a then-not-out homosexual, outweighed by a bored-looking misogynist whose opinions were allowed to colour most of twentieth-century Scottish literature, and who put himself at the centre of the very un-Scottish idea of canon-formation itself.

A canon like the gran canyon

Alan Riach's *Representing Scotland* is one of the most ingenious and enter-taining books on Scottish literature of recent decades. It uses Walter Scott as a crux to show that Scottish bifurcated characters have not merely become 'nostalgic' in the face of Jacobitism versus Union, but have inau-gurated a double heroism which becomes a pioneer or 'cowboy' attitude, travelling trans-Atlantic both ways.[36] Riach sets out by suggesting that the production of 'Scotland' is tied to the mechanics of the production of the popular itself. This leads on to a claim that Scott's collecting was the inception of a 'popular' which shadowed Shakespeare as the 'literary'; the silhouetted and oft-repeated double hero, pre- and post-Jacobite rebellion, repeats mid- and post-empire, and returns in guises as various as John Buchan, Ian Fleming, spaghetti westerns (of which he provides a fascinating collection) and Bud Neill, author of the Glasgow/Wild West fusion cartoon *Lobey Dosser*: thus the title of this section.[37]

For Riach (try finding this on the average undergraduate literature class), James Bond is 'the most important character in post-war fiction'.[38] He points out that when Fleming wrote the 1962–67 Bond films, both he and the audience had Sean Connery in mind.[39] This fits perfectly with the argument drawing on Scott which relates to Scotland's ability to don the mask rather than fitting into some prior catergory of *über*Scottishness:

> subversively, Connery's infiltration of a Scots identity – self-ironising, comically reductive yet self determined and independently minded – off-set the excesses of sordid violence and pornographic exploitation which, however occasionally they are explicitly present, always remain the hinterland of a James Bond story. A different reading from the conventional one of Bond as imperialist metaphor was possible – indeed, an anti-imperialist reading was now imaginable.[40]

Thus '[a]n Englishman could neither speak nor act so honestly on behalf of all of Her Majesty's British Subjects (nor embody them so well), as a Scot in Her Majesty's Service'.[41] As recent research has shown, Scots' place in empire was deeply ambivalent; they were among *both* the most ruthless and the most radical, as well as being quite often the most famous. That 007's nationalist tattoo is briefly visible in *Dr. No* is deeply significant: he is working on behalf of a government which the actor himself will go on to undermine, and anyone who sees the film has this duality tattooed on her brain.[42] In Bond's 1962 my-it's-hot-better-get-the-sleeves-up version, this is an *active* duplicity, where for the Edinburgh *literati* of the late eighteenth century it had been a passive and jealous one. But the groundbreaking argument Riach makes is to conjoin the two in international actions of national resistance. Bond is symbolically and phonetically ('the enemy is in shite') needling this empire while working on its behalf, and making it work for him, instead of remaining within an Anglo-British field.

Also slightly leftfield from the 'this generation of novelists' approach, Duncan Petrie's 2004 book builds on his earlier celebrated history of Scottish film[43] to show us how Scottish cultural tropes can be gathered round 'fictions' rather than individual figures, whether the handful of greats by which we remember the Renaissance, or the conveniently famous handful of novelists of the 1990s who propelled Scotland to fame, including Irvine Welsh, Janice Galloway, A. L. Kennedy and Alan Warner (all writers who wouldn't touch 'theory' with a pole), rather than Great Men, types of narrative, or types of reading of narrative.

Petrie and Riach come at a multi-media critique from different angles: for Riach, general editor of the definitive series of works of MacDiarmid, and risking the irritation of the elder statespersons of Scot. Lit., 'film is literature', and furthermore, '[t]elevision is literature'.[44] Even comics, jings crivvens, are literature. (MacDiarmid, so far as I know, was not a great reader of comics.) For Petrie, coming from film studies, film and TV have always been primary text, and his thematic bunching to include literary works is an opposite form of branching out. And while Riach's might be a study which re-reads literary classics in an attempt to prise open modern Scot. Lit. in a uniquely sharp manner, and Petrie's study is both more general and more identitarian and 'thematised', they both have the effect of saying that what we now call Scottish Literature need not be described in terms of centrality to a group of figures defined as 'the canon'.

In charting the rise of Scottish post-genre, Riach uses the TV series *Edge of Darkness* (1985) to show how an 'underground' will to look forward was growing even during the darkest political times:

> [t]he scripts were written at a time of political pessimism, but a moral optimism seemed to be gaining strength underground, so that a mythic dimension of earthly rootedness and the authority of the earth itself might legitimately be called up.[45]

Riach is, unlike a surprisingly large number of post-1945 critics, mindful of the context of the Cold War in mapping out Scottish critical thought, whether it be in the folk songs tirelessly collected by Hamish Henderson, true to a Scottish balladic and semi-anonymous tradition, or the way in which making half of Scotland a nuclear target removed it even further from the London government, and called for an articulation of this place in which Scots lived, which was in a reversal of the late eighteenth century, beginning to look light years away. Riach notes repeatedly, and via various ruses including the important one of showing that 'everyone's favourite novel' is open to frequent change, that in Scotland, '[t]he canon quickly accommodates change',[46] and that whenever a canon looks like it might close over, it becomes 'open to revision when the impulse to subversion remains as essential as the recognition of authority of co-ordinates'.[47]

This is a movement on from an 1980s/1990s tendency Eleanor Bell and others have identified in which the cultural body of Scotland is still seen as an effect of a Scottish historical-economic 'base':

> there has been a tendency in Scottish studies to equate history with literature, so that literature tends to be regarded as the *effect* of cultural processes, rather than as an intervention into those processes, of indeed as a relatively autonomous act of aesthetic, ethical, or political engagement. Subsequently, there is a certain factor of reducibility at work, where texts produced by Scottish authors must in the first instance be explained in terms of their Scottishness.[48]

As the book progresses it turns out that Bell is questioning certain tendencies in the Cairns Craig of *Out of History*.[49] In any case, the idea of an informant economic 'base' once seemed more powerful than that of a 'canon', whether at the local, or for our purposes here, national level: there are no great names, no perfect models, no properties to which every colonial subject is glued. Nor is any base needed in the traditional Marxist sense, a tendency towards which critics have been drawn, perhaps despite themselves. What remains is a set of principles, a shifting literariness which shows strong similarities to 'French' theory. This is partly why, as I have argued elsewhere, the *process* of devolution (whatever the fate and activities of the MSPs and their over-priced new Parliament) is oriented towards a democracy which is, in Derridean terms, both perfect and unattainable.[50]

Neo-Marxism, Neo-situationism and play

As its author is doubtless aware, *The Play Ethic* owes a lot to earlier Scottish ideas of inventiveness, interdisciplinarity and, following Trocchi, Situationism. And this is a literary field: Pat Kane insists that 'a socius of play requires a *rhetoric of play*, a need to embrace the vocabulary of ambiguity'.[51] New terms are needed to indicate a new type of connection – a faculty that comes naturally to children, who learn through play – as in the early 'child-centred' theories of the Scottish educator A. S. Neill. Neill would have concurred that a 'feedback loop' should be in place between educators and the creative input of children (like the loop of the author-as-DJ).[52] Kane thus questions the increasing anti-play tendencies in education (school league tables again come to mind). Central to his thesis is the idea that children *already* understand networks in a way that the adult 'networking' can't quite encapsulate.[53] This argument also gives the lie to the Lad o' Pairts pride in lottery-like access to a literary education by stressing that play-education demands a whole, easily accessible network.[54]

For Kanein Foucauldian terms, the *invention* of childhood has gone together with the trivialisation of play, with its consignment to the nursery-room.[55] From the nineteenth century, for adults an 'efficient' play based on partnership with work became dominant, and also the stuff of dystopias, of which Aldous Huxley's *Brave New World* (1931) is exemplary, describing how rigid social control is maintained using work and specific, consumerist, distracting recreations.[56] This reliance on the division of play from the serious stuff of the work ethic would intensify during the Welfare State's division of work and the many new forms of post-1945 leisure.[57]

Kane identifies an entirely different tradition of play, one which for the radical P. B. Shelley helped overcome the alienation felt by Romantics of both stripes (Scottish and English),[58] and which runs through to the idea, as we have seen from the radical elements in the Scottish 1960s, that has more to do with the process of becoming oneself. The fourth paper of the Sigma Portfolio talks of an aesthetic which is 'essentially ludic', and its next paper identifies the major literary question of the time as '[w]hat are the possibilities of the leisure situation? What are its dangers?'[59] Kenneth White similarly concerns himself with the interstices of work, play and people, seeing these lived combinations as giving rise to a new interdiscpinarity beyond extant genres.[60] And although he does not make the connection explicitly, Kane speaks with Laingian tongue: when he sat with a patient for extended periods in incomprehensible states or speaking schizophrenic babble, Laing was demonstrating that the patient was following the rules of the institution but had kept personal faculties which could be maximised in ludic behaviour, which the clinic then turned into a symptomology.[61] With an even wider arc, Kane traces the ludic self created in Renaissance poetry, for example in Donne, to the frequently ironic ego of hip-hop.[62] Between the seventeenth and twenty-first centuries, play has always been on the fringes, albeit at times pushed there, of adult interaction.[63]

One place in which Kane finds adults in a world of play is in gambling, a subject directly pertinent to Scottish literature (as in the early stories of James Kelman), but one which is linked to inaction. What was left of a consolidated British government already knew this in the 1990s: when people complained about the dismantling of the Welfare State, one of the first reactions was to set in place the National Lottery as funding, via which everyone could abandon themselves to the 'forces of play': but '[f]ateful play is a largely passive, not active, practice – a truth accepted by even the most skilful poker player or adept horse fancier, waiting for their luck to change'.[64] As I have suggested elsewhere,[65] a Derridean understanding of play is blocked here by the fact that the Lottery is an insidious bottom-up form of taxation, and furthermore that the bookie is also the state. The Lottery is an anti-disestablishment punt aimed at the tabloid-fuelled dreams of the increasingly isolated poor. Kane refuses to recognise the Lottery as play in his terms; play is, for example, too ambiguous to acknowledge the Lottery's deafening proclamation of 'victory'.[66] We might remember here that in Derrida *jeu* means both 'play' and 'give', where 'give' is not an exchange or a tax on emotion, but a one-way act of generosity.[67] The gift is both impossible as exchange and utterly necessary as *jeu*:[68] games don't have taxing or funding motives behind them.

Thus the hoary old truism about the empire being 'won' on the playing-fields of Eton must be dismissed at, as it were, a stroke. For Kane a more fitting analogy for play is the festival, where large numbers of people come together to behave in unexpected ways. Like many others I have drawn links between the UK festival circuit and Bakhtinian carnival; festivals, at least during their music sessions, have a large element of strangers playing (non-sexually) with touch.[69] In part historically this has to do with ecstasy, rediscovered in the 1980s as a 'play' drug (none of the Scottish or American 1960s thinkers was really 'playing' with LSD; they were 'experimenting'), one which stimulates visual senses but sets up a hunger for the tactile. At turn-of-the-1990s raves, it was not uncommon to see complete strangers hug one another with no sense of unease. Moreover, while an older corporate idea of 'networking' can get in the way of human contact, now more horizontal networks are possible; or, to put this more simply, old top-down enforced leisure may be falling apart in favour of a play-*dominated* model in which people are connected roughly along the lines of the Deleuzian rhizome.[70] Play exists somewhere between project – horizontal – and protest – vertical; it has no topology as yet familiar to Scottish literature.[71] Play is voluntary and yet complex, and again, in a phrase which could have been taken directly from *A Thousand Plateaus*, is a 'generation of multiplicities'.[72] One example examined by Kane is Paul Laverty/Ken Loach's *Sweet Sixteen*, in which the entrepreneurial adolescent drug-dealer addresses inequality by using the capitalist rules of the game against itself, in Greenock (and as Duncan Petrie has shown, Greenock has been a key location for Scottish documentaries and short films, economically dependent on the Clyde and representing a smaller-town Glasgow).[73]

Protests from the height of rave onward have thus had more to do with the Situationist than the stand-off:

> pranksterish behaviours in front of armed police, the costumed prancing and soft toy throwing typical of the usual protest . . . this 'scrambling of the

conventional categories' of street protest, this explicit deployment of play rhetorics, reveals a deeper point about the kind of society envisaged by anti-corporate protesters.

[David] Graeber claims that the creativity and playfulness inherent in the protesters' activities is a kind of 'prefigurative politics' – a politics which gives people a tangible experience of the new society they are struggling for. In this sense, the protestors are practising [sic] a kind of 'adaptive potentiation', in the sense as defined by our general theory of play: they are testing out other worlds in their activities, yet not regarding any of these experiments as definitive programmes for social order.[74]

This Sigma-like reading puts play in a new unplagiarised space which could outflank the work/leisure dichotomy of the Welfare State:

> [a] creative democratic politics, which presumes that startling new alliances and shifts are implicitly possible in a dynamic, emergent, networked world, could be a complement to a *defensive* democratic politics which aimed to restore social and cultural stability by pressing the pause button on dynamism, to enable a moment of reflection. The play ethic might then occupy a space between the poles of the protest ethic and the work ethic.[75]

But the loss of the Scottish Protestant work ethic leaves the county with a vacuum, a 'spectre' (one wonders whether Kane deliberately uses a Derridean term here). The work ethic was strongest at the height of the British empire – a path is traced from Thomas Carlyle, for whom in *Past and Present* 'labour is life',[76] to Gordon Brown, who has, since the beginning of the Blair administration, stressed the work ethic, seeing 'the work continuing'.[77] Brown has, for example, an almost pathological fear of benefit fraud: '[t]he whole New Right rhetoric of "dependency" (enthusiastically employed by Brown and others in New Labour) is driven by the notion that those without employment are using state benefit to live "leisurely" lives'.[78]

Brown's imaginary bouncy castle-style 'leisure' is carried out by an underclass (since Brown, New Labour-style, does not really believe in full employment) 'between the bars' of the old work ethic.[79] *Trainspotting*'s Renton, Kane reminds us, is most telling when he doesn't 'choose life', as the overblown film trailer has it, but chooses his own particular and dangerous form of play.[80] Brown's transmission of the tradition of *Thomas* Carlyle is neo-Calvinist, and Cultural Studies, *mea culpa*, breaks its rules by playfully incorporating other media into a conception of Eng. Lit. running from early empire to F. R. Leavis: 'of course, this is exactly the role that media and cultural studies has tried to play in the Western education over the last twenty-odd years – and never has a subject been more vilified, mostly by the remaining representatives of an industrial-age mindset'.[81]

Welfare State work practice has not sufficiently adapted to the fact that large chunks of organised 'leisure', Orwellian hiking groups and Huxleyesque Community Sings, have disappeared, as have Peckham Rye's Humphrey's intra-class distinctions. Vulgar Marxists, in other words, underwrite their own alienation when they stick to stable hours one-man work bolstered by compulsory leisure.[82] And the loss of control of the worker in a post-Welfare State environment is also the loss of the pre-Laingian family, as the old work ethic refuses to grasp people's need for a sense of fulfilment in their work.[83] Kane's Deleuzian machine is pointedly proactive, a 'homeostat':

> [s]o the machine metaphor, *pace* our general theory of play, can be improved – but only slightly. Instead of being a cog in the corporate mechanism, you can become something more meaningful. Like those magical little gadgets that automatically keep your room at a constant temperature, you can become a self-regulating mechanism – a 'homeostat', if you like – that can strike a balance between what you want, and what the company requires, in the working environment.[84]

This critique is, like Situationism and Deleuzianism, and like Spark if we see her early novels in the light of the *nouveau roman*, a post-Sartrean cultural theory:

> It's not difficult to imagine a policy platform for the play ethic twenty-first century Europe. So much of its essential argument – that work should be 'decentred' from its dominant ethical position in society and placed in context with other, equally value-adding activities – is already accepted, and has in some places been implemented. When the political philosopher Jürgen Habermas (a major influence on the Social Democratic Party in Germany) talks of 'conserving the great democratic achievements of the European nation-state, beyond its own limits', or when the recent French Prime Minister Lionel Jospin spoke of 'market economy, not market society', both drew some kind of line between a civilization entirely defined by work, and one in which the '*arts de vivre*' – the arts of living – are many and varied.[85]

In 1997, then, Demos's mistake was to *revive* the work ethic even while claiming to move towards a Third Way for New Labour.[86] Kane instead broadly follows Lawrence Lessig in seeing the network as the locus of a real ethical community, a 'dot-commons'.[87] The dot-commons is even an alternative commonwealth, and dot-commer will demand a sovereign coin:[88] '[t]he prospect of players using their bandwidth to spend the "social currency" of friendship and mutual interests, perhaps more avidly than they would spend hard cash, clearly requires a drastic, neo-socialist response'.[89] Elsewhere I have questioned whether visibility and advertising power could set up a loop whereby people became unable to avoid watching ever more spectacular news.[90] However, this could be countered by an agreed play agenda (thus avoiding American culture's indebtedness to advertising money), and by admixing cultures on- and offline. Besides this, as Kane points out, the BBC, the company begun in painfully correct Received Pronunciation for the purposes of education and enlightenment by the Scot John Reith, based on a technology largely invented by another Scot, John Logie Baird, is, while remaining 'nationalised' to a large extent, highly net-invested.[91] One outcome is that peer-to-peer broadcasting will become much more common, creating (my phrase) rhizomic groups of people who are able to ignore the top-down model for long periods and even turn off their screens and interact. The last battles of the Scottish Enlightening mission in the form of the early BBC may have self-destructed into unpredictable, changing communities in which, again in the post-Eng. Lit. tradition suggested throughout this book, no one is entirely producer or consumer.

Moreover Kane writes within the welfare tradition that demands that all should be cared for, despite the withering of the Welfare State: the play ethic could also guarantee a minimum wage. The example given is Tom Paine's 1796 *Agrarian Justice*;[92] another might have been Adam Smith's 1776 *The Wealth of Nations*, which insists that trade must be for the common good, that is, the mutual fulfilment of humankind.[93] Smith has to wait till later, however, when Kane, outflanking the third way, points out that Smith recognised the need for some kind of market (heavily inscribed as play rather than profit) *plus* guaranteed social care. Moreover, in Smith no split can be detected between theory and practice: engaging in pure 'practice' is an idea as nonsensical as engaging in pure theory.[94]

In a final chapter which has become even more timely since its publication, Kane insists that *all* religious fundamentalism is anti-play. Of course, we have 'our' Calvinist fundamentalism, which comes in for heavy attack, but this fundamentalism, one hopes, now has little to do with literary-cultural practice.[95] In demonstrating how discursive flux leads to spiritual liberation, the Muslim thinker Ziauddin Sardar convincingly shows that the Koran was devised as a ludic problem-solving tool until it was taken over by Islamic states and the tradition of *itijihad* was closed down from the fourteenth century.[96] Until the religious coup, mainstream Islam was as interdisciplinary as the tradition of G. E. Davie. Thus, Islam is ambiguous, ground-shifting and playful. Hakim Bey, guru to the rave generation, has thus described Islam as carnival.[97] Bey has also more famously identified iconoclasm as necessary for liberation of the imagination, and thus for creativity.[98] In Hinduism, moreover, Kane finds that the very warp and woof of existence is made of play.[99] In Christianity, '[Don] Cupitt's deeply performative and creative vision of religion asks us to place our faith in the incessant flux of language and discourse – signs and images being our earthly kingdom of eternal plenitude'. What is finally at stake is the possibility of change in the self, the very condition of Bakhtinian dialogics.[100] Kane himself links it in his 'outro' to (Algerian) deconstruction, lamenting the loss of *itijihad*.[101]

It would not even occur to Kane's netizens to separate out practice and theory, or genres of production; new 'genres' rise and disappear as a matter of practice, and this is part of the aesthetic – as the likes of Trocchi realised to an extent extraordinary for their time. I look forward to the revival of *itijihad*, and *Daily Mail* readers who fret about the loss of 'a thousand years of history' (there are, of course, no thousand years: these people have an infantile grasp of history) are on the wrong page entirely: Arabic workers from the increasing populations of the Middle East and North Africa *will* be 'imported' as time goes on, if only to pay for ageing Britons' pensions. When generations of Scottish *literati* in the near future contain names unpronounceable to others who still think of themselves as 'native' Scots, we will be better placed to look at the 'twenty-first-century situation'.

Notes

1. Gregg Lambert, 'On the Uses and Abuses of Literature for Life', in Ian Buchanan and John Marks, eds., *Deleuze and Literature* (Edinburgh: Edinburgh University Press, 2000), pp. 136–66: 158.
2. Introduction to Buchanan and Marks, *Deleuze and Literature*, pp. 1–13: 11.
3. Introduction to Gilles Deleuze, trans. Daniel W. Smith and Michael A. Greco, *Essays Critical and Cultural* (Minneapolis: University of Minnesota Press, 1997 [1993]), p. xii.
4. Jean-Luc Nancy, 'The Deleuzian Fold', in Paul Patton, ed., *Deleuze: A Critical Reader* (Oxford: Blackwell, 1996), pp. 107–13: 111.
5. Jacques Derrida, trans. Geoffrey Bennington and Rachel Bowlby, 'This Strange Institution Called Literature', interview with Rachel Bowlby, in Derek Attridge, ed., *Acts of Literature* (London: Routledge, 1992), pp. 33–75.
6. Gilles Deleuze and Felix Guattari, trans. Robert Hurley, Mark Seem and Helen B. Lane, *Anti-Oedipus: Capitalism and Schizophrenia* (Minneapolis: University of Minnesota Press, 1983 [1972]), pp. 223–6.
7. Ibid., pp. 150–63: 64.
8. Ibid., pp. 323–5; Gilles Deleuze and Felix Guattari, trans. Brian Massumi, *A Thousand Plateaus: Capitalism and Schizophrenia* (London: Athlone, 1988 [1980]), p. 504.
9. Deleuze and Guattari, *A Thousand Plateaus*, pp. 197–9.

10. Lambert, 'On the Uses and Abuses of Literature for Life', p. 141.
11. Bruce Baugh, 'How Deleuze can help us Make Literature Work', in Buchanan and Marks, *Deleuze and Literature*, pp. 34–56: 36 (his own quotation is from Alan D. Shrift, *Nietzsche's French Legacy* (London: Routledge, 1995)), p. 63.
12. Ronald Bogue, *Deleuze on Literature* (London: Routledge, 2003), p. 93.
13. Ibid., p. 99.
14. Cf. Timothy S. Murphy, 'Only Intensities Subsist: Samuel Beckett's *Nohow On*', in Buchan and Marks, *Deleuze and Literature*, pp. 229–50: 232.
15. Deleuze and Guattari, *Anti-Oedipus*, pp. 113–14.
16. See Frantz Fanon's 'tripartite' model in *The Wretched of the Earth*, trans. Constance Farrington (Harmondsworth: Penguin, 1967 [1963]), pp. 167–73; Lambert, 'On the Uses and Abuses of Literature for Life', pp. 148–50.
17. Gilles Deleuze, 'He Stuttered', in trans. Daniel W. Smith and Michael A. Greco, *Essays Critical and Clinical*, pp. 107–14; see also Daniel W. Smith's introduction, ' "A Life of Pure Immanence": Deleuze's "Critique et Clinique" ' Project', pp. xi–lvi: xlvi–xlvii; Lambert, 'On the Uses and Abuses of Literature for Life', p. 163.
18. See Michael Gardiner, 'British Territory: Irvine Welsh in English and Japanese', *Textual Practice* 17.1, Spring 2003, pp. 101–17.
19. Gilles Deleuze, 'The Exhausted', in *Essays Critical and Clinical*, pp. 152–74.
20. Deleuze and Guattari, *A Thousand Plateaus*, pp. 3, 4, 504, 508.
21. Paul Patton, 'Future Politics', in Paul Patton and John Protevi, eds., *Between Deleuze and Derrida* (London: Continuum, 2003), pp. 15–29: 15.
22. Jacques Derrida, *Psyché: l'invention de l'autre* (Paris: Galilée, 1987); see Patton, 'Future Politics', pp. 18, 24.
23. David McCrone, *Understanding Scotland: The Sociology of a Stateless Nation* (London: Routledge, 1992); Craig Beveridge and Ronald Turnbull, *The Eclipse of Scottish Culture* (Edinburgh: Polygon, 1989); Eleanor Bell, *Questioning Scotland: Literature, Nationalism, Postmodernism* (Basingstoke: Palgrave, 2004), p. 80.
24. Cf. Michel Foucault, *The Order of Things; An Archaeology of the Human Sciences* (London: Routledge, 2001 [1970]).
25. Miles Glendinning and Aonghus MacKechnie, *Scottish Architecture* (London: Thames and Hudson, 2004), p. 125.
26. *The Glasgow Mechanics' Magazine* 1824, quoted in Geoffrey Batchen, 'Guilty Pleasures', in Thomas Y. Levin, Ursula Frohne and Peter Weibel, eds., *CTRL [SPACE]: Rhetorics of Surveillance from Bentham to Big Brother* (Boston, MA: MIT Press, 2002), pp. 447–59: 447.
27. For a report on the CCTV cameras' installation and 'effectiveness', see http://.scotland.gov.uk/cru.resfinds/crf0800.htm.
28. Alasdair Gray, *Lanark: A Life in Four Books* (Edinburgh: Canongate, 1981), p. 30; discussed in *Bell, Questioning Scotland*, p. 106.
29. Stuart Kelly, 'Canons to the Left of Him, Canons to the Right of Him: Kenneth White and the Constructions of Scottish Literary History', in

Gavin Bowd, Charles Forsdick and Norman Bissell, eds., *Grounding a World: Essays on the Work of Kenneth White* (Glasgow: Alba, 2005), pp. 186–96: 188.

30. Ibid., p. 188.
31. Ibid., p. 188.
32. Ibid., p. 189.
33. Ibid., p. 189.
34. See Robert Crawford, *Devolving English Literature* (Edinburgh: Edinburgh University Press, 2002 [1992]).
35. Edwin Morgan, 'Creator and Critic: Jekyll and Hyde?', 1979 lecture repr. in Edwin Morgan, ed. Hamish Whyte, *Nothing Not Giving Messages: Reflections on Life and Work* (Edinburgh: Polygon, 1990), pp. 236–49.
36. Alan Riach, *Representing Scotland in Literature, Popular Culture, and Iconography: The Masks of the Modern Nation* (Basingstoke: Palgrave, 2005).
37. Ibid., p. xiii.
38. Ibid., p. 174.
39. Ibid., p. 180.
40. Ibid., p. 180.
41. Ibid., p. 181.
42. Ian Fleming, dir. Terence Young, *Dr. No* (Eon, 1962).
43. Duncan Petrie, *Scottish Fictions: Film, Television and the Novel* (Edinburgh: Edinburgh University Press, 2004); Petrie, *Screening Scotland* (London: BFI, 2000).
44. Riach, *Representing Scotland*, pp. 195, 206.
45. Ibid., p. 206.
46. Ibid., p. 232.
47. Ibid., p. 242.
48. Bell, *Questioning Scotland*, p. 2.
49. Cf. e.g. Ibid., p. 89.
50. Cf. Jacques Derrida, trans. George Collins, *The Politics of Friendship* (London: Verso, 1997), p. 306; A. J. P. Thomson, *Deconstruction and Democracy: Derrida's Politics of Friendship* (London: Continuum, 2005); Thomson, 'So What's New about British Politics? Devolution, Democracy, and Deconstruction', paper presented to the Devolution in Comparative Perspective conference, University of Strathclyde, 7–9 January 2004.
51. Pat Kane, *The Play Ethic* (London: Macmillan, 2004), p. 40.
52. Ibid., p. 201.
53. Ibid., pp. 190, 195–8.
54. Ibid., p. 40.
55. Michel Foucault, trans. Robert Hurley, *The History of Sexuality* (London: Allen Lane, 1979 [1976]).
56. Aldous Huxley, *Brave New World* (London: Vintage, 2004 [1931]).
57. Kane, *The Play Ethic*, pp. 46, 50.
58. Ibid., p. 45.
59. Alexander Trocchi, 'Potlach', Sigma Paper 4 (1963), p. 1; Sigma Paper 5 (1963), p. 3.
60. Kenneth White 'Looking out: From Neotechnics to Geopoetics', in

White, *On Scottish Ground* (Edinburgh: Polygon, 1998), pp. 129–46: 138, 141.

61. Kane, *The Play Ethic*, p. 46; cf. R. D. Laing, *The Divided Self: A Study of Sanity and Madness* (London: Tavistock, 1960), and many of Laing's subsequent clinical descriptions.
62. Kane, *The Play Ethic*, p. 48.
63. Ibid., p. 49.
64. Ibid., p. 51.
65. Michael Gardiner, *The Cultural Roots of British Devolution* (Edinburgh: Edinburgh University Press, 2004), pp. 141–2.
66. Kane, *The Play Ethic*, p. 52.
67. Jacques Derrida, trans. Geoffrey Bennington and Rachel Bowlby, 'This Strange Institution Called Literature', in Derek Attridge, ed., *Acts of Literature* (London: Routledge, 1992), pp. 33–75.
68. Jacques Derrida, trans. Peggy Kamuf, *Given Time: 1. Counterfeit Money* (Chicago: Chicago University Press, 1992), pp. 12–29.
69. See Gardiner, *The Cultural Roots of Devolution*, p. 124.
70. Kane, *The Play Ethic*, p. 63, cf. p. 205.
71. Ibid., p. 87.
72. Ibid., pp. 87–8.
73. Ibid., pp. 207–9; Duncan Petrie, *Screening Scotland* (London: BFI, 2000).
74. Kane, *The Play Ethic*, p. 316.
75. Ibid., p. 317.
76. Ibid., p. 71.
77. Ibid., p. 71.
78. Ibid., p. 73.
79. Ibid., p. 75, cf. the high jinks of the band Happy Mondays, as portrayed in Frank Cottrell Boyce, dir. Michael Winterbottom, *24 Hour Party People* (Channel Four et al.: 2002), and the opening credits to the TV series *Shameless* (Channel 4: 2004–present): 'all of them to a man know first and foremost one of the most vital necessities in this life is, they know how to throw a party'.
80. Kane, *The Play Ethic*, p. 76.
81. Ibid., p. 199, cf. p. 212.
82. Ibid., p. 193.
83. Ibid., pp. 79, 81.
84. Ibid., p. 82.
85. Ibid., p. 293.
86. Ibid., p. 312.
87. Ibid., p. 294.
88. Ibid., p. 304.
89. Ibid., p. 304.
90. Michael Gardiner, 'Endless Enlightenment: Eye-Operated Technology and the Political Economy of Vision', *Reconstruction* 4.1 (2004): http://www.reconstruction.ws/041/gardiner.htm.
91. Kane, *The Play Ethic*, p. 299.
92. Ibid. on Paine, pp. 305–6, Thomas Paine, *Agrarian Justice, Opposed to Agrarian Law, and Agrarian Monopoly. Being a Plan for the Condition of Man, by Creating in Every Nation a National Fund . . .* (London:

T. Williams, 1797 [1796]).

93. Adam Smith, *The Wealth of Nations, Books 1–3*, ed. Andrew Skinner (London: Penguin, 2003 [1776]).

94. Kane, *The Play Ethic*, p. 353.

95. Ibid., p. 324.

96. Ibid., p. 339; see also various essays in Sohail Inayatullah and Gail Boxwell, eds., *Islam, Postmodernism and Other Futures: A Ziauddin Sardar Reader* (London: Pluto, 2003).

97. Kane, *The Play Ethic*, p. 339.

98. Ibid., p. 340; cf. Hakim Bey, *T.A.Z.: The Temporary Autonomous Zone, Ontological Anarchy, Poetic Terrorism* (New York: Autonomedia: 2003 [1991]).

99. Kane, *The Play Ethic*, p. 343.

100. Ibid., p. 345.

101. Ibid., p. 339.

Index

Hubbard Tom, 33, 34, 35
Hume, David
America and, 142
Burns and, 26
Deleuze and, 11–14, 22, 177
Finlay and, 134, 135, 139
Kelman and, 159
MacDiarmid's essay on, 38
on Scots language, 25
on space, 7, 9, 73
Reid and, 157
Rousseau and, 3, 139
Trocchi and, 77, 80, 82
White and, 99
humour, 2, 26, 65, 66, 113, 139, 160
Hurt, John, 74
Huxley, Aldous, 187

Imlah, Mick, 100
Ionesco, Eugene, 72

Jakobson, Roman, 117
Jargon Group, 5, 74
Jargon Papers, 74, 85, 99, 113
Jordan, Neil, 57
Jospin, Lionel, 190

Kafka, Franz, 3, 159
Beckett and, 178
Deleuze and, 163, 164, 169, 177
Derrida and, 161
existentialism, 20, 159, 161
Georgianism and, 170
Kelman and, 20, 159–64, 165, 166, 168, 169, 171
Laing influenced by, 20
Muirs' translation of, 20, 30, 31, 32
Reid and, 159
Trocchi influenced by, 20
voice, 159–60, 163
Welsh and, 171
Kamensky, Vasily, 109
Kane, Pat, 58, 76, 78, 186–92
Kant, Immanuel, 82, 140
Kearns, Cleo McNelly, 138
Kelly, Stuart, 100, 181, 182
Kelman, James, 3, 127, 152, 153–72
'Block, The', 171
Busconductor Hines, The, 10, 152, 164
Deleuze and, 3, 160, 164–72
Disaffection, A, 161
drama, 87
Galloway and, 141, 145, 147, 159
Glasgow and, 74, 123, 124, 153–7
How Late, It Was, How Late 164–6, 167–9, 171
Kafka and, 20, 159–64, 165, 166, 168, 169, 171
Kane and, 187
Scots language, 26, 74, 123, 161, 164, 167, 179
Spark and, 46, 59, 66, 172
voice, 141, 159, 160, 161, 164, 166, 168
Kennedy, A. L., 185

Kermode, Frank, 49
Kinloch, David, 100
KLF (Kopyright Liberation Foundation), 96
Koran, the, 191
Kristeva, Julia, 79, 124–5

L=A=N=G=U=A=G=E poetry, 83, 93, 117, 133
Laing, R. D., 6
Burroughs and, 83
concrete poetry and, 171
Deleuze and, 78, 83, 92, 98, 164, 171, 172
Divided Self, 59
drugs, 78, 83, 92
eastern thought, 99
existentialism, 83, 171, 172
Galloway and, 145
Kafka's influence on, 20
Kane and, 187
logical positivism, 80
MacDiarmid and, 95
Macmurray and, 83
Morgan and, 171
on play, 98
Sartre and, 164, 171
Scottish personalism, 58
Spark and, 46, 59
Trocchi and, 37, 78, 86, 92, 95
Trocchi's Sigma Portfolio, 82–3, 94
Trocchi's Sigma Project, 76
White and, 92, 99, 100
Lallans, 33; *see also* Synthetic Scots
Lallans, 33, 35
Lally, Pat, 156
Lambert, Gregg, 178
language, 2, 3
Deleuze on, 177, 178, 179
education and, 24, 55–6, 119, 191
in *The Ballad of Peckham Rye*, 56–7
MacDiarmid and, 121, 183
Morgan and, 37–8, 121–3, 183
Muir on, 23
nations and, 121–2
see also English language; Gaelic language; minor languages and literatures; Scots language; 'three languages' model
Larkin, Philip, 113, 116
Laverty, Paul, 188
Law, T. S., 33, 34, 35
Lawrence, D. H., 23
Le Play, Frédéric, 98, 99
Leary, Timothy, 85, 92
Leavis, F. R., 23, 32, 152, 183, 189
Lenin, Vladimir, 126
Leonard, Tom, 26, 38, 123, 159
Lessig, Lawrence, 190
Lettrism, 72, 79
Lewis, Percy Wyndham, 38
Lindsay, Maurice, 35
literary canons, 32, 100, 115, 181–6

literature
Deleuze on, 9, 12, 170, 177, 178, 179
Derrida on, 178, 179
Gaelic literature, 33
philosophy and, 177–8
Riach and Petrie on, 184–5
Spark on, 45
Trocchi on, 78–9, 80, 81
see also English literature; language; minor languages and literatures
Little Sparta, 134, 135, 136, 138, 139
Little Spartan medallions, 139–40
Lloyd George, David, 77–8
Loach, Ken, 188
Lochhead, Liz, 123, 182
Lodge, David, 66–7
Lotringer, Sylvère, 6

McCaffery, Steve, 117
MacCaig, Norman, 35
McClure, Michael, 84–5
McCordick, David, 100
McCrone, David, 180
MacDiarmid, Hugh
Akros and, 36
antisyzygy and, 19
Borders and, 56
Burns and, 25
Burroughs and, 37, 88, 95
essay on Hume, 38
definitive edition of works, 185
Finlay and, 37, 123, 134
Gaelic and, 33
Geddes' influence on, 20
Glasgow and, 27, 34–5
imperialism, 21–2
in *Poets' Pub*, 182
Laing and, 95
language and, 121, 183
Law and, 34, 35
McGrath on, 36, 125
Mayakovsky and, 109
modernism, 36
Morgan and, 37–8, 95–6, 121, 122–3, 126, 131
Muir and, 20, 22, 24, 25, 32, 110, 140
nationalism, 30, 56, 94, 95, 119
organic communities and, 40n
Pound and, 36, 93, 94, 96, 112, 125, 183
Russian literature, 109
Scots language, 25, 26, 37, 110, 123, 127
Second Renaissance, 33, 34, 35, 36–8
Seurat and, 99
Synthetic Scots, 20, 21, 22, 37, 38, 95, 97, 123
Tom Scott and, 34
Trocchi and, 37, 85, 88, 94, 95
whisky in works of, 167
see also Synthetic Scots
McDonald, Gus, 119